W9-AMP-007

THE
HISTORY OF
MEXICO

ADVISORY BOARD

THE
HISTORY OF
MEXICO

Burton Kirkwood

The Greenwood Histories of the Modern Nations
Frank W. Thackeray and John E. Findling, Series Editors

Greenwood Press
Westport, Connecticut • London

Library of Congress Cataloging-in-Publication Data

Kirkwood, Burton.
    The history of Mexico / Burton Kirkwood.
        p.   cm.—(The Greenwood histories of the modern nations,
    ISSN 1096–2905)
    Includes bibliographical references and index.
    ISBN 0–313–30351–7 (alk. paper)
    1. Mexico—History. I. Title. II. Series.
    F1226.K57   2000
    972—dc21   99–33688

British Library Cataloguing in Publication Data is available.

Library of Congress Catalog Card Number: 99–33688
ISBN: 0–313–30351–7
ISSN: 1096–2905

First published in 2000

Greenwood Press, 88 Post Road West, Westport, CT 06881
An imprint of Greenwood Publishing Group, Inc.
www.greenwood.com

Printed in the United States of America

The paper used in this book complies with the
Permanent Paper Standard issued by the National
Information Standards Organization (Z39.48–1984).

10 9 8 7 6 5 4 3 2

Contents

Series Foreword

The Greenwood Histories of the Modern Nations series is intended to provide students and interested laypeople with up-to-date, concise, and analytical histories of many of the nations of the contemporary world. Not since the 1960s has there been a systematic attempt to publish a series of national histories, and, as series editors, we believe that this series will prove to be a valuable contribution to our understanding of other countries in our increasingly interdependent world.

Over thirty years ago, at the end of the 1960s, the Cold War was an accepted reality of global politics, the process of decolonization was still in progress, the idea of a unified Europe with a single currency was unheard of, the United States was mired in a war in Vietnam, and the economic boom of Asia was still years in the future. Richard Nixon was president of the United States, Mao Tse-tung (not yet Mao Zedong) ruled China, Leonid Brezhnev guided the Soviet Union, and Harold Wilson was prime minister of the United Kingdom. Authoritarian dictators still ruled most of Latin America, the Middle East was reeling in the wake of the Six-Day War, and Shah Reza Pahlavi was at the height of his power in Iran. Clearly, the past thirty years have been witness to a great deal of historical change, and it is to this change that this series is primarily addressed.

With the help of a distinguished advisory board, we have selected nations whose political, economic, and social affairs mark them as among the most important in the waning years of the twentieth century, and for each nation we have found an author who is recognized as a specialist in the history of that nation. These authors have worked most cooperatively with us and with Greenwood Press to produce volumes that reflect current research on their nation and that are interesting and informative to their prospective readers.

The importance of a series such as this cannot be underestimated. As a superpower whose influence is felt all over the world, the United States can claim a "special" relationship with almost every other nation. Yet many Americans know very little about the histories of the nations with which the United States relates. How did they get to be the way they are? What kind of political systems have evolved there? What kind of influence do they have in their own region? What are the dominant political, religious, and cultural forces that move their leaders? These and many other questions are answered in the volumes of this series.

The authors who have contributed to this series have written comprehensive histories of their nations, dating back to prehistoric times in some cases. Each of them, however, has devoted a significant portion of the book to events of the past thirty years, because the modern era has contributed the most to contemporary issues that have an impact on U.S. policy. Authors have made an effort to be as up-to-date as possible so that readers can benefit from the most recent scholarship and a narrative that includes very recent events.

In addition to the historical narrative, each volume in this series contains an introductory overview of the country's geography, political institutions, economic structure, and cultural attributes. This is designed to give readers a picture of the nation as it exists in the contemporary world. Each volume also contains additional chapters that add interesting and useful detail to the historical narrative. One chapter is a thorough chronology of important historical events, making it easy for readers to follow the flow of a particular nation's history. Another chapter features biographical sketches of the nation's most important figures in order to humanize some of the individuals who have contributed to the historical development of their nation. Each volume also contains a comprehensive bibliography, so that those readers whose interest has been sparked may find out more about the nation and its history. Finally, there is a carefully prepared topic and person index.

Readers of these volumes will find them fascinating to read and useful in understanding the contemporary world and the nations that comprise it. As series editors, it is our hope that this series will contribute to a heightened sense of global understanding as we enter a new century.

Frank W. Thackeray and John E. Findling
Indiana University Southeast

Preface

The good news is that interest in Mexico has risen in recent years. The North American Free Trade Agreement, the important role of Mexico in the international war on drugs, the arrival of Mexican immigrants seeking employment in the United States, and the attraction of Mexico as a vacation destination have created a desire to learn more about our southern neighbor. The bad news is that many people only have a cursory knowledge about Mexico and hold continuing stereotypes about it.

The goal of this book is to introduce secondary school students and the mainstream public to the history of Mexico. The text offers a more readable and in-depth analysis than traditional world history books or texts on Latin America in which discussion of Mexico is limited to a relatively few pages. But this should only be the beginning. It is my hope that after reading this book the reader will engage in further study of Mexico.

Writing solely about Mexico is a daunting task. To devote an entire book to any country's history forces the author to determine what to introduce and, of course, what to omit. This study of Mexico follows the chronological development of prominent themes in the nation's political, social, and economic evolution. The early chapters discuss the arrival of the first peoples in the Western Hemisphere and their successful creation of political, economic, and social institutions; the destruction of a significant portion of these indigenous systems when Spanish explorers arrived at the end of the fifteenth century; the implementation of the Spanish colonial system; and Mexico's attempts at self-rule in the nineteenth century. The latter chapters focus on the emergence of the dictator Porfirio Díaz in 1876; the Revolution of 1910; and the ensuing struggles to implement the goals of the revolutionary period.

The reader will find supporting material in the form of a timeline with important events and their corresponding dates. Brief biographical sketches of some of Mexico's more influential historical figures provide the reader additional information that may not exist in the main text.

Because many readers may not be familiar with Spanish, I have kept the use of Spanish terms and phrases to a minimum. Where necessary, however, Spanish terms are italicized. In each case an accompanying explanation of the term follows.

This work represents the collective efforts of numerous people. I want to thank John Findling and Frank Thackeray at Indiana University Southeast for their support in preparation of the manuscript. Barbara Rader, my editor at Greenwood Publishing Group, provided support and guidance for this project and, above all, patience. At the University of Evansville, Dr. Larry Colter, Dean of Arts and Sciences, provided me with financial support so that I could devote a summer to writing. Colleagues at the University of Evansville—Jennifer Bell, Brad Cohen, Dan Gahan, Annette Parks, and Anthony Tuck—in their own quiet ways supported my efforts. In particular, Anthony Tuck read sections of the manuscript and offered suggestions to improve the writing.

My students also assisted in the development of this project. The majority of them aided this book by taking my classes and thereby serving as sounding boards for different ways by which to introduce topics about Mexico. Others played a more direct role. Cindy Meyer reviewed certain sections of the manuscript for clarity.

Although all these people aided in the project, the errors and weaknesses of this book are mine alone.

Finally, three other people deserve mention. Rodney D. Anderson introduced me to Mexico and early on shaped my views of the country and its people. C. Peter Ripley, friend and mentor, has consistently listened to my complaints and shared in the minor victories; for that I am indebted. My father, Jim Kirkwood, will probably be shocked to read his name in his son's book, but he must know that he has had a lot to do with the decisions I have made.

Timeline of Historical Events

35,000 50,000 B.C.	First peoples cross Bering Strait and enter Western Hemisphere
pre-3500 B.C.	Emergence of sustainable agriculture
700 B.C.	Appearance of Olmec civilization
A.D. 200–800	Teotihuacán
500 B.C.–A.D. 700	Monte Albán
400 B.C.–A.D. 800	Mayan civilization
A.D. 900–1200	Toltec civilization
1400–1521	Aztec civilization
1440–1468	Moctezuma I
1492	Arrival of Spanish explorers in Western Hemisphere
1502–1520	Moctezuma II
1519	Jerónimo de Aguilar (shipwrecked Spaniard found by Hernán Cortés); Doña Marina (introduced to Cortés); Spanish land at Veracruz and

	establish city; encounter with Tlaxcalans; massacre at Cholula
November 8, 1519	Arrival at Tenochtitlán (Aztec capital city)
1519	Arrest of Moctezuma II
July 1, 1520	*La noche triste* (the sad night)
August 13, 1521	Fall of Tenochtitlán
1521	Settlement of New Spain begins
1522	Arrival of missionaries
1529	Arrival of Bishop Juan de Zumárraga
1531	Juan Diego and the Virgin of Guadalupe
1535	Arrival of first viceroy—Don Antonio de Mendoza
1540s	Bartolomé de las Casas protests Spanish practices toward Indians
1542	Founding of Guadalajara
1542	New Laws protect Indians against exploitation
1553	Establishment of University of Mexico at Mexico City
1651–1695	Sor Juana Inés de la Cruz
18th century	Bourbon reforms
September 16, 1810	Father Hidalgo and the Grito de Dolores
February 24, 1821	Plan de Iguala
September 1821	Independence
May 1822–February 1823	Mexican empire
1794–1876	Antonio López de Santa Anna
1836	War with Texas
1838	Pastry War
1846–1848	U.S.-Mexican War
1848	Treaty of Guadalupe-Hidalgo
1854	Revolution de Ayutla

1857	Constitution of 1857
1858–1861	War of the Reform
May 5, 1862	Battle of Puebla (Cinco de Mayo)
1862–1867	French occupation
June 19, 1867	Execution of Hapsburg prince Ferdinand Maximilian
1872–1876	Presidency of Sebastian Lerdo de Tejada
1872	Veracruz–Mexico City railroad is completed
1876–1911	Dictatorship of Porfirio Díaz (the Porfiriato)
1880–1884	Presidency of Manuel González
1906	Strike at Cananea textile facility
1907	Strike at Río Blanco
1908	Creelman interview
1909	Francisco Madero publishes *The Presidential Succession in 1910*
1910	Porfirio Díaz wins his last presidential election; Francisco Madero is jailed; Plan de San Luis Potosí
February 1913	Assassination of Madero
1914	United States occupies Veracruz; convention at Aguascalientes
1915	Battle of Celaya; United States recognizes Constitutionalists
1916–1917	Constitution of 1917 is created
1919	Assassination of Emiliano Zapata
1920	Plan de Agua Prieta; assassination of Venustiano Carranza
1920–1924	Presidency of Alvaro Obregón
1923	Bucareli Agreements; De la Huerta revolt; assassination of Pancho Villa
1924–1928	Presidency of Plutarco Elias Calles
1928	Assassination of Obregón

1926–1929	Cristero Rebellion
1928–1934	Maximato (period of dominance by *jefe máximo* Plutarco Elias Calles)
1929	Creation of Partido Revolucionario Mexicano and origin of Partido Revolucionario Institucional (PRI)
1934–1940	Presidency of Lázaro Cárdenas
1937	Nationalization of railroads
1938	Nationalization of oil industry
1940–1946	Presidency of Manuel Avila Camacho
1942	Mexico declares war against Germany
1946–1952	Presidency of Miguel Alemán Valdés
1952	Expansion of National University of Mexico
1952–1958	Presidency of Adolfo Ruiz Cortines
1958–1964	Presidency of Adolfo López Mateos; expansion of land distribution programs
1964–1970	Presidency of Gustavo Díaz Ordaz
1968	Tlatelolco massacre; Olympic Games at Mexico City
1970–1976	Presidency of Luis Echeverría
1976–1982	Presidency of José López Portillo
1980	Mexico's oil reserves grow
1980s	Oil crisis
1982–1988	Presidency of Miguel de la Madrid
1982	Nationalization of bank industry
1985	Mexico City earthquake
1988	Election of Carlos Salinas de Gortari
1994	North American Free Trade Agreement; EZLN rebellion; assassinations of Luis Donaldo Colosio and José Francisco Ruiz Massieu; election of Ernesto Zedillo Ponce de Léon

1997	Cuauhtémoc Cárdenas wins Mexico City mayoral election
1999	Pope John Paul II visits Mexico; conviction of Raúl Salinas for conspiracy in murder of Ruiz Massieu

1

Mexico Today

Although today it is a distinct nation, Mexico has been shaped by a wide variety of factors. Initially climate, geography, and geology combined in myriad ways to affect the population of this land. Mexico is a nation of ancient indigenous peoples whose distinct languages, religion, and technology predated the arrival of the Europeans. They in turn brought their own languages, religion, and technology, which melded over the centuries with those of the indigenous cultures and guided the development of the country. The result is a nation formed from the processes of conflict, revolution, and resolution and yet tempered by centuries of cultural evolution.

This work surveys Mexico's history from the arrival of the first people in the Western Hemisphere to current issues at the close of the twentieth century. To understand Mexico's history one must examine its economic, social, and religious institutions, all of which have influenced its political institutions.

GEOGRAPHY

Geography, climate, and geological events such as earthquakes and volcanoes have equally influenced and illuminated Mexico's history. For

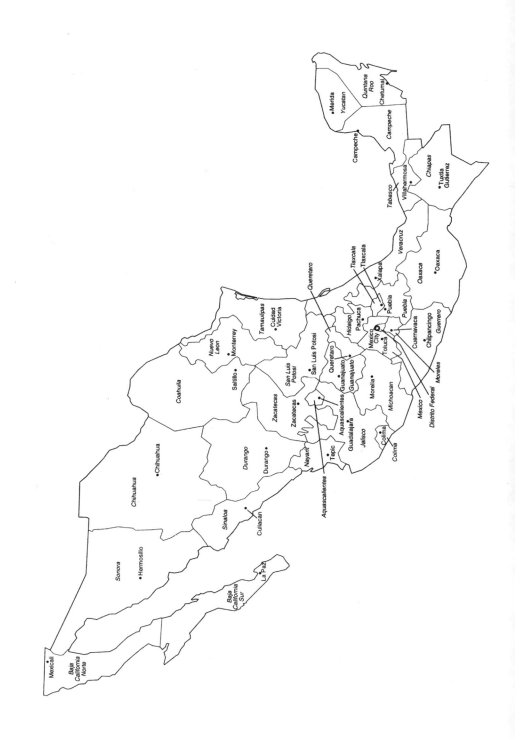

example, in 1985 a devastating earthquake struck Mexico City, killing thousands. The damage to the capital and the nation was immediately evident not only in the destruction of buildings but also in the political and social arenas because the government was unable to offer basic relief. Shortly after the earthquake destroyed buildings, people witnessed what had only before been rumor: torture chambers in government buildings (their existence had been consistently denied). Discovery of the government's lies compounded the growing realization that the government's corruption made it unable to provide even rudimentary aid to the people of the capital. Instead, grassroots organizations mobilized to provide food, water, medicine, and material for rebuilding. These new civil groups proved more capable than the government. This resulted in challenges to the authority of the national ruling party, the Partido Revolucionario Institucional (PRI).

The geography of Mexico features two large mountain chains running roughly parallel in a northwest to southeast pattern. To the west lies the Sierra Madre Occidental, and to the east lies the Sierra Madre Oriental. In southern Mexico, bordered by Guatemala, is the Sierra Madre del Sur. The highest peak tops 18,000 feet, and the size and depth of the deepest canyon, that of Santiago, are comparable to that of the Grand Canyon. Each mountain range influences the climate of its region. Within the three mountain regions, the diverse geography is shaped by rugged peaks and steep valleys. One consequence of Mexico's geography is a long-time regional identification (*patria chica*) that has been just as important as national identification.

In recent times the geography has made construction of an internal transportation system difficult. For example, the first railroad line connecting the important east coast port city of Veracruz with Mexico City (located in the central highlands at nearly 7,000 feet) had to climb more than 9,000 feet over the Sierra Madre Oriental and cross huge canyons, some more than 300 feet deep. The explorer Hernán Cortés's legendary attempt to describe the land of Mexico was dramatic. The conquistador (conqueror; the Spanish name used to describe the men who conquered the Indian population in the Western Hemisphere) balled up a piece of paper and let it partially unfold; "there," he said, "is what the land looks like." The complexity of the terrain continues to make public works construction projects difficult and expensive.

Geography has also played an important and complex role in the development of modern Mexico and its relationship with the United States. Because of their proximity both nations have influenced and been influenced by each other, but the relationship has left a legacy of familiarity combined with suspicion. Certainly in the twentieth century both have moved closer through the adoption and adaptation of cuisine, language, economics, social practices, and marriage. However, suspicion remains, as is evident in U.S. immigration policies and Mexico's views of U.S. economic policies. The North American Free Trade Agreement (NAFTA) signed between Mexico, the United States, and Canada will test whether Mexico and the United States can put aside their old traditional hostilities and work within the cooperative spirit of the agreement.

Geography and climate conspire to complicate life in Mexico. In the north, vast sweeps of arid land can barely support a single cow. In contrast, the southern states of Chiapas, Guerrero, and areas extending into the Yucatán receive so much annual rainfall that it is measured in feet, not inches. Central Mexico, where the capital is located, contains some of the nation's richest agricultural lands and receives moderate rainfall. Yet inconsistent rain and large areas of arid land result in less than 10 percent of Mexico's total land producing crops annually. There are only two significant river systems: On the east coast the Papaloapan River drains the states of Veracruz and Oaxaca; in the west the Balsas River drains the states of Michoacán and Guerrero. Geographic complexity and uncertain rainfall have historically prevented the creation of an internal transportation network utilizing these river systems. The nation contains a rich diversity of flora and fauna that in many ways reflects the country's geographical diversity, encompassing the arid region of the north and the rainforest of the south.

Mexico's 756,000 square miles amount to only one-quarter the size of the United States. The capital and largest city, Mexico City, has an estimated population of 20 million. In comparison Guadalajara, the second largest city, has an estimated population of 5 million. Other large cities are Monterrey and Puebla.

POPULATION AND LANGUAGE

Mexico's population in 1999 stood at 100 million with an annual growth rate of 1.8 percent. The population is primarily urban, with 71 percent living in cities and only 29 percent in rural areas. Nothing dramatizes Mexico's urban growth more than its capital, Mexico City, which has an estimated population of 20 million. Historically the area where the capital is located—the Valley of Mexico—has been a magnet for people, first as a place for abundant game and a region capable of growing substantial crops. Now the city attracts people with the lure of jobs and money, an elusive myth for the many unemployed residing there.

The ethnic makeup of the nation represents the fusing of diverse peoples. With the arrival of the conquistadors in the early sixteenth century, followed by Africans who came first as slaves, a process of race blending, or miscegenation, began. An almost immediate consequence was the ethnic categorization known as mestizo, a person with both European and Indian blood. Numerous other categories followed, but mestizo remains the predominant classification. Today approximately 60 percent of the population is mestizo, with Amerindians (Indians living within the Western Hemisphere) making up 30 percent and whites making up 9 percent. Less than 1 percent of the population falls outside these three categories.

Life expectancy in Mexico is catching up with that of first world nations. As a result of improved health care and dietary enhancements, life expectancy has nearly doubled from an average of 36 years in 1930 to 70 years for men and 77 years for women today.

Spanish and Amerindian dialects are the dominant spoken languages, with Spanish being the official national language. As in many other countries, English is increasingly important in the major industrial centers, the tourist locations, and the educational system. Some 200 or more Indian ethnic groups remain in Mexico speaking more than 50 Amerindian dialects.

RELIGION

Fully 89 percent of the population of Mexico identify themselves as Roman Catholic. Protestant denominations have made inroads since the late nineteenth century, aided by the anti-clerical features of the Constitution of 1917. These features restricted the number of priests, required that they register with the government, and limited the presence of the Catholic Church in the nation's educational arena. Today 6 percent of the population consider themselves Protestant. Less than 5 percent identify with other religions. Not surprisingly, the Catholic Church exercises tremendous influence in Mexico despite consistent challenges by the government ever since the colonial era. Crowds numbering as high as one million greeted Pope John Paul II in his January 1999 visit, a testament to the continued influence of Roman Catholicism in Mexico today.

The 1917 constitution prohibited the clergy from educating the workers or the peasants. Despite this restriction the enrollment in private schools, nearly half of which were operated by the Roman Catholic

Church, grew to nearly 1.5 million between 1940 and 1979. Until recently the existence of these schools was in violation of the law. In fact, the willingness of the Church and many Mexicans to defy the anti-clerical position of the 1917 constitution illustrates the tradition of accommodation that operates in Mexico. It was easier, and perhaps more politically savvy, for the government to overlook these violations as long as the Church remained relatively supportive of the government. Since the 1980s and the presidencies of Miguel de la Madrid and Carlos Salinas de Gortari, the restrictions imposed by the government on the Catholic Church have been abandoned. As of 1992 Mexican priests can vote, the Church can own property, and religious education is allowed. Diplomatic relations with the Vatican have been reinstated as well.

Despite this relatively recent accommodation, the Church has not remained quiet on the issue of poverty. Historically, as the government failed to care for the people, the Church assumed greater responsibility and became more vocal in complaining about the government's shortcomings. Today the Church, which once strove mainly to preserve its own authority, has emerged as an outspoken opponent of the government. Yet aggressive Church actions were evident early in the century, both in opposition to the anti-clerical language of the 1917 constitution and in the violent Cristero rebellion of the 1920s. From 1926 to 1929 Mexico faced strong resistance by Catholics who opposed the anti-clerical component of the Constitution of 1917 that regulated the affairs of the Catholic Church. After the emergence of liberation theology among Latin American Catholic priests in the 1970s, Mexican clerics became vocal in their condemnation of oppressive government policies. In 1991 clerical officials leveled a broad range of charges against the government including torture, abuse of prisoners, political persecution, corruption, and electoral fraud. These charges were repeated by Pope John Paul II in his 1999 visit when he called for an end to "violence, terrorism, and drug trafficking." The Church has been critical of the government by supporting the rebellion in the southern state of Chiapas. Tension between church and state emerged again as recently as 1994 when the government attempted to blame the Chiapas uprising on the language and actions of various clerics.

EDUCATION

Education has become an important component of reform in recent decades. The national government has committed the equivalent of millions of dollars to improve educational opportunities; at the same time individual states, supported by the federal budget, have directed the development of curriculum, school building, hiring of teachers, and assessment.

For Mexicans between the ages 6 and 18, school is mandatory. However, the economic reality for many families makes this impossible. As late as 1994, only 59 percent of this age group attended school. This reflects the need of many families to have their children work rather than attend school. Yet other signs are more positive. Since 1970 there has been a dramatic increase in the number of students attending primary, secondary, and postsecondary schools. Primary school attendance rose from around 10 million to 17.5 million students, secondary school attendance rose from 1.4 to 4.5 million, and university attendance skyrocketed from 62,000 students in 1959 to 1.2 million in 1994. The overall increased enrollment has raised adult literacy to an estimated 89.6 percent. Nevertheless the task of public education remains daunting; although educational expenditures have risen to meet the demands of increased numbers of students, per capita investment in education has declined. If the amount of money spent on public education is not increased, the number of uneducated Mexicans will grow beyond the current level of 2 million.

POLITICAL AND MILITARY SYSTEMS

The Constitution of 1917 established a federal republic with three branches of government: executive, legislative, and judicial. The executive is both chief of state and head of the government and serves a six-year term. The president cannot be elected to two consecutive terms.

The legislative branch comprises a Congress with a Senate and Chamber of Deputies. As with the president, consecutive reelection is not permitted. In the Chamber of Deputies the elected officials, called deputies, serve three-year terms. Of the 500 members of the Chamber of Deputies, 300 are elected as representatives of individual districts; voters choose the remaining 200 proportionally from five electoral regions. The Senate's 128 members are elected to six-year terms; like the president, senators cannot be elected to consecutive terms in office.

Since World War II the democratization of Mexico has received increasing attention. Most significant is the emergence of opposition parties that compete with the official national party, the Partido Revolucionario Nacional (PRI). The oldest and most successful opposition party is the Partido Acción Nacional (PAN), formed during the late 1920s. Since 1989

PAN candidates have captured gubernatorial seats in the states of Baja California Norte, Chihuahua, Guanajuato, and Jalisco. The challenge to PRI's dominance in the Senate is reflected in the increased number of opposition senators; now 33 out of 128 Senators represent the opposition parties.

The Partido Revolucionario Democrático (PRD) evolved from grass-roots organizations that were formed after the 1985 earthquake in Mexico City. Created in 1988, but not formally established until 1990, the PRD elected Cuauhtémoc Cárdenas as its president. He was the leading opposition candidate in the 1988 national presidential campaign. Although he was defeated in 1988, Cárdenas and the PRD won Mexico City's mayoral election in 1997. Clearly this is a challenge to the PRI and an indication that democratization is gradually being achieved in Mexico.

The nation's military is composed of an army, navy, and air force totaling approximately 175,000 personnel. The national government spends roughly 0.9 percent of the annual budget to support the military, whose primary responsibilities included national defense, public works projects such as road construction, disaster relief assistance, narcotics policing, and search and rescue operations. Since the 1920s the federal government has pursued policies that limit the level of the military's political influence. Consequently the military's political power has diminished from its prominence in the nineteenth century.

ECONOMY

Mexico's diverse economy is dominated by petroleum, automobiles, consumer electronics, steel, textiles, coffee, cotton, fresh and processed foods, and tourism. Since 1988 there has been an economic liberalization campaign under the leadership of former president Carlos Salinas and current president Ernesto Zedillo. In 1994 Mexico entered the North American Free Trade Agreement (NAFTA), under which tariffs among the United States, Mexico, and Canada are to be eliminated over a fifteen-year period. Most people remain optimistic about the nation's sustained economic growth, but in early 1995 the devaluation of the peso had devastating consequences for the nation's financial infrastructure, with purchasing power dropping precipitously. As a result, the United States and other international lending agencies provided an estimated $40 billion in aid. Subsequently substantial gains in 1996 caused an economic growth rate of approximately 6 percent. Despite this stabilization, prices remain high. In fact, the middle class has seen its purchasing power decline dramatically. Annual per capita income is about $4,000 in comparison to almost $26,000 in the United States. In early 1999 under free trade policies the Zedillo government ended the subsidies on tortillas, a staple of the Mexican diet. Such economic decisions may ultimately have serious consequences for the nation's long-term political health.

CULTURAL LIFE

One of the most disturbing phenomena facing Mexico since World War II is the growing effect of "Americanization"—the imposition of American culture through food, television, movies, music, clothing, sports, and even language. For example, phrases such as "happy hour" and "okay" have become part of the spoken language. Large multinational food chains have made significant inroads since 1985, when McDonald's first opened in Mexico City; Pizza Hut, Kentucky Fried Chicken, and Denny's have followed suit. The cultural invasion reached a point of logical absurdity when Taco Bell first opened in 1992!

U.S. consumer practices have moved into Mexico in numerous other ways. In the wealthier neighborhoods of Mexico's large cities people are induced to buy U.S. cars with banners proclaiming "You are in Dodge country!" Wal-Mart, cell phone companies, Kodak, and providers of consumer goods are arriving at a dizzying pace. Even large *supermercados* such as Gigante, offer one-stop shopping for products ranging from food, clothes, and tools to electronic goods. As in the United States, these large stores threaten to consume the local community structure provided by small family businesses.

It is significant that the Mexican economy is absorbing some of the worst elements of American mass consumerism. Since Mexico's acceptance of NAFTA, this process of cultural imperialism may accelerate.

Sports have also crossed the border. American football has become widely popular, and the National Football League now plays preseason exhibition games in Mexico. Increasingly Mexican television stations telecast these games, and at the same time the number of Mexican viewers of the Super Bowl has increased. Moreover, audiences watching games by the National Basketball Association (NBA) and the National Collegiate Athletic Association have increased in the last two decades. In Mexico's public parks the basketball rim is becoming as ubiquitous as the soccer field, with young ball players wearing the jerseys of popular NBA stars. Baseball was introduced earlier in the twentieth century. As it maintains a significant fan base, an increasing number of Mexican players, such as Fernando Valenzuela, are entering the major leagues. In return Mexico has contributed to sports in the United States, with football—or soccer, as it is known in the United States—becoming the fastest growing team sport.

STATUS OF WOMEN

Mexico has witnessed significant changes in the status of women. Although they played an important role in the Mexican Revolution and other conflicts, they remained peripheral figures in the political arena. It was not until 1955 that women received the right to vote. Momentum followed, with a law ultimately presented by President Echeverría in 1972 granting women equality in jobs, pay, and legal standing.

Traditionally regarded as a woman's issue, birth control has become a mainstream political issue since the 1970s. After all, through the combined effects of cultural expectations to raise large families and the Catholic Church's ban on birth control, the population grew dramatically. Women who chose not to have children resorted to crude abortions. In 1970, the year Luis Echeverría became the first Mexican president to call for a reduction in the nation's population, as many as 32,000 Mexican women died from abortion complications. Although discussions of population control have long been taboo by the Catholic Church, 1972 saw a reversal when Mexican clerics called for reduced family size. Thereafter government support enabled family planning clinics and educational programs to be developed. By 1988 the Mexican annual population growth rate was nearly halved, to 1.8 percent.

Women in Mexico have been pushing for significant changes within the political and social arenas, and they are slowly gaining access to previously male-dominated spheres. For example, they are now elected as state governors and as representatives in the Chamber of Deputies. Increasingly they are leaving bad marriages in spite of condemnation from the Church and hostility from their own families. Indeed, there is growing liberation from the traditional roles and expectations for women in Mexican society.

Meanwhile Mexico continues to evolve. Its rich cultural and historical identity is experiencing increasing integration into the global community. The latest manifestation of this cultural evolution is in the changing perspective on the 1910 revolution. The revolutionary process has been substantially weakened by the consequences of free market reform and the view that revolutionary institutions have not delivered the promises enunciated by the constitution. Yet Mexico survives. Its people have demonstrated a remarkable resiliency that bodes well for the nation's future.

2

Mexico's Early Inhabitants

At the end of the fifteenth century Spanish explorers stumbled upon the peoples of Mesoamerica, finding sophisticated societies with advanced political, social, economic, and religious systems. In writing about their impressions of the Indians, the Spanish were both impressed by and contemptuous of the native population. But as they took over Indian land, wealth, and control of the people, the Spanish succumbed to a condescending viewpoint. Imbued with the zealous spirit of Catholicism and flush with military victory over the Muslims who had controlled the Iberian peninsula for centuries, they regarded the indigenous peoples of Mesoamerica as inferior.

When Christopher Columbus encountered the Arawak peoples on the islands of the Bahamas in 1492, he wrote admiringly yet ominously about this meeting. He spoke of their willingness to provide for the Spanish: "they willingly traded everything they owned." He described their striking features: "they were well built, with good bodies and handsome features . . . they do not bear arms, and do not know them, for I showed them a sword, they took it by the edge and cut themselves out of ignorance. They have no iron. Their spears are made of cane." Columbus described their behavior with a new implement as ignorant. His contemptuous view of the Arawaks was further revealed when he wrote, "they would make fine servants . . . with fifty men we could subjugate them all and make them do whatever we want."[1]

Although historians can be precise about the meeting of European Christians and the Mesoamerican peoples, they cannot be as accurate about when the first peoples of Mexico emerged. Through radiocarbon dating, computers, and the technology used by botanists, it has become possible for ethnologists, geologists, and geographers to generate positions of general agreement. The prevailing view places human beings in the Americas approximately 35,000 to 50,000 years ago. The ancestors of today's Mexican people crossed the Bering Strait between Siberia and Alaska traveled down through North America into Central America, and arrived at the southern tip of South America about 8,000 to 10,000 years ago.

The period during which Mexican ancestors wandered across the Bering land bridge and into present-day Mexico was dominated by nomadic hunter-gatherers whose life revolved around the precarious acquisition of food. Because information about how these people lived remains fragmentary, one can only speculate on the nature of their existence. However, the process of migration appears to have occurred in two phases. The first wave of people crossed the Bering Strait in pursuit of small animals and plants, whereas the second wave sought larger game. Archeological evidence indicates that the early hunters used sophisticated stone weapons to kill and butcher various animals. For example, in central Mexico scientists have found stone arrow points embedded in the bones of a mastodon. Stone, bone, and wooden tools; evidence of crude living arrangements and cooking; and limited textile and pottery implements suggest early manufacturing skills and rudimentary social organization.

Potsherds and figurines enable archeologists to re-create how the early people lived and to develop hypotheses about their social organization. Moreover, where clay potsherds have been unearthed scientists have discovered other ways to understand the early existence of human beings. Potsherds are the remnants of ceramic pottery discovered by archaeologists when they excavate ancient historical sites. The remains of mud or stick dwellings indicate a settled lifestyle, yet other evidence indicates that extensive trading occurred between groups. For example, shells, turquoise, jade, and obsidian objects found beyond their place of origin indicate that some form of trade took place among the various populations in Mesoamerica.

Much as climatic conditions made possible the presence of human beings in the Americas, so changes in the climate altered how they lived. During the last Ice Age, the lower temperatures caused the present-day area of the Bering Sea to freeze over, thus allowing a bridge over which people could cross from Asia to the Western Hemisphere. It was a rare and unique opportunity that began the population of this region with Mexico's ancient ancestors. Climatic changes also caused people to make the transition from hunter-gatherers to agriculturists around 10,000 years ago when rainfall decreased, resulting in limited vegetation and reduced water supplies. This proved disruptive for Mexico's early inhabitants, as the traditional food supplies declined. In particular, climatic changes probably contributed to the extinction of large game. As a result, the early peoples looked for alternative sources of food.

Chronological Divisions of Early Mexicans

Division	Period	Characteristics
Pre-Agricultural	to 5,000 B.C.	early nomadic stage
Archaic	5,000 to 1,500 B.C.	initial attempts at agriculture
Pre-Classic	1,500 to 200 B.C.	initial village life
Classic	200 B.C. to A.D. 900	established/stratified villages
Post-Classic	900 to 1521	emergence of militaristic societies, ending with defeat by the Spanish

PRE-AGRICULTURAL AND ARCHAIC PERIODS

During the pre-agricultural period the early peoples responded to climatic changes. As a result of drier conditions and the loss of large game for hunting, they adopted new methods of acquiring foodstuffs. Unquestionably the most significant action taken during this period was the deliberate cultivation of plants for consumption. Around 7,000 B.C. maize, or corn, was planted. Because it was capable of growing almost anywhere, corn quickly evolved as a central component of the Mexican diet and became the most important crop. Other plants soon followed, including squash, beans, chili peppers, pumpkins, and various tuber plants.

Over the next 5,000 years during the archaic period, cultivated agriculture developed to the extent that reliable foodstuffs allowed people to transition from a semi-nomadic to a stationary existence. In central Mexico in the modern state of Puebla, agrarian villages have been uncovered dating back nearly 4,000 years. The significance of this transition cannot be overstated. Now, free from the almost constant search for food, people turned their attention to other activities—including the manufacture of textiles, pottery, and stone and metal tools.

PRE-CLASSIC PERIOD

By around 1,500 B.C. established agricultural communities existed throughout Mexico as the development of farming tools from wood, stone, bone, and horn assisted cultivation. Other practices to enhance productive output included the terracing of slopes on hillsides and the construction of floating gardens, or *chinampas*. These were actually elevated mounds of earth constructed in lakebeds or swampy areas. Anchored to the lake bottoms with sticks and filled with the rich soil from the bottom of the lakes, they proved extremely fertile. More than the new farming implements, the construction of terraced slopes and *chinampas* suggests an orderly, organized society necessary to oversee these building projects.

Those who knew how to construct the terraced fields and *chinampas*, and increasingly those who provided direction for the villagers to supplicate the various deities who were believed responsible for the erratic behavior of nature, emerged as leaders. In particular, the priest class developed an important and mysterious role within the community. Soon the priests began calling for the construction of structures to serve as a place where presentations to the gods could be made. As their role grew, priests initiated the practice of requiring the population to pay tribute to benefit the society religiously and economically. Under this approach the governing system collected different products and foodstuffs grown or manufactured within its area of control; these were later distributed as necessary.

Olmec and Mayan Civilizations

The advances in agricultural techniques and the rise of the priest class facilitated the evolution of a stratified social organization. From about 1500 B.C. to 200 B.C. the first stratified civilizations appeared in Mexico, including the Olmecs and the people of Monte Albán. For our purposes, *civilization* means an urban society possessing a complex social organization of labor, politics, and religion as well as the ability to write. Debate has swirled around which group was the "first" civilization in Mexico.

The prevailing view claims that the Olmecs, who settled in what are now the modern states of Tabasco and Veracruz, were probably the first civilized people in Mexico. Their cities appeared around 1200 B.C., with the zenith of their power occurring around 700–400 B.C.; this bridges the archaic and classic periods. The center of the Olmec civilization was the city of La Venta, constructed out of the swamps of Tabasco. Two other important Olmec sites were Tres Zapotes and San Lorenzo. All three urban centers influenced people only within their immediate vicinity, thereby suggesting that the Olmecs lacked a centralized political organization. In an organizational model found elsewhere in Olmec sites, the urban area at La Venta included a ceremonial center where priests placated the various gods. They also practiced a form of hieroglyphs (a pictorial type of writing, a key stage in creating a writing system), and the city supported a substantial population numbering around 18,000.

La Venta demonstrated certain characteristics necessary for an urban area to expand. Not the least was the production of surplus foodstuffs, which freed a portion of the population to engage in other activities (e.g., the construction of ceremonial centers and irrigation systems) conduct trade, and pursue a variety of art forms. The size of the city also suggests a highly organized religious and political leadership with a ruling elite that governed the city and its population.

In the Olmec civilization, various art forms emerged as an important indicator of a stratified society. Two distinct art forms were large stone heads—measuring nearly nine feet in height and weighing an estimated 40 tons each—and figurines made of jade. The large heads' Negroid characteristics have caused speculation regarding migration from Africa to the Americas, but that theory has not received widespread support. More likely, as Nigel Davies, author of *The Ancient Kingdoms of Mexico*, suggests, migrants from Asia would have included peoples with Negroid characteristics.[2] In the jade figurines and other artifacts, the jaguar was the central feature; at times the jaguar face was combined with human bodies to create "were-jaguars." Political leaders blended jaguar and human imagery to demonstrate their power over their people. The were-jaguar represented a complex array of religious beliefs associated with the gods of rain and fertility, and also with the god of the earth. Recent work on the murals found in the Mayan city of Bonampak, painted in the eighth century A.D., reveals the presence of the were-jaguar. This suggests that the were-jaguar imagery was widespread across time and geographic region in early Mexico.

Toward the middle of the first millennium B.C. the Olmecs disappeared for reasons that remain a mystery: Either another group gained control over them, or the surrounding area failed to support their existence. Nonetheless the Olmecs played a vital role in shaping human civilization in Mesoamerica, because many of the civilizations that followed adopted their ideas, practices, and values. For example, jade was valued more highly than gold; other groups appreciated the quality of the Olmecs' beautifully skilled carvings; the ritual handball game became an important component of future civilizations; and human sacrifice, believed to have been practiced by the Olmecs as offerings to the gods, became a key feature of subsequent civilizations.

As the Olmec civilization declined, the people in Monte Albán (located just outside of present-day Oaxaca City) rose to prominence. Established on a high mountain top, by 200 B.C. Monte Albán displayed features of an organized urban society with a system of writing. The existence of similar art carvings in the principal Olmec cities of Tres Zapotes, La Venta, and San Lorenzo and the people of Monte Albán suggest that important contacts, perhaps even some form of trade, were taking place between these peoples and places.

CLASSIC PERIOD

During this period two groups emerged in Mesoamerica that represented the flowering of cultural, architectural, and scientific developments: the people of Teotihuacán in the Valley of Mexico; and the Mayans, who established their centers in the Yucatán extending into present-day Guatemala.

Teotihuacán

In the Valley of Mexico, Teotihuacán emerged as the most important and largest city of the era. Called by the Aztecs "the place of the gods," it bridged the pre-classic and classic periods. Its location along the route to the valley of Puebla was probably important for trade or military purposes. Eric Wolf, author of *Sons of the Shaking Earth*, maintains that the size and location of Teotihuacán helped deter the migration of nomadic tribes, often referred to as barbarians, from descending into the Valley of Mexico. Only after Teotihuacán collapsed around the eighth century A.D. do signs appear suggesting that nomadic groups began to move freely in and out of the valley. Moreover, murals on the walls at

Teotihuacán include imagery of jaguars and coyotes—"predatory beasts" that "marks the coming of a new style of life, borne by new peoples."[3]

Around 600 B.C. early residents of the area around Teotihuacán initiated construction of what eventually became the most spectacular city in ancient Mexico. By 200 B.C. the focus was on major construction projects that included the Pyramids of the Moon and Sun, and the Temple of Quetzalcóatl. By the time of Teotihuacán, Quetzalcóatl had become the dominant deity and was widely worshipped in Mesoamerica. Quetzalcóatl was believed to have instructed the ancient peoples in agricultural practices and was revered as a benevolent god, but the people of Teotihuacán practiced human sacrifice, contradicting the long-held position that he opposed this practice.

Archeologist Nigel Davies argues that by any definition Teotihuacán was a true city because all classes of people lived and worked there, making its role different from that of the Olmec cities. They had served a primarily ceremonial and religious function. In contrast, Teotihuacán played a crucial role as a manufacturing and trading center. Researchers there have uncovered evidence of trade relations with Monte Albán in Oaxaca, and remnants of the Mayan peoples in Veracruz also suggest trade with Teotihuacán. The widespread practice of painting murals on the walls of ceremonial buildings and the places where people lived and worked gave rise to what Davies calls a "painted city," one with broader purposes than ceremonial or religious ones.[4] Walls were adorned with pictures of gods, people, and animals; images of the countryside with trees and flowers; and representations of violence with war insignias and imagery of sacrifice and blood. (Militaristic symbols came late to Teotihuacán as the city faced growing pressure from threatening external forces.) Depicting customs and ceremonies, style of dress and adornments, and evidence of ball games, the murals suggest a diversity of themes extending beyond the religious. Recently the mural art has been reinterpreted in a manner that abandons the previous view of the city as peaceable in favor of one that practiced a significant number of human sacrifices.

By the fifth or sixth century A.D. Teotihuacán had a huge population, numbering approximately 200,000. At the top of the social order stood the priests and kings. These were supported by a large artisan group, an agricultural working base, and a substantial merchant class. The agricultural laborers, assisted by slaves, provided the necessary foodstuffs to feed the population. The artisan class manufactured products in pottery, construction, weaving, and obsidian. Finally, the merchant group distributed these manufactured goods across a wide breadth of ancient Mexico. There is evidence of trade among Teotihuacán, Monte Albán, and the Yucatán, although of the three civilizations Teotihuacán exerted the greatest influence on the others.[5] In fact, it was more influential in terms of trade than military power.

Political rule rested on the leadership of a theocracy, that is, a ruling elite with such a close relationship between political and religious aspects that the two cannot be separated. The priests, with their knowledge of when to plant crops, the working of calendars, and how to construct irrigation systems, soon became vital in directing the city's planning. Indeed, the need for adequate irrigation systems required a strong and central political infrastructure.

The priest caste also helped perpetuate the religious myths that continued to evolve in the pre-Hispanic experience. Some themes appeared with a fair degree of consistency in the various civilizations that rose and fell in Mesoamerica. The jaguar became an important element in the Aztec Smoking Mirror god. The legend of Quetzalcóatl, also known as the Feathered Serpent or Plumed Serpent, first appeared at Teotihuacán and was later adopted by the Aztecs. The names for Quetzalcóatl evolve from the Nahuatl words *coatl*, meaning serpent, and *quetzalli*, meaning green feather, the highly prized quetzal feathers.[6] The brilliant green colors of the quetzal feathers were highly regarded and were used in the making of ceremonial dress for the Aztec rulers. The symbolism was vital in the Mesoamerican experience because the bird-serpent represented the land and sky, connected in this case by this deity. Quetzalcóatl assumed numerous responsibilities ranging from leading the people into the Valley of Mexico, to demonstrating proper irrigation techniques and showing how to plant crops. The benign aspect of Quetzalcóatl appears to be contradicted by evidence from the codices of human sacrifice for his benefit. At Tula, the city that arose following the collapse of Teotihuacán, Quetzalcóatl appeared as the patron of the warrior society. By the time of the Aztecs, however, Quetzalcóatl had re-assumed a benign image.

Even though information about the history of Teotihuacán continues to grow, exactly why the city collapsed remains a mystery. It appears that Teotihuacán experienced a rising level of apprehension, with its power over its neighbors beginning to wane in the fifth and sixth centuries A.D. As its political and economic influence declined, the role of the military grew. Wolf points out that the increased prevalence of weapons and militaristic themes at Teotihuacán represent a twofold possibility. One, the military increased in response to threatened attacks by external forces. Two, a larger military presence was required for the ruling class to exercise control over the populace.

It is certain that the city was overrun in the eighth century A.D., with ample evidence that buildings were burned down or torn down. The ceremonial centers were targeted in particular, suggesting that the people may have grown disillusioned with their gods. Moreover Teotihuacán, like other Mesoamerican cities (and, for that matter, other cities in ancient history), faced almost constant threats from barbarian groups roaming on the outskirts of the city or the frontier. But what made it ripe for attack by nomadic forces? One theory is that the region around the city that provided the necessary foodstuffs was no longer capable of feeding the growing population. Yet critics of this theory point out that food could have been imported from regions on the periphery of Teotihuacán's control. A more commonly accepted theory is the "giants with feet of clay" hypothesis, which posits that the agricultural system may not have advanced technologically to keep up with the demands of the growing population. Despite the splendor of the city's buildings, arts, and crafts, the farmers around Teotihuacán did not develop advanced farming techniques. They still planted with the digging stick, did not utilize the technology of the wheel, and did not enrich the soil.

Pressured by a growing inability to feed itself, the city likely faced increasing social tensions. Such conditions, with a populace angry with the leadership, would have made them vulnerable to external aggression. This is but one argument used to explain the collapse of some of the ancient civilizations that existed in Mexico prior to the arrival of the Spaniards. Future evidence may well render this argument invalid.

Mayan Civilization

A few centuries after the fall of Teotihuacán, the Mayan civilization flourished. Often considered the most brilliant of the classic groups and the most advanced scientists of ancient America, the Mayans probably entered their own classic stage around A.D. 300. Although they are not credited with the invention of writing or calendars, the Mayans improved both these systems. In fact, their method of recording dates on *stelae* or stone pillars has been deciphered by specialists, thus allowing scientists to convert Mayan dates to the Judeo-Christian calendar. Once believed to serve a distinctly religious purpose, Mayan hieroglyphic writing is now thought to record the Mayan historical past. Their concern with calendars led to extensive observation of the stars and planets. They constructed their cities so that buildings were aligned with the activity of the stars, enabling the Mayans to determine equinoxes and solstices. Moreover, their knowledge of calendars enabled the Mayan priests to direct the planting and harvesting cycles. In this way the priests gained positions of authority and cemented their role as social leaders.

Much of our knowledge about the Mayans comes from the work of the Spanish bishop Diego de Landa, who wrote the *Relation of Things of the Yucatan* (1566). Diego de Landa reported that the Mayan social order was complex and highly stratified; close cooperation existed to ensure the preservation of the greater order. Ironically, much of what Diego de Landa wrote came after he had participated in the widespread destruction of symbols of the Indian cultural and religious life.

The nature of Mayan rule differed markedly from that of Teotihuacán due to the decentralized political system. The Mayans did not have one central political/religious center; rather several important centers were scattered around the Yucatán, southern Mexico, and reaching down into the isthmus of present-day Central America. In many ways the development of the Mayan civilization mirrored that of the Olmecs, who also did not have a centralized political organization. For example, the decentralized political system contributed to stability and longevity. Because there was no central city to attack it, it was difficult for invading forces to make significant inroads into the Mayan civilization.

Evidence points to a well-established trade between the Mayans and the peoples of Monte Albán and Teotihuacán. Diego de Landa reported that the Mayans produced cloth and pottery, which allowed their influence to extend throughout Mesoamerica via trade. Extensive trade underscored the role of Mayan economic practices, including the concept of market days and a system of credit. The dual role of trade and religion promoted a strong urban focus.

Experts have long believed that the Mayan cities' primary function was ceremonial, partly because this was the nature of Olmec cities. Recent work, however, has revealed that the Mayan cities had functions closer to that of Teotihuacán in that they were well-established urban centers with substantial populations that supported the religious/political leaders or the theocratic social order. In order to support widespread trade among the Mayan cities as well as with Monte Albán and Teotihuacán, the Mayan urban populations had to have served a role beyond support for ceremonial functions.

One of the long-standing positions on the Mayans was that they were not given to warfare and were in fact a peaceful people. Yet recent scholarship and research—in particular, based on evidence from recently excavated Mayan tombs—reveals that violence and sacrifice were central to the Mayan religious practices. Because they valued human blood as a supreme offering to their gods, the Mayans employed a variety of practices to present blood to them. This included the piercing of body parts such as ears, noses, tongues, and genitals. Moreover, growing evidence suggests that the Mayans practiced forms of cannibalism as a way to demonstrate supremacy over those they consumed as well as to acquire some of their victims' strength.

Toltec Civilization

Following the collapse of Teotihuacán the first occupants of the destroyed city were probably the Nahuas, who had participated in its destruction. Because power no longer emanated from Teotihuacán, another group known as the Toltecs soon dominated the area north of Teotihuacán called Tula. Even though they had helped bring down the city of Teotihuacán, the Toltecs adopted many of the practices established prior to its collapse.

In particular, they adopted religious practices surrounding Topiltzin-Quetzalcóatl. According to legend Topiltzin-Quetzalcóatl moved his people to Tula, where a significant struggle between the gods took place. The story of that struggle provided the basis for one of the most important pre-Hispanic legends in the Amerindian pantheon of gods.

Although they were willing to follow Topiltzin-Quetzalcóatl to Tula, the Toltecs brought with them the worship of Tezcatlipoca (in Nahua his name meant Smoking Mirror.) According to the Toltecs, Tezcatlipoca demanded human sacrifice, a practice that Topiltzin-Quetzalcóatl attempted to stop. In many ways their differences represented the symbolic struggle between good and evil, and in fact the ensuing contest between the two gods indirectly helped Hernán Cortés in 1519. According to the later Aztec interpretation, Topiltzin-Quetzalcóatl consumed too much alcohol, thus humiliating himself and his family. His response was to flee to the east, where he marked his way by shooting arrows through saplings (which created the symbol of the cross, the same symbol the Spanish would be wearing and carrying when they arrived). He vowed to return in the Aztec year One Reed, which corresponded to the European calendar year 1519.

Tula represented a paradox of contradictions. The city became iden-

tified with the ideals of civilization in the period after the fall of Teotihuacán, yet those ideals represented the achievements of Teotihuacán
rather than innovations by the Toltecs. The nature of Toltec rule emphasized a powerful militaristic theme. Tula maintained its control through
taxes and tribute from its subordinate people. As the Aztecs also discovered later, the Toltec practices created resentment among their subjects.

By the middle of the twelfth century the Toltec rule extended over
twenty cities. Evidence suggests that in the decade around 1150 rainfall
decreased substantially enough to weaken the ability of the city to feed
itself. This agricultural crisis, coupled with the people's resentment at
having to pay taxes and tribute, weakened the Toltecs' ability to rule.
Increasingly they became vulnerable to aggressive attacks from nomadic
groups, including the Chichimeca (barbarians armed with advanced
weaponry of bows and arrows), who were the Aztecs' ancestors. Civil
instability, coupled with pressure from the barbarians, contributed to the
fall of the Toltecs.

Aztec Civilization

Knowledge of the Aztecs comes from the Aztecs themselves, and thus
the information remains uncertain. The Aztecs began to systematically
rewrite their history in the early days of their empire to justify their
dominant role in the Valley of Mexico and the expansion of their frontier
with their practice of human sacrifice. Known as the Mexica, they were
part of the nomadic groups called the Chichimeca who appeared in the
Valley of Mexico sometime in the twelfth century. It was during this
century that the Aztecs first established a home in the area around Chapultepec hill located in present-day Mexico City. They spoke Nahuatl,
one of the languages within the pantheon of Amerindian languages.
Some researchers suggest that this may not have been their native language but, like other aspects of their culture, was adopted as they moved
around and ultimately settled in the Valley of Mexico.

The Aztec chroniclers maintained that they left "Aztlán" when their
god Huitzilopochtli instructed them to leave their ancestral home. Huitzilopochtli demanded that human sacrifices be performed in his name.
Most likely the Aztecs came out of northern Mexico, as did their predecessors in the Valley of Mexico. During the collapse of Teotihuacán they
probably descended into the valley, where they wandered around during
the height of the Toltec rule at Tula. Those who had established control

in the valley disregarded the Aztecs as uncivilized, although they recognized their ability as mercenary soldiers.

Their early years were ones of almost constant wandering and flight from enemies. Repeatedly the Aztecs would do something that horrified their neighbors around the valley, and they were forced to live in the most inhospitable regions around Lake Texcoco. Their neighbors criticized them for stealing women and practicing human sacrifice. Nevertheless their skill as fierce warriors caused many neighboring groups to hire them even knowing the nature of their behavior.

One story highlights the Aztec barbarity. The Aztecs hired on as mercenaries to their neighbors of Culhuacán. The Culhuacán leader, Coxcox, pledged the Aztecs their independence if they and the people of Culhuacán were victorious. After the victory Coxcox kept his promise and even gave the Aztecs one of his daughters, in the mistaken belief that they were about to bestow a great honor on her. When Coxcox returned to the Aztec village he discovered that she had been sacrificed and flayed; one priest was even dancing in her skin! Attacked by Coxcox and his soldiers, the Aztecs once again fled, this time settling in a most inhospitable place—the mud flats located around the lake in the Valley of Mexico. Their crude existence, coupled with the nearly universal dislike of the Aztecs by the people along the lakeshore, forced the Aztecs to develop an attitude of self-sufficiency rather than reliance on their neighbors.

Out of the mud flats grew the center of the Aztec empire. Two cities first appeared: Tlatelolco and Tenochtitlán. It is believed that Tlatelolco was the first city settled by the Aztecs, but Tenochtitlán soon became the center of their power. The re-founding of Tenochtitlán has been surrounded by numerous and sometimes conflicting legends. The long-standing story maintained that the Mexica wandered aimlessly until they spotted an eagle perched on a cactus clutching a serpent in its beak. According to the Aztec chroniclers, the eagle was sighted at the site of Tenochtitlán following their flight from the soldiers of Coxcox. More recent archaeological evidence suggests that this romantic view was a myth manufactured by the Aztec chroniclers. Despite being forced to relocate, their services as successful fighters always brought them back into contact with the powers around the lake.

Mexica Religion

The religion adopted by the Aztecs represented a synthesis of religious elements indigenous to Mesoamerica. The Mexicas' identification with previous political/religious organizations ensured stability and continuity. According to the Mexicas the world had existed previously in periods divided into "suns." During four earlier suns human beings had appeared and food products and animals had evolved for human consumption; each time improved on the development in earlier suns.

The Mexica believed the fifth sun was due to collapse. Operating under this fatalistic outlook, they established practices to further the life of the sun. Believing that their gods had made sacrifices to create and set in motion the sun, they felt it was incumbent on the Mexica people to provide an equally valuable and significant sacrifice to the sun in return. In understanding the value of human blood to sustain human life, the Mexica believed that the offering of human blood was essential to further the life of the sun as well. Thus they regarded their victims as messengers to their gods who would express the reverence and sincerity of the Mexica people. The need for sacrificial victims soon underscored the role of military, political, and social conditions. In particular it necessitated the practice of ritual war, whose primary purpose was to acquire sacrificial victims.

The practice of human sacrifice has made it difficult for people to evaluate the Aztec religion in a balanced manner because their brutality prevents objective analysis. Yet the Aztecs' intent was to placate their gods by offering the most valuable gift they could. Shooting a victim with arrows so that his blood dripped on to the ground was believed to symbolize falling rain and a manner by which to revitalize the soil.

Political Evolution

After 1431 and the defeat of the allied tribes over the city-state of Atzcapotzalco, the Aztecs (as the Mexica were now known) initiated a process of total domination over the Valley of Mexico and the surrounding lands. In part this occurred through the political foresight of the Mexica elite leader Tlacaélel, who was the power behind the throne in Tenochtitlán from 1431 until his death in 1480. He twice turned down the throne, having decided that he could wield greater power behind the scenes. He was a cunning, ruthless, and brilliant manipulator of leaders and men.

Almost immediately after the victory over Atzcapotzalco, Tlacaélel and the ruler of Tenochtitlán, Itzcóatl, began to acquire land and tribute payments. The two men also created a well-orchestrated military aristocracy that was loyal to the new state, in this case the city of Tenochtitlán. Their method involved two approaches. One, they gave land to those who demonstrated prowess on the battlefields and authority to govern the people who lived on those lands; these grants were for life. Two, they rewarded success on the battlefields with hereditary awards, thereby in a rapid and sweeping manner creating an aristocracy that was loyal to the state.

Below the new elite class were those who sustained the city-state: the *mayeque*, or serfs, who worked the land and paid tribute; and also slaves, artisans, and merchants. Unlike the European system of slavery, Aztec slaves possessed certain rights. For example, they could purchase their freedom, and their children were born free. The origins of the Indian slave caste system also differed from the European model. In Tenochtitlán many slaves were criminals whose penalty did not merit death, prisoners of war who were not used for human sacrifice, or people who could not honor their debts (they became slaves until they were capable of purchasing their freedom).

Culture and Mythology

The Aztecs created distinctive pottery and were highly skilled in weaving. They also produced valuable works in feathers and made tools of obsidian (a volcanic rock). Their ability to work with obsidian was extensive, as evidenced in the many archaeological finds of obsidian products manufactured by the Aztecs and traded widely throughout Mexico. The merchants who managed this trade served a dual purpose for the empire. They obtained goods desired by the elite while at the same time acting as the eyes and ears of Tenochtitlán when they traded with other regions of the empire.

The Aztec empire was a highly ordered civilization. It featured impressive buildings and temples as well as important public works projects such as aqueducts and drainage systems that surpassed European achievements. These works are especially significant in light of thus they were built without advanced technological knowledge such as the wheel.

Within Tenochtitlán gender roles were highly structured and promoted the interest of the community over that of individuals. Boys began at an early age to train daily for war and to support the demands of the gods. They were instructed by the warrior-priests about religion, history, and Aztec customs and ceremonies.

Educational opportunities for young girls were limited, partially because they did not play a significant political or religious role in the community. Taught by their mothers about religion and domestic skills, young women learned to play a subordinate role in Aztec society.

The military offered upward social mobility for anyone living within the Aztec realm. Military prowess brought the rewards of land and labor. It was also from this group that judges, palace officials, priests, and bureaucrats were chosen.

To justify their constant expansion, the Aztecs rewrote their own history and the demands placed on them by their gods. Their god Huitzilopochtli had been a powerful force in their religious pantheon ever since allegedly ordering them to leave Aztlán, their ancestral home. Through their nomadic wanderings they adopted other gods, including the Toltec god Tezcatlipoca. Under the manipulations of Tlacaélel, Huitzilopochtli soon became an equal to the Toltec god.

Huitzilopochtli demanded that human blood be provided for him through various forms of sacrifice. Through the interpretation of Tlacaélel, the Aztecs were given a new purpose that justified their expansion and the rising practice of human sacrifice. According to Tlacaélel the Aztecs were to unify all the surrounding peoples for the purpose of worshipping the Sun god with human blood. By providing human blood the Aztecs ensured the preservation of the sun and thus the earth would continue to provide them with necessary foodstuffs. This goal dominated the ten-year period following the defeat at Atzcapotzalco that saw the Aztecs come to dominate the Valley of Mexico under the leadership of Itzcóatl and the machinations of Tlcaélel.

Itzcóatl died in 1440 and was replaced by Moctezuma I, who ruled for the next twenty-eight years. Under his leadership war became the dominant activity of the Aztecs. They focused the direction of their expansion on what is the present-day state of Veracruz. During their acquisition of territory they encountered one group they could never defeat, the Tlaxcalans, a group that later served as a valuable ally for the Spanish.

Another ominous situation evolved under Moctezuma's reign when a series of climatic disasters severely decreased the food supply. Believing their gods to be angry and needing to be appeased, the Aztecs stepped up the number of sacrifices. Yet finding enough people for the religious sacrifices was a problem. Not to be thwarted by such logistical issues, the Aztecs developed the Flower Wars. These carefully choreographed battles were designed to obtain victims for sacrifice, not to destroy an enemy. The climatic conditions ultimately abated, but the ominous consequence was the belief that through violence the Aztecs had won the gods' approval.

For the remainder of the fifteenth century, the Aztecs expanded their realm until they were unquestionably the dominant power in the Valley of Mexico and beyond. Following the death of Moctezuma I, fairly unimpressive kings ruled the Aztecs. In all likelihood, the Aztecs were ruled more by Tlacaélel, the individual who determined who would be king and perhaps which poor leaders should be removed. Regardless of weak leadership in the position of king, the Aztecs expanded their realm and unquestionably were the dominant power in the Valley of Mexico and beyond. At the time of their expansion the practice of human sacrifice grew dramatically, forcing the Aztecs to look further away from the Valley of Mexico for the necessary victims. In 1502 Moctezuma II came to power. His ascension to the throne resulted from the death of his brother on the battlefield. Initially, Moctezuma trained for the priesthood while his brother learned how to lead the Aztecs in war, carry out territorial expansion, and ensure that the gods were suitably appeased.

Moctezuma II came to the throne of an empire that included between 11 and 20 million people. Control over such an empire required an enormous political system, or what has been called a palace bureaucracy. Although some of the tribute-paying states exercised a certain degree of control within their own realm, they answered to the bureaucracy located at Tenochtitlán. The Aztec political organization was not a loose confederation of semi-independent states, but rather a highly centralized political entity. One way in which this control can be seen is by understanding that by the beginning of the sixteenth century Nahuatl was the dominant language of the Valley of Mexico and one of the few native elements to survive the subsequent conquest.

The control the Aztecs held over their neighbors was fierce and relentless, and it created enemies within the empire. After approximately 1450, in their attempts to expand territorially and increase the number of sacrifices the Aztecs faced extensive resentment and hostility. Dissension within the empire ultimately allowed the Spanish, led by Hernán Cortés, to obtain important allies against the Aztecs.

At the beginning of the sixteenth century, the Aztecs watched with increasing interest a variety of strange events that they believed portended trouble for the empire. Observers grew nervous when a comet streaked across the sky around 1509, and they were particularly disturbed when the towers on top of the temple of Huitzilopochtli burst into flames and were completely destroyed. Finally, reports from the east of men with two heads and great castles floating on the water alarmed many, including Moctezuma himself.

The worst fears of the Aztecs were realized with the arrival of the Spanish. The sun did not die as their religious leaders had portended,

but what lay ahead was the destruction of their way of life at the hands
of the Spanish.

NOTES

1. Howard Zinn, *A People's History of the United States: 1492–Present*
(New York: Harper Perennial, 1995), 1.

2. Nigel Davies, *The Ancient Kingdoms of Mexico* (New York: Penguin
Books, 1987), 26–27.

3. Eric Wolf, *Sons of the Shaking Earth: The People of Mexico and Guatemala—Their Land, History and Culture* (Chicago: University of Chicago
Press, 1959), 102.

4. Davies, *The Ancient Kingdoms of Mexico*, 78.

5. Ibid., 89.

6. Ibid., 138.

3

The Conquest

Following the establishment of Spanish control in the Caribbean, expeditions went forth searching for gold, slaves, and advanced, wealthy civilizations. In 1517 the Spanish governor in Cuba, Diego Velázquez, ordered Hernández de Córdoba to search neighboring Caribbean islands for more slaves and wealth. In doing so the expeditions made contact on the Yucatán peninsula. The people they encountered there, descendants of the Mayans, initially received them warmly and showed the Spanish their well-built towns that demonstrated considerable community organization, more than the Spanish had discovered in the Caribbean. But the cordial reception was short-lived. The Indians attacked the Spanish in a fierce manner, unlike anything they had experienced on the Caribbean islands. Numerous Spaniards died, including Córdoba, who succumbed to his wounds after returning to Cuba.

Following Córdoba's return and stories of the Indians, Velázquez sent Juan de Grijalva. He landed north of where Córdoba had landed, in the present-day state of Tabasco. Grijalva made contact with a group of Indians and learned that a larger, established empire lay to the west. However, lacking aggressiveness to make an independent decision to expand the directives of his mission, Grijalva did not pursue any more information about this empire.

Although the Grijalva exploration did not yield great returns except in the form of information, his reports induced Governor Velázquez to send out more expeditions. This time he sent Hernán Cortés, who he believed possessed great initiative and loyalty to the Spanish Crown. Velázquez's decision to send Cortés was a brilliant move in terms of Spanish imperialistic goals but an unwise choice in terms of the future success of the Cuban governor, and a fatal step for the Indians. By departing Cuba free from the authority of Governor Velázquez, Cortés was able to bypass the authority of the governor and ensure great wealth and prestige for himself rather than share it with Velásquez.

Cortés had been in the Indies for fourteen years when Velázquez selected him to explore the mainland and confirm both Córdoba's and Grijalva's reports. Cortés had grown up in a poor family from Extremadura, the poorest section of sixteenth-century Spain. He had studied law but soon grew bored with it and decided to sail for the Indies at age 19. There he established a reputation as an able administrator and soldier. Ultimately, and reluctantly, he accepted an *encomienda* (a grant that allowed a Spaniard to control the people living on the land) and began growing sugar destined for trade in Europe. However, lacking the drive to be a successful agriculturist, Cortés grew tired of raising sugar in Cuba and considered alternative ways to direct his energy.

Meanwhile he heard the rumors about a well-established kingdom on the mainland, so he began recruiting men to accompany him on an exploratory trip to the Yucatán. His plans, however, disturbed the Cuban governor, who feared he could not control Cortés or pay for the cost of the expedition. Moreover, Governor Velázquez received reports that Cortés might initiate a rebellion and sail for the mainland without permission. Hoping to thwart Cortés, Velázquez rescinded his authority to leave Cuba and ordered his arrest. Cortés defied the governor and on February 10, 1519, departed for the mainland, stopping along the Cuban coast to obtain more men and supplies. Three days after leaving Cuba, Cortés took stock of his men and supplies: He had 508 men, 32 crossbowmen, 13 gunmen, 10 bronze guns, and 16 horses; the expedition also included some Indian women and blacks.[1] Other ships joined the Cortés expedition in the summer of 1519, bringing much needed supplies, men, and war material.

THE CONQUISTADORS

Information about the conquistadors has been shrouded in the myth of the conquest and, in particular, the myth surrounding the leadership and behavior of Cortés. Because of the lack of reliable documentation, it is difficult to explain the actions of a relatively few men in the New World, Spain's evolution as an international power, and the violence used to conquer the Aztec empire. Also, it is important to understand that the well-known names from the historical record are "not truly representative of the great majority of the conquistadores."[2]

Who were these men, and what were their motives for engaging in the highly dangerous actions that constituted the conquest? The majority of the conquistadors came from Spain, but some were from Portugal and Italy. Foreigners in Spain, such as Jews and Conversos (i.e., Jews who had been forced to convert to Catholicism), had to bypass restrictions prohibiting their participation in overseas travel. The existence of foreigners in the ranks of the conquistadors, and their eagerness to defy royal edict, suggests that an organizer of an expedition would take nearly anyone willing to take great risks. Most of the conquistadors were relatively young: More than 60 percent were between the ages of 20 and 40, and the oldest recorded age was 72! Women, probably as many as twenty, accompanied the explorers of New Spain,[3] the name by which the Spanish referred to Mexico in the colonial era.

More than twenty-seven occupations have been listed for the conquistadors; sailors and soldiers constituted less than half. Many occupations had logical connections to the conquest. For example, blacksmiths, carpenters, surveyors, tailors, gunsmiths, doctors, craft workers, and others used their skills to keep the conquistadors supplied with tools, clothing, and so on. Significantly, these men did not represent the elite elements of Spanish society (or European society, for that matter). Instead they constituted social elements that regarded the explorations as an avenue for social or economic advancement. Ironically many of these individuals did not experience either economic or social advancement; instead approximately 60 percent died during the conquest of Tenochtitlán. Of the survivors, "a fair number eventually lost part or all of their personal wealth"; it remained for the children of the first conquistadors to obtain the success that their fathers sought.[4]

THE SPANISH AT VERACRUZ

As Cortés and his men made their way from the Yucatán toward what is now the city of Veracruz, a chance encounter occurred that became significant in influencing the Spanish success during the conquest. On one of their landfalls Cortés's expedition encountered a Spaniard, Jerónimo de Aguilar, who had lived on the mainland since surviving a shipwreck in 1511. Fortunately for Cortés, he knew the local Mayan dialect. Near Veracruz another piece of the linguistic puzzle was completed when local tribesmen gave the expedition several women. One had grown up speaking Mayan but since her early adult years had learned Nahuatl, the language of the Aztecs. The Spanish christened her Doña Marina (although Mexicans later called her La Malinche, because her role with the Spanish has been regarded as treasonous). Thus through de Aguilar and Doña Marina the Spanish could converse with the Aztecs.

When the Spanish landed at Veracruz, Cortés's legal position was tenuous at best. He needed to legally cement his position to continue exploring independently of Cuban governor Velázquez, who had tried to stop him from leaving. All Spanish expeditions required royal approval; without such authorization further explorations were considered illegal. Therefore the Spanish established Veracruz in the king's name and appointed councilmen and other officials to whom Cortés officially resigned his authority. The newly established town officials promptly elected him captain with full judicial and military authority until royal orders arrived.

AZTEC KNOWLEDGE OF THE SPANISH PRESENCE

Meanwhile reports filtered back to Tenochtitlán of strangers in the land. Evidence suggests that the Aztecs knew of the Spanish explorations that reached the Yucatán in 1511, 1517, and again in 1519 when Cortés landed there. Miguel Leon-Portilla, author of the Aztec account of the conquest entitled *The Broken Spears*, writes that messengers informed Moctezuma of light-skinned strangers with beards who arrived from the east in "towers or small mountains floating on the waves of the sea."[5] Aztec uncertainty regarding the Spanish apparently led them to employ an appeasement strategy: Moctezuma presented gifts to the Spanish while trying to convince them not to come to Tenochtitlán. The policy of delay allowed two things to occur. One, the Aztecs hoped to learn whether the Spanish were the embodiment of the legendary Quetzalcóatl or his representatives. Two, the Aztec indecisiveness gave the Spanish time to learn about the Aztecs and establish alliances with several neighboring Indian factions who were dissatisfied with Aztec control. The Aztecs hesitancy also gave Cortés time to learn about and exploit the legend of Quetzalcóatl and turn it to the Spanish advantage.

An important component of the conquest was the legend of Quetzalcóatl. The most popular explanation is that the Aztecs (including Moctezuma) believed the Spanish (in particular, Cortés) were either Quetzalcóatl himself or his representatives returning to reclaim his authority over the Mexica peoples. According to Aztec mythology Quetzalcóatl had been light skinned, occasionally wore a beard, and was a benign, generous leader of the Mexica who abhorred human sacrifice. In a struggle between various deities Quetzalcóatl had been humiliated and fled to the east, vowing to return someday. The appearance of the light-skinned, bearded Spanish from the east, on the water, in the year that Quetzalcóatl had been prophesied to return, has been used to explain the Aztec hesitancy.

Latin American historian J. H. Elliott writes that Moctezuma may have hesitated in dealing with the Spanish out of uncertainty about their religious position, or he may have simply employed the standard Aztec treatment of immunity toward ambassadors of other lords and allowed the Spanish entry into Tenochtitlán.[6] Regardless of the reasons, the Spanish made it to the center of the vast Aztec empire rather easily.

The Aztecs possessed a numerical military advantage that should have allowed them to defeat the Spanish, but they failed to do so. Why the Aztecs allowed the Spanish to so easily enter Tenochtitlán remains a mystery, but the evidence implies that the Aztecs believed the Spanish were somehow connected to Quetzalcóatl. Also, the Spaniards' Indian allies played an important role in providing sanctuary, food, shelter, and most significant, numerical strength on the battlefields. The various tribal groups facilitated the ease with which the Spanish moved from the coast to the Valley of Mexico.

THE MARCH TO TENOCHTITLÁN

Armed with dubious legal authority granted by the newly created Veracruz town council, the explorers moved inland toward the Totonac city of Cempoala. At the Indian city the Spanish learned that the Aztecs had recently established control over the Totonacs. The Cempoalan leader informed Cortés about the Aztecs' oppressive practices against his people, but announced they "dared do nothing without Moctezuma's orders."[7] They operated in fear of the Aztecs, reluctantly providing tribute as demanded of them.

The hostility expressed by the Totonacs toward the Aztecs became a recurring theme as the Spanish marched toward the Aztec capital. Indeed, internal divisions within the Aztec empire served Cortés well as he attracted Aztec opponents to his side. He recognized the value of political instability early on, stating that "every kingdom divided against itself will be brought to desolation."[8]

Shortly after the Spanish entered Cempoala, Aztec tribute collectors arrived. According to Bernal Díaz del Castillo, a Spanish conquistador who accompanied Cortés to Mexico, their primary purpose was to observe the Spanish and to express Aztec displeasure at the Totonacs for welcoming the Spanish. Cortés encouraged the Totonac leaders to seize the tribute collectors, emphasizing that he would protect the Totonacs. Because imprisonment of an Aztec collector was viewed as a deliberate affront to Aztec authority, the Cempoalans' action created a de facto alliance with the Spanish. Later that evening Cortés released two of the collectors, presenting himself as a friend. He told them to return to Tenochtitlán with his best wishes to Moctezuma and insisted that he wanted to meet with the Aztec leader.

When the Totonacs discovered the two collectors had left, they feared punishment from Tenochtitlán; but Cortés still promised protection. According to Bernal Díaz, the Totonacs announced "they would join their forces with ours against Moctezuma and all his allies."[9] Neighboring towns, which also resented Aztec hegemony, stopped paying tribute and declared their support for the Spanish and opposition to the Aztecs.[10] Leaders at Tenochtitlán responded by sending a force to Cempoala to punish their defiance, but the Spanish and their new allies defeated the Aztec advance.

From Cempoala, Cortés and his men met the Tlaxcalans who had repeatedly opposed Aztec domination. Twice during Moctezuma's reign the Aztecs had attempted to destroy the Tlaxcalans, and twice the Aztec warriors had limped back to Tenochtitlán defeated. Initially the Tlaxcalans were suspicious of the Spanish because of their early contact with Moctezuma's representatives. The Tlaxcalans also viewed the Cempoalans as tacit supporters of the Aztecs because they had failed to demonstrate open hostility to Aztec control. When the Spanish and the Tlaxcalans met, a fight broke out. The Spanish won, but their psychological edge was somewhat dampened when two of their horses were killed.

The image of a man on horseback unnerved the Indians. Because the horse was not native to the Western Hemisphere, initially the Indians regarded man and horse as a two-headed creature. The man on horseback was but one of the weapons possessed by the Spanish that created consternation among the Indians. The war dogs that European armies had used for centuries were also used with great effectiveness.

The Spanish brought them in the early days of exploration and they proved indispensable in suppressing indigenous armies. Large-framed, aggressive, and presumably fairly wild, these dogs caused genuine fear. Moreover, the Spanish guns and cannons, although difficult to fire and highly inaccurate, produced loud reports and, of course, could kill from a great distance. These weapons added to the Indians' sense of insecurity.

The Spanish victory over the Tlaxcalans had two significant results. One, the Spanish defeated a group that had twice defeated the Aztecs. This earned them respect from the neighboring tribes. Two, after losing to the Spanish, the Tlaxcalans agreed to ally with them. Once again the Spanish were building allies as they moved toward the Aztec capital. As mentioned earlier, the role of the Indian allies has been overlooked in the traditional, romantic view of the conquest. Yet there is no doubt that internal divisions within the Aztec empire, and thus the Indians who supported the Spanish, proved the difference in the Spanish victory. The conquest must be understood as being as much an "Indian conquest" as a Spanish conquest. As J. H. Elliott writes, "Cortés' conquest was as much a revolt by a subjugated population against its overlords as an externally imposed solution."[11]

Noting the Spanish determination and success following their victory over the Tlaxcalans, Moctezuma invited the Spanish to Cholula, where he planned to meet with Cortés. The Cholulans were to take care of the Spanish until Moctezuma arrived. The Spanish were suspicious about this arrangement and their concerns were echoed by the Totonacs and Tlaxcalans who accompanied them to Cholula.

What followed remains open to debate, as the records of the Spanish and the Aztecs differ. The Spanish maintain that their suspicions (supported by Tlaxcalan fears of the Cholulans) were confirmed by a woman who befriended Doña Marina and informed her of a plot to seize the Spanish. Hearing about the plan from Doña Marina, Cortés called the Cholulan leaders to the central square in front of a religious temple, where he had assembled his men and weapons. Once they arrived, at a pre-arranged signal the Spanish and their allies attacked, killing as many as 6,000 Cholulans. The Aztec record, revealed in *The Broken Spears*, accuses the Spanish of carrying out a brutal surprise attack. It does not mention a plot to destroy the Spanish.

Nevertheless the attack resulted in a significant number of Indian deaths and the destruction of much of the city. Moctezuma was apparently amazed at the extent of human and physical destruction. The amount of property destroyed and lives lost—and, more significant, the fact that the attack occurred in the central square in front of a religious temple, caused Moctezuma and his advisors to believe that this was not the action of Quetzalcóatl. The Aztecs did not believe that Quetzalcóatl would sanction such aggressive action in proximity to a religious site. Despite his uncertainty, the Aztec leader continued to discourage the Spanish from coming to Tenochtitlán, arguing that the trip was dangerous and that the city did not have adequate means to house or feed them. But the Spaniards viewed his requests differently. Emboldened by the recent successes and angry over the alleged deception at Cholula, Cortés informed Moctezuma that the Spanish would continue to Tenochtitlán, arriving as friend or foe; the choice was up to Moctezuma. Frightened and falling under an increasingly fatalistic view regarding the Spanish arrival, and fearing that the gods had deserted his people, Moctezuma reluctantly invited the Spanish to Tenochtitlán.[12]

The events at Cholula constituted one of the uglier episodes of the conquest that bolstered later charges of Spanish brutality leveled by European critics. The Dominican friar Bartolomé de Las Casas argued that the massacre served only terrorist purposes. Contemporary observers argue the same position, maintaining that the Spaniards wanted to instill fear in the belief it would assist their domination.[13] One must ask whether the Tlaxcalans acted of their own accord or only with the confident assurance of protection from their new and powerful allies. Probably it was a combination of both; after all, the Tlaxcalan hostility against Tenochtitlán had long been established. Despite these questions it is evident that the incident at Cholula reflected a pattern employed by the Spanish. They deliberately used violence and allowed revenge to influence the behavior of their Indian allies.

Doña Marina's notification of the threat at Cholula has also become an important element in the story of the conquest. To some she embodies a traitor to everything that was indigenous to Mesoamerica. Doña Marina, as Cortés had christened her, had no sense of identification with or loyalty to the Mexica at Tenochtitlán. Instead she chose to protect those who had released her from the slavery she had been cast into by her own people. Moreover, because her protection by the Spanish depended on her role as a translator, she probably sought to elevate her standing by notifying the Spanish of the imminent danger. In all likelihood she had no sense of racial identification or any premonition that her actions would contribute to the decline of the civilization at Tenochtitlán.

From Cholula, Cortés and the explorers marched to Tenochtitlán to meet with Moctezuma and bring word from the Spanish king. As the

Spanish descended the mountain slopes toward Tenochtitlán, they were awestruck by what they saw. Bernal Díaz wrote a glowing report about the size, color, and order of the Aztec capital: "and when we saw so many cities and villages built in the water and other great towns on dry land and that straight and level causeway going towards Mexico, we were amazed and said that it was like the enchantments they tell of in the legend of Amadis, on account of the great towers and cues and buildings rising from the water, all built of masonry. And some of our soldiers even asked whether the things that we saw were not a dream."[14]

In Cortés's *Letters from Mexico* he echoed Bernal Díaz but also expressed a pejorative view shared by many of the conquistadors. "I will only say that these peoples live almost like those in Spain, and in as much harmony and order as there, and considering that they are barbarous and so far from the knowledge of God and cut off from all civilized nations, it is truly remarkable to see what they have achieved in all things."[15]

On November 8, 1519, in one of the great meetings between civilizations, Hernán Cortés and Moctezuma met on one of the causeways linking the mainland to Tenochtitlán. On the water canoes carried hundreds who observed this meeting, and many more people lined the route. Cortés rode on a horse, whereas Moctezuma was carried in a litter. In many ways the manner in which the two men arrived represented important differences in their civilizations' achievements at that moment in history. The Spanish had taught the horse to labor for them, whereas the Aztecs continued to rely on human labor. Moctezuma gave a short speech of greeting to the Spanish that was laboriously translated through Doña Marina and then into Spanish. It is not certain how much either man understood the other, but each replied in friendly terms. It is significant that although the Spanish informed the Aztecs that they were arriving as friends, Moctezuma spoke to Cortés in a manner indicating that the Aztecs still associated the Spanish with Quetzalcóatl. Moctezuma presented the Spanish with gold necklaces and prostrated himself before the visitors before he gave his address. When Cortés dismounted he attempted to greet Moctezuma with an abrazo (a vigorous hug used to express affection between men) but was stopped by those who attended the Aztec leader.

Following more speeches the Spanish marched into Tenochtitlán, where the Aztecs treated them to food, clothing, and lodging. Soon the Spanish concern for what has been called the trilogy of God, Glory, and Gold revealed itself. The Spanish have justified their actions because they brought Christianity to the Indians and eliminated human sacrifice and cannibalism; thus they claim their atrocities were necessary. But the conquest was more about acquiring wealth and improving one's social status. Cortés supposedly said, "I and my companions suffer from a disease of the heart which can be cured only with gold."[16] They demanded that gold be brought to them. Soon the Aztecs presented to the Spanish beautiful pieces of Aztec gold art and jewelry. Not appreciating the intrinsic value of the indigenous art work, the Spanish melted the gold into bars for easier transport.

The Spaniards remained in Tenochtitlán for at least four days before undertaking one of the more symbolic events of the conquest: taking Moctezuma prisoner. The Spanish justified this by arguing that the Aztecs had attacked Spanish forces at Veracruz. The seizure of Moctezuma followed established Spanish patterns employed in the Caribbean and introduced during their early days on the mainland. But the Aztec society was so complex, that the empire did not fall with his arrest. Francis J. Brooks writes that although Moctezuma was clearly a prisoner of the Spanish, the "political structure remained largely intact."[17] Perhaps the population did not understand that their leader was a prisoner. The Aztec account, found in *The Broken Spears*, reveals that the other principal chiefs were angry at Moctezuma after he capitulated to the Spanish arrest; they "no longer revered or respected him." Cortés later explained that Moctezuma ruled "in the style of a prisoner."[18] Dissatisfaction manifested itself in a variety of ways; not insignificantly, few Aztecs visited their leader. They adjusted to his capture but soon disagreed over how they should act. Were they to continue their functions with their lord as a prisoner, or were they to resist the Spanish challenge to their state? In the end, resistance evolved over the continued demands by the Spanish for more gold and for the Aztecs to end the practice of human sacrifice. Even as the arrest of Moctezuma provided the opportunity for the Aztec political leaders to consider changes within the Aztec political infrastructure, another event accelerated these changes.

THE NARVÁEZ EXPEDITION

In April 1519 Cuban governor Diego Valázquez received instructions from the Spanish king extending his authority to the Yucatán. Armed with this royal decree, Velázquez sent a large force under Pánfilo de Narváez in April 1520 to arrest Cortés. Narváez's force was made up of men who had not profited in the Caribbean and regarded the mainland as an opportunity to enhance their status. Hearing of their arrival, Cortés tried to discover if Narváez represented the Spanish king or the Cuban governor. Meanwhile, when the Narváez expedition arrived at Cempoala they immediately portrayed Cortés as a traitor. Without Cortés's knowledge, Moctezuma offered Narváez presents of "food, gold, and cloth" and instructed surrounding villages to supply the Spaniards with food. In truth, Moctezuma attempted to drive a wedge between the two Spaniards, perhaps hoping that Narváez's soldiers would capture Cortés or that the two groups would destroy each other. Soon ambassadors from Narváez met with Cortés, who realized the Spaniards were there to arrest him. After learning what he could—in particular, who had ordered them to Mexico—Cortés sent them back to Narváez. Before they departed he employed a tactic that served him well with Narváez's men: He gave them gold with the implicit promise that more was forthcoming. These bribes tempted the men with dreams of future wealth and raised their doubts as to whether Narváez should arrest Cortés.

Leaving a contingent of men at Tenochtitlán under Pedro de Alvarado, Cortés struck out for Cempoala. He explained to those accompanying him that Narváez was attempting to undermine everything the Cortés expedition had achieved to that point in Mexico. In a night attack during a rain storm, Cortés's forces attacked the Narváez camp and easily defeated the troops; wounded in an eye, Narváez capitulated to Cortés. In negotiations with Narváez's men, Cortés convinced them of the great opportunities that awaited them if they were to join the actions against Tenochtitlán. Thus what began as a potential crisis for Cortés turned to his advantage. When the Spaniards who had been sent to arrest him decided to join him instead, they provided more men (nearly 900 men had sailed with Narváez), horses, and supplies for Cortés's forces in Mexico.

Yet precisely as Cortés turned this event into a positive gain, the expedition received word that Pedro de Alvarado and his men had been surrounded, seven soldiers had been killed and many others wounded, and they desperately needed assistance.

Back in Tenochtitlán, as soon as Cortés departed to respond to the Narváez threat the Aztecs began preparations to reassert their control. Aztec nobles held a ceremony that Colin MacLachlan and Jaime Rodriguez suggest was an attempt to return "the rhythm of life, to demonstrate that the institutional structure continued to function."[19] Specifically they held a ceremony to honor the war god Huitzilopochtli. Elliott suggests that the actions of the priests were an attempt to preserve their own position, which had been threatened by the Spanish proselytizing and efforts to tear down Aztec religious shrines.[20] Cortés had approved the ceremony before heading to the coast to respond to the Narváez expedition. Alvarado concurred with Cortés's decision allowing the Aztecs permission to hold the ceremony, but with the caveat prohibiting human sacrifice. As preparations continued, Alvarado grew nervous about the Aztec behavior and the potential threat toward the small Spanish garrison in Tenochtitlán. Fearing that the massing of native peoples would threaten the Spanish forces, Alvarado ordered an attack against the participants in the ceremonies and they were brutally cut down. Spanish monk Bernardino de Sahagún, who compiled a collection of the Indian version of the Conquest, later wrote, "the blood of the chieftains ran like water."[21] The Spanish attack was the beginning of the battle between the Aztecs and the Spanish forces.

Cortés returned to Tenochtitlán, where he quickly surmised the difficulty of the Spanish situation. The garrison held out for a few days under the increasingly aggressive Aztec attacks, but then, in a move that was disturbing to the Spanish, the Aztecs elected a new lord, Cuitláhuac. Now Moctezuma did not enjoy any influence with the people of Tenochtitlán. Recognizing the danger of their own situation, Cortés decided the Spanish should leave the city. He persuaded a reluctant Moctezuma to speak to the crowds and convince them that the Spanish should be allowed to leave. However, before Moctezuma could finish addressing the crowd, some began throwing stones at him. At least three struck the Aztec king, and his wounds proved fatal. With his death, the Spanish lost any bargaining chip they may have had with the Aztecs while Moctezuma was alive.

Realizing the futility of their situation, the Spanish planned to leave the city at night on July 1, 1520. In earlier struggles with the Spanish, the Aztecs had cut gaps in the causeways to prevent an escape. The Spanish therefore built temporary, light bridges that could be placed across each gap and then moved to the next gap, thus enabling the conquistadors to cross to the mainland. Prior to departing, the Spanish divided up the gold acquired during their stay in Tenochtitlán. Once again Spanish greed revealed itself, and many died as a result. Despite Cortés's warning not to overburden themselves, some of his men carried too much gold. It hindered their ability to move, and it had even worse consequences for those who fell into the water surrounding the causeways. Moreover, despite the Spaniards' having wrapped their horses' hooves in cloth to quiet their sounds as they moved out of the city, Aztec sentinels discovered their attempted escape and sounded an alert. A bloody battle followed as the Spanish fought their way out of the city at considerable cost to themselves and the Aztec population. At least 450 people died that night in the attempted escape; Bernal Díaz estimated that 860 died that night and in the ensuing flight from Tenochtitlán until they reached safety with the Tlaxcalans.[22] The Spanish have since referred to this event as *la noche triste,* or the sad night.

After *la noche triste* the Aztecs, now led by Cuitláhuac, failed to gain allies with the eastern groups whom the Aztecs had never defeated. In all likelihood these groups refused, fearing that their previous support of the Spanish would haunt them if they agreed to an alliance with the Aztecs and the Aztecs were ultimately victorious. It is significant that the failure of Tenochtitlán to secure other allies revealed the level of hostility within their empire toward the Aztec leadership.

Cortés fled to Tlaxcala with the remainder of his men, now numbering a little over four hundred. They remained there from July 1520 until April 1521 recovering from the devastation of *la noche triste* and making preparations to attack Tenochtitlán. The role of the Tlaxcalans after *la noche triste* cannot be overstated. With their assistance the Spanish escaped what might have been total disaster. The Tlaxcalans obtained from Cortes promises of what would be forthcoming should Tenochtitlán fall; in particular, they wanted an end to future tribute requirements. The Spaniards' predicament left them with little choice but to promise whatever was demanded of them. Following the king's request that Cortés return to Spain in 1528, an investigation by the Spanish Royal Court of Cortés behavior was conducted in 1529. This inquiry revealed that "if the natives of Tlaxcala had risen against the Spaniards, they [the latter] would have all been killed, because many Spaniards were wounded and had been badly injured."[23]

Despite the Spaniards' and their allies' losses at the Aztec capital, they never thought about conceding the city. The Tlaxcalans provided additional supplies, and more Spaniards joined the effort when word of the Aztec wealth reached them. By the end of 1520 Cortés had over nine hundred Spanish soldiers and more than one hundred horses. Moreover, the Spanish began to construct ships for deployment on the water surrounding Tenochtitlán against the canoes used by the Aztecs.

Another phenomenon contributed to the weakening response from Tenochtitlán: an outbreak of smallpox that devastated the native population in September 1520. Even Cuitláhuac died from this epidemic, which lasted a little over two months. Known in Europe for centuries, smallpox

was particularly devastating to the Mesoamerican indigenous populations, who had not acquired immunities to it. Most likely the Narváez
expedition introduced the disease to Mexico, and in the end it created
physical weakness and undermined the leadership in Tenochtitlán.
Cuautéhmoc, the last surviving Aztec ruler who replaced Cuitláhuac,
attempted to rally the city against the Spanish but failed to achieve this
goal, as many former members of the Aztec alliance abandoned them
and turned to support the Spanish.

Once the Spanish completed building their ships and organized their
soldiers and allies, they began the assault against Tenochtitlán in May
1521. Initially Cortés hoped to seize the city without destroying it, but
the nature of the battle soon made that idea impossible. With their ships
the Spanish quickly controlled the lake and imposed a blockade to starve
the city into surrender. However, as countless other foreign invaders
have learned, besieged populations possess ways to defeat such tactics;
at Tenochtitlán the Aztecs used their canoes to bring in supplies from
shore at night. Other factors extended the conflict and caused increased
devastation in the cities along the lake. For example, the architectural
design of the houses, with courtyards, narrow streets, and plazas, meant
the Spanish and their allies fought from house to house, resulting in
almost total destruction of the city.

Despite the technological advantage of the Spanish, the people at Tenochtitlán fought bravely and suffered serious casualties as a result. Recognizing that the fighting was not going to be easy, the Spanish
repeatedly urged the Aztecs and their allies to surrender. Later Spanish
defenders suggested that the Aztec determination prolonged the fighting, and thus they claimed the Aztecs shared the responsibility for the
extent of destruction. Rather than risk the lives of his troops through
more house-to-house fighting, Cortés deployed the siege—one of the
most brutal forms of warfare—against Tenochtitlán with awful consequences. The Spanish cut the aqueduct leading into the city, forcing the
inhabitants to rely on the unhealthy water from Lake Texcoco. Thereafter
the city's inhabitants became increasingly sick from drinking the unclean
water.

In June 1521, while the Spanish attempted a massive frontal attack,
the Aztecs counterattacked and captured more than fifty Spaniards. To
the horror of their compatriots, the Aztecs sacrificed them in view of the
Spanish. Bernal Díaz captured the horror felt by the Spaniards in his
description: "We saw them place plumes on the heads of many of them
. . . and for them to dance . . . and after they danced they immediately

placed them on their backs on some rather narrow stones . . . and with stone knives they sawed open their chests and drew out their palpitating hearts and offered them to the idols."[24] These sacrifices and the sheer struggle to escape from Tenochtitlán weakened the morale of Cortés's men so much that he halted all activities in order to regroup.

The fighting continued for the next two months. By August much of the once beautiful city had been reduced to rubble and the stench of decaying bodies hung in the air. On August 12, 1521, many residents of Tenochtitlán began to flee the city, even though this meant exiting through a corridor of Spanish troops and their allies who subjected them to humiliating abuses (e.g., branding them as slaves taken in war, and raping the women). On August 13, 1521, the eightieth day of the siege, the Spanish entered the city. Cuitláhuac was captured by the Spanish, although versions of the story differ. Some suggest that Aztec nobles delivered him to the Spanish or that he was captured while attempting to flee across the lake in a canoe paddled by his warriors, only to be overtaken by a Spanish ship outfitted with sails. Regardless, Cuitláhuac became a prisoner of the Spanish.

The fatalistic outlook of the Aztecs surfaced in the post-conquest period. For many, their defeat represented the failure of their gods. Some scholars have argued that believing in the defeat of their gods enabled them to readily accept the new, victorious European god. Others have suggested that the failure of the Aztec gods facilitated the Spanish domination because following the collapse the Aztecs lost not only their religion but their will to live.

In the passage from the Gulf of Mexico to Tenochtitlán, the Spanish employed brutal methods of torture and fighting to achieve their goal. Through their detailed reports we know the Spanish had some Aztec leaders burned alive when it was revealed that they had killed Spanish soldiers. Others faced torture as the Spanish attempted to learn where the supposed riches of Mesoamerica were located; Cuitláhuac's feet were burned in an attempt to force him to reveal the location of Aztec wealth. After the fall of the Aztec empire, the tribute-paying tribes also fell under the control and violence of the Spanish. The brutality of the conquest illustrates the sixteenth-century European method of warfare and territorial acquisition that included cruel and destructive behavior on the part of the victorious power. The poorly paid and often poorly controlled soldiers routinely destroyed the areas through which they passed. In other words, the behavior of the Spanish in Mesoamerica was no different from that of other European armies at the time.

NOTES

1. Bernard Grunberg, "The Origins of the Conquistadors of Mexico City," *Hispanic American Historical Review* 74:2 (1994): 263–264.

2. Ibid., 259.

3. Ibid., 275–279.

4. Ibid., 276–283.

5. Miguel Leon-Portilla, *The Broken Spears: The Aztec Account of the Conquest of Mexico* (Boston: Beacon Press, 1992), 13.

6. J. H. Elliot, "The Spanish Conquest," in *Colonial Spanish America*, ed. Leslie Bethell (Cambridge: Cambridge University Press, 1987), 33.

7. Bernal Díaz del Castillo, *The Discovery and Conquest of Mexico* (New York: Noonday, 1956), 88.

8. Hugh Thomas, *Conquest: Moctezuma, Cortés, and the Fall of Old Mexico* (New York: Touchstone, 1993), 245.

9. Ibid.

10. Ibid.

11. Elliot, "The Spanish Conquest," 35.

12. Colin M. MacLachlan and Jaime E. Rodriguez O., *The Forgings of the Cosmic Race: A Reinterpretation of Colonial Mexico* (Berkeley: University of California Press, 1980), 72. See also Thomas, *Conquest*, 263–264.

13. Thomas, *Conquest*, 262.

14. Bernal Díaz, *The Discovery and Conquest of Mexico*, 190–191.

15. Francis J. Brooks, "Moctezuma Xocoytl, Hernán Cortés, and Bernal Díaz del Castillo: The Construction of an Arrest," *Hispanic American Historical Review* 754:2 (May 1995): 156.

16. Elliot, "The Spanish Conquest," 32.

17. Brooks, "Moctezuma Xocoytl, Hernán Cortés, and Bernal Díaz del Castillo," 165.

18. Thomas, *Conquest*, 307.

19. MacLachlan and Rodriguez, *Forging of the Cosmic Race*, 73.

20. Elliott, "The Spanish Conquest," 34.

21. Thomas, *Conquest*, 390.

22. Bernal Díaz, *The Discovery and Conquest of Mexico*, 295–326.

23. Thomas, *Conquest*, 428.

24. Bernal Díaz, *The Discovery and Conquest of Mexico*, 436.

4

The Colonial Era, 1521–1821

With the fall of Tenochtitlán, the military conquest of the Indian population was complete. What lay ahead was the conquest of the people in
virtually all other areas of their lives. During this period the Spanish
established the basic pattern of colonization. It differed throughout Spanish America according to the conditions of earlier Indian civilizations,
the complexity of colonial development, and the time in which such development occurred.[1]

Military conquest was but one arena in which the Spanish changed
the Indian way of life. In virtually all areas changes occurred as the
Indians' and European's languages, social customs, economic practices,
religions, and political organizations were blended. In the religious arena
the conquest introduced Christian worship that was combined with indigenous practices. Unknowingly the Spanish defeat carried with it seeds
of earlier practices employed by the Indians. In the pre-Hispanic era,
victory often involved replacing the defeated religious institutions with
those of the victorious religion; this was the case with the Spanish victory
as well. As part of the physical destruction of Tenochtitlán the Spanish
destroyed the Aztec temples, statues, murals, and hieroglyphic records.
Cleric Juan de Zumárraga, the first Christian bishop in Mexico, claimed
to have directed the destruction of some 500 temples and more than

20,000 symbolic representations of Aztec idols.[2] In the center of Mexico City, or the Zocalo, the Spanish built the National Cathedral on top of the ruins of the defeated Aztec temples utilizing material from the destroyed city. This practice was similar to that previously employed by victorious Indians who imposed their gods on their defeated foes, or by Christians in medieval Europe who built their sanctuaries over pagan sacred sites.

Not all the destruction of the indigenous buildings and institutions was actually done at the hands of the Spanish; much of the destruction of native temples and Aztec codices (pictographic representations that recorded the historical record of the Aztecs) was carried out by the defeated Indians at the behest of the Spanish, reflecting a native group dissatisfied with the political and religious direction of their former leaders and gods. Indeed, the authority of the native priests and politicians had decreased with the Spanish arrival. Despite these changes, significant elements of the pre-Hispanic systems survived the Spanish: village societies, agricultural systems, numerous customs and foods, and aspects of Indian language.

THE CHURCH IN THE COLONIES

In many ways the conquest of the indigenous population meant a religious conquest. Ever since the days of the *reconquista* (the reconquest of Spain from Islamic rule) when the Christian serfdoms overthrew the Muslim domination on the Iberian peninsula, the Spanish had acted in the manner of recent zealous converts, committed to spreading Catholicism. Consequently they regarded any non-Christians as heathens who would benefit from the clear light of Catholicism. Thus priests traveled with Cortés in the early days of the march to Tenochtitlán, and the conquistadors' control over the Indians was quickly followed by a systematic effort at conversion to Christianity.

The religion that emerged from the ashes of Tenochtitlán contained elements of Aztec and Christian religious practices. Just as a new race (the mestizo, or mixed blood) and a new nation appeared following the conquest, so followed a religion blending elements of each. As with the Indian political system, a close relationship between church and state existed under the Spanish. Both cultures featured a combined authority between political and religious sectors, and both had comparable practices and similar ideological issues.

Both the Aztecs and Catholics practiced baptism by bathing the infant and naming the child. The Catholic practice of communion with the consumption of wine and wafer to symbolize the blood and body of Christ had similarities to the Aztec practice of eating symbolic images of their gods exposed to sacrificial blood. In both religions people burned incense, utilized the imagery of the cross, fasted, went on pilgrimages, did penance, and accepted the idea of a powerful, supreme mother figure and the concept of a virgin birth. The ancient Mexicans worshipped Coatlícue, the mother of Huitzilopochtli who gave birth after having been "impregnated by an obsidian knife." Coatlícue also was regarded as the mother of the moon and the stars.[3]

The goal of converting the Indians to Catholicism rested on the religious issues stemming from the *reconquista* and the authority vested in the Spanish Crown by Pope Alexander VI, who in 1493 established guidelines to provide a religious explanation for the conquest. Under a series of agreements culminating in the *patronato real*, the Spanish crown acquired extensive authority over the Church in Spanish territories. In 1508 Pope Julius II redefined the *patronato* as it was to be employed in the New World. The Spanish appointed church officials, allowed those officials to immigrate freely without any restrictions from Rome, and gave the Spanish colonial bureaucracy authority to reject papal bulls (official orders from the Pope to his followers) in the colonies. The Church used the tithe to enrich itself and fund its existence, although the Spanish Crown had great liberty with finances that it collected. Meanwhile the Church supported the Spanish political influence, national unity, and absolute royal power by creating a unified and monolithic religious system. Church and state remained intimately connected well into the twentieth century; no other colonial device so profoundly affected the cultural structure of Mexico.

Role of the Missionaries

The first friars in the New World represented the reformist goals of the Catholic Church and combined a sincere social conscience with a love of learning. The early missionaries viewed the native population favorably, admiring their lifestyle that was free from the greed and ambitions of the Europeans. On the other hand, the ascetic lifestyle of the missionaries, together with their willingness to learn native dialects, appealed to the Indians. According to Charles Gibson in his work *The Aztecs under*

Spanish Rule, the Indians accepted much of what the missionaries introduced about Christianity, especially "the great churches, the ceremonies, the processions, and the images of the saints."[4]

The missionaries carried out an important component of the Spanish imperialistic mission: to convert the Indians to Catholicism. Implicitly this meant the destruction of the Indian religious institutions. The emphasis on converting the native population represented a response to Pope Alexander VI's papal bull that required the conquistadors to convert the Indians to Christianity. Spanish efforts to eliminate Indian religious practices resulted in the rampant destruction of anything Indian. Diego de Landa, bishop of Yucatán, destroyed all the Mayan artifacts he could find, although before their destruction he studied and wrote about them. Thus, ironically, he provided historians with one of the most significant insights into pre-Hispanic Mayan civilization.

Following the collapse of Tenochtitlán, Cortés sent for more missionaries to assist in the conversion of the Indians. The first of the orders, the Franciscans, arrived in 1522 armed with a papal bull giving them extraordinary authority. In effect, the papal bull gave the religious orders authority that was independent of the secular state. Such a position marked the origin of discontent between the religious and secular institutions, particularly as the religious orders increasingly criticized colonial practices toward the Indians. The independence of the religious orders provided the means by which clerics could voice their complaints on a wide range of issues.

In 1524 twelve more Franciscans arrived at Veracruz and traveled to Mexico City. They demonstrated their piousness and humility by wearing simple garb and walking barefoot to the capital. When Cortés greeted them "by falling to his knees and kissing the friars' hands," it mightily impressed the Indians that such a powerful leader would bow to poor representatives of the religious order. Thus, as Bernal Díaz later wrote, "when the friars come, the Indians receive them with the same reverence and respect." Among this initial group of Franciscans was Toribio de Benavente, identified by the Indians as "Motolinía or the Poor Little One," arguably one of the most popular priests in Mexico's colonial era. The Dominicans arrived in 1525, bringing a reputation as intellectuals and participants in the Inquisition.[5] Begun in Spain, the Inquisition was a court established by the Catholic Church to try individuals suspected of religious heresy. The Inquisition would also be used in Mexico beginning in 1571. The Dominicans became, perhaps, the most outspoken of the missionary brotherhoods against the poor treatment handed out by the Spanish against the Indians. Bartolomé de las Casas, a Dominican, criticized Spanish Indian policy and has been credited with the Spanish crown's decision to adopt the New Laws in 1542 designed to protect the Indians. Clerical critique of the treatment of the Indians revealed the problems between church and state as the Catholic Church attempted to provide protection while the colonists exploited Indian labor.

Led by Juan de Zumárraga, the first bishop of Mexico City and a man known as the Protector of the Indians, the Franciscans joined the Dominican fight to aid the Indians. The Franciscans introduced a variety of educational opportunities to the Indians. Vasco de Quiroga, another Franciscan, established communities modeled on Thomas More's ideal discussed in his *Utopia*. A sixteenth-century British social and political critic, More's publication influenced a number of European idealists. In these communities the Franciscans taught the Indians technical skills and religious training. Also, the sons of native Indian priests were trained for the Catholic priesthood. Clearly the Franciscans believed Indians could become priests, but other clerics rejected this position, which led to a temporary ban on Indians serving as priests between 1555 and 1591. The Franciscan communities became the models for missions established by different clerics who operated on the Spanish colonial frontier.

Juan Diego

In the conversion of the defeated Indians to Catholicism, nothing so helped the missionary orders as the vision witnessed by Juan Diego, a young Indian, in 1531. At the ancient Aztec religious site of Tepeyac (the temple site of the Aztec earth goddess) Juan Diego claimed he saw the vision of the Virgin Mary. According to the story she spoke to Juan Diego in Nahuatl and instructed him to have a church constructed at this spot so that she could aid the Mexican people. After repeated attempts he finally received an audience with Bishop Juan de Zumárraga, who was convinced only after Juan Diego produced roses from Tepeyac and an image of a dark-skinned Indian woman was found on Diego's cloak. Juan Diego's vision, adopted by the Church, became known as the Virgin of Guadalupe. She became the patron saint of Mexico and thereby elevated the role of Mexico and its population, because many believed the Virgin had specifically chosen to appear in Mexico and before an Indian.

One problem facing the early clerics was the difference in language. Many religious missionaries quickly learned the indigenous languages and thus presented the ideas of Christianity in the native dialects of the people. For example, clerics in the area north of present-day Mexico City received instructions to learn the native dialect so they could preach in the native language and receive confession from the Indians; all this occurred in six months. As an offshoot of this process, some priests began to record Indian oral history.

Depth of Conversion

An issue that has disturbed historians of Mexico ever since the conquest is whether the Indians actually converted to Christianity and, if they did, to what degree they fully accepted its tenets. In the attempt to address this issue, many took the position of early priests who wrote that it was better to have a shallow conversion than none at all. It is not clear in many cases whether conversion was forced or voluntary. Nevertheless the early clerics maintained that they converted a huge number of Indians.

The religion that emerged represented the blending of Aztec and Christianity in a process known as *syncretism*: literally, the fusion of various elements from each religious experience. As a result, any form of conversion implied a not entirely strict acceptance of European Catholicism. Early on, Spanish clerics allowed worship to take place at familiar Indian sites, often at former sites of worship for the indigenous religion. The construction of the National Cathedral in Mexico City on top of the ancient Aztec religious temples was an example. Religious officials also tolerated worship on familiar Aztec religious dates. This pattern of tolerance was designed to ensure a significant number of converts.

As with the Conversos in Spain, it was decided that the Court of the Inquisition was needed in the New World to ensure conversion. The Inquisition soon expanded beyond its original concerns within the religious realm and became an important tool supporting the Crown. In a nation where the church played such a profound role, a charge before the Court of the Inquisition served to tarnish one's reputation. Moreover, to defend oneself required a great deal of time and money.

As it did in Spain, in New Spain the Court of the Inquisition exposed heretics. In the colony the Holy Office of the Inquisition could investigate and punish those charged with religious crimes. A similar device had been utilized in the colony prior to 1571 but had been criticized for aggressive behavior against the Indians that included torture and execution. When the Inquisition was established in 1571 the status of the Indians had been the subject of long debate, and many thought that because of their recent conversion the Indians should not be held to as rigorous a standard as Spanish Christians. The lenient position underscored an important debate among Europeans: Were the Indians human? If they were not, could they be held responsible to understand the tenets of Christianity? Between 1570 and 1820 the Courts of Inquisitions in the colonies heard 6,000 cases, resulting in 100 individuals being burned at the stake. Few of those brought before the Court were Indians, the majority being Protestant or those who had recently converted from Judaism and who were suspected of heresy toward the Catholic Church. Some who appeared before the Court were tried for moral or political offenses.

Many of the institutions the Spanish introduced in their colonies evolved from the Spanish *reconquista*. At the same time, the Spanish utilized pre-existing Indian institutions and practices to ensure the dominance of the victor and ease the administrative demands assumed by the Spanish. A practice familiar to both Spanish and Indian was the rewarding of successful soldiers with land and the authority to direct the labor of the people who populated those lands. The Spanish called these grants *encomiendas*. The recipient (the *encomendero*) was responsible to collect tribute, direct Indian labor, and ensure that the Indians converted to Catholicism. Theoretically, receipt of an *encomienda* did not imply the acquisition of the land, but it underscored the inferior status of the Indians in comparison to that of the Spanish.

Spanish law required that the *encomendero* provide the people with food, clothing, shelter, and religious training. But as would be repeatedly demonstrated throughout the colonial era, the implementation of laws did not mean enforcement. The Spanish argued that the system did not regard the Indians as slaves; the reality, however, suggested that it was slavery in everything but name. The population that lived within a specific *encomienda* was regarded as free, although prohibited from leaving the *encomienda*.

An important function of the *encomienda* was the collection of tribute. This was paid in the delivery of particular products (or, later, payments in cash) or in the form of labor; both were patterns of tribute known to the Indians prior to the Spanish arrival. As noted earlier, the Aztecs had utilized the tribute system. The debilitating effect of the tribute collection grew following the conquest as great numbers of the Indian population died. Yet the rate of population loss was not matched by a decrease in Spanish tribute demands. As a result, the level of delivery became increasingly onerous on the surviving population. Frequently Indian villages sought to have their tribute levels lowered or eliminated as they lacked the ability to meet the demands. Soon the problems caused by the demands of tribute collection added to the growing debate over the Spanish treatment of the Indians.

Dominican missionaries led the attack against the treatment of Indians governed by the *encomienda* system shortly after its establishment. Two suggestions were made. One, as proposed by Bartolomé de las Casas, suggested importing African slaves to reduce the workload expectations of the Indians. The other idea was a radical departure from the European practices toward the Indians. As early as 1510 Father Antonio Montesinos protested the practices employed on the island of Hispaniola. He said he was "the voice of Christ crying in the wilderness of this island" and in doing so raised questions over the right and responsibility the Spaniards had over the conquered people that would be debated over the next half-century. Criticizing the Spanish behavior, Father Montesinos declared, "Are they not men? Do they not have rational souls? Are you not bound to love them as you love yourselves?" Montesinos condemned the Spanish, concluding that "you can no more be saved than the Moors or Turks who do not have and do not want the faith of Jesus Christ."[6]

INDIAN SLAVERY

The institution of slavery had roots in both the Spanish and Indian background. Aztecs and other Indian societies had held slaves; however, a greater sense of freedom existed for Aztec slaves than it did within the European system. During the *reconquista* Spaniards enslaved Muslims, and this practice followed them across the Atlantic, where they began enslaving Indians almost as soon as they arrived. Spaniards speciously justified the enslavement of Indians for a host of reasons. As has been noted, Columbus viewed the peoples of the Caribbean as fitting candidates for slavery the moment the European fleet arrived. Europeans regarded the Indians as pagans who could be enslaved.

Without a doubt the enslavement of Indians sped up the process that disease and murder initiated in the rapid demise of the Indian population. The declining Indian population and the loss of available labor necessitated, from the European viewpoint, a new source of labor. Slowly the Spaniards overcame the lack of capital and lack of control of ports in Africa from which to export African slaves to New Spain. Although the implementation of policy was slow, the idea was not. Ironically, Bartolomé de las Casas, the man who acquired a reputation as the defender of the Indians, proposed supplementing African slaves to replace Indians. Spain first imported Africans into the Caribbean in 1518, and Africans accompanied Cortés in the conquest of the territory that became New Spain.

The primitive technology and lack of sufficient capital available to the Spanish required abundant labor in the agricultural fields and soon in the mines as well; in particular, the colonial agricultural demands necessitated a substantial labor force. As colonial agricultural products (e.g., indigo and cochineal, two dye products in demand by the textile industry) entered the international market, labor demands increased. Moreover the labor force needed on sugar plantations was significant. It is not surprising that to meet the international market demands the Europeans turned to slavery as a means of ensuring a permanent labor force.

Father Montesinos's condemnation resulted in the Crown's search for a legal justification to continue Indian enslavement. Sixteenth-century Europeans justified slavery by adhering to two principles: A person captured in war and an individual already in slavery could be sold into or kept in slavery. As the Spanish conquest continued, they allowed slavery for those who engaged in cannibalism, resisted Catholicism, and opposed Spanish settlements.[7] The Spanish formalized these conditions with the creation of the Laws of Burgos in 1512. Failure to accept any or all of these provisions gave the Spanish the legal justification to enslave the Indians, occupy their lands, and ultimately destroy their very existence.

The laws led to extensive discussions by theologians culminating with the *requerimiento*. It was stipulated that the Spanish read the text of the *requerimiento* to the Indians demanding their acceptance of Christianity and the Catholic Church, as well as the supremacy of the Spanish Crown and the Pope. The Spanish chronicler Gonzalo Fernández de Oviedo y Valdés wrote in 1514 that the Spanish did not attempt to explain the language of the *requerimiento*, "apparently because it was superfluous or inappropriate."[8] The Dominican friar Bartolomé de las Casas reportedly did not know whether to laugh or cry when he heard about the *requerimiento* and its supposed use. He had hoped the Indians and Spanish could peacefully co-exist, with the Spanish gradually teaching the Indians the ideals of Christianity. In his work entitled *Breve Relación de la destrucción de las Indias occidentales*, de las Casas argued that the Spanish treatment caused the deaths of more Indians than did disease.

The debate over the condition of the Indians at the hands of the Spanish continued, perhaps even escalated, as a result of the *requerimiento*.

Regulations appeared in the 1530s regarding tribute and Indian labor, but the pattern of ignoring the law had been long established. In 1542 the Crown established the New Laws of the Indies ending slavery and allowing the release of those enslaved. The New Laws revealed the Crown's concern about the Spanish colonists when it declared that existing *encomiendas* were not hereditary.

Regardless of the attempts by the Crown to employ a labor policy that provided adequate labor for the colony and preserved Indian health, poor conditions continued. De las Casas noted that the Crown had the right to impose tribute-collecting procedures, but that the "unjust, excessive and tyranical" damages imposed on the Indians rendered tribute unjustifiable. In 1552 he announced that if the Indians had been treated well and not suffered "irreparable injuries, [the tribute] could well be justified . . . they should pay the king a certain quantity of gold and other things . . . as a sign and acknowledgement of his universal and sovereign lordship."[9]

With the passage of the New Laws, the *encomienda* system began to wane as an important labor policy. Ending the system reflected the Crown's desire to control the population. For Spain to achieve its mercantilist goals, the Crown needed Indian labor to insure high profits in the colonial economy. What followed was the *repartimiento* that provided labor for colonial enterprises; it also ensured a continuation of colonial Indian exploitation. It demanded that Indian communities deliver adult men to work on public works projects, in the mines, on the haciendas, and even in the *obrajes*, or early textile factories. Theoretically the Indians were paid for their labor, but wages were abysmally low and the exploitation of the *repartimiento* by unscrupulous private industry continued.

One other change influenced the Indian role in the economy and the move from a payment in a particular product to payment in cash. Tributes in cash forced Indians to become more connected with the economy. The impact of cash in the economy has been viewed as having "altered the traditional economy." Although some have bemoaned the changes that were wrought, the Indians did not placidly sit by. They adapted quickly to the cash-driven economy; some even earned wages using the technical skills they learned from the Spanish. Others utilized their artisan skills to participate in the growing capitalist economy. The introduction of cash into the economy provided a new means for Indians to advance their social condition, but many soon found themselves controlled by the European guild system. Initially a device to protect artisan skills and quality of the product, as well as provide an identity, the guilds soon became a controlling device to limit Indian access to the highest ranks. Regardless of these impositions, Indians continued to function in an increasingly important manner within the colonial economy.

WAGE LABOR

The *encomiendas* and *repartimiento* were similar to labor systems utilized among Indians to work for a specific time on public works projects. But the Spanish demand for gold and silver led to greater exploitation of Indian labor. With the explosion of mining, more Indians were required to labor for longer periods of time away from their native homes and in awful conditions. Exploitation of the Indians destroyed the *repartimiento* and the ability of local Indian villages to provide labor. Responding to these changes, the owners of haciendas or mines began paying wages for labor. Initially a temporary arrangement, wage payment soon became a permanent system. As Indians lost their lands or failed to meet the financial responsibilities of the tribute payments or wished to obtain some income, they hired out to the *hacendados*, owners of *obrajes*, or mine owners.

By the early seventeenth century the wage system had replaced all other forms of labor arrangements. Wage labor developed an institutionalized form of control through the debt peonage system. To ensure a stable labor pool, the owners of haciendas, mines, or *obrajes* occasionally advanced their workers wages. Owners also provided workers with necessary tools, clothing (occasionally), shelter, and food, all of which were all advanced against future wages. In the Bajío region, employees often owed their employers as much as six months' wages in accumulated debt.

Historians have traditionally viewed debt peonage as an evil. Little protection existed for the workers because wages remained artificially low. As the system became more institutionalized, owners of haciendas, factories, and mines paid wages in currency that was only acceptable in the company store (the *tienda de raya*). Thus they manipulated wages to keep workers in debt and limit their ability to freely leave. John Tutino's analysis of the debt system has suggested that the arrangement may not have been as onerous as has traditionally been observed. Instead, Tutino argues that the high incident of debt reveals the acute shortage of labor, so that owners actually advanced wages operating from a position where they did not initially expect repayment.[10]

COLONIAL LATIN AMERICAN RACIAL HIERARCHY

Conquest produced four racial categories: Europeans (Spaniards), Mestizos, Indians, and slaves, who eventually created further distinctions in Latin American colonial society. Initially one's position in colonial society was determined by having participated in the conquest. A two-tiered social order followed the conquest, distinguished by conquerors versus conquered. Few experiences in history have offered the opportunity for such a rapid advance in social mobility, because the majority of the conquistadors were not from the elite of Spain. Most came from the working class: tailors, carpenters, masons, shoemakers, and others. In the early days after the conquest they were in a privileged position in Mexico because of their role against the Indians. But with time and the rapid arrival of other Spaniards, one's position or relation to a participant in the conquest became less relevant. Other factors became more important. For example, a Spaniard born in Spain had a higher social standing than an individual with Spanish parents born in the New World. Soon a rigid racial hierarchical structure was established and became so pervasive that any attempt at equality between whites and Indians failed.

The conquest introduced to the Western Hemisphere both the European and the African; the combination of these three races produced what has been called the *mestizo*, initially regarded as a blend of European and Indian. Martín Cortés's birth from the union of Hernán Cortés and Doña Marina symbolized the beginning of this new race. The role of race in determining one's status in colonial Mexico remained important throughout much of the colonial era. Even in the late twentieth century, Indians in Mexico continue to find themselves in a second-class position. With the emergence of early capitalism, lines of racial stratification began to weaken as economic wealth played an increasingly greater role in determining an individual's social position. In other words, wealth proved to be a social leveling device as individuals acquired social status based on wealth.

Europeans dominated the colonial infrastructure. In general, of course, the Iberian born and their offspring born in the New World enjoyed the greatest power and prestige. Many owned large haciendas as well as urban property. Haciendas were large estates that used wage labor to meet the growing demands by the colonial population for foodstuffs. From their position as the landed elite they extended their dominance by controlling the important ministerial and bureaucratic positions, clerical offices, military officer corps, and merchants.

Spaniards

They composed the elite of post-conquest society. Although the Crown limited the authority of the conquerors, Spaniards dominated positions in colonial society. The top of the social ladder contained important divisions determined by place of birth. Spaniards born in Spain were known as Peninsulares. They were regarded as superior to the Spaniards born in New Spain, known as Creoles. A sharp antagonism divided these two groups. Although physically indistinguishable from the Peninsulares, the Creoles' subordinate status limited their access to the top bureaucratic offices.

Able to utilize their access to the Royal Court, the Peninsulares dominated high-ranking and lucrative colonial positions. Many in Spain believed in the inferiority of the colonial environment, arguing that the atmosphere produced an individual who was physically, mentally, and morally inferior. Peninsulares thus viewed the Creoles as lazy, irresponsible, and lacking in physical and intellectual vigor. Pregnant women even returned to Spain so their children would escape the stigma of being born in New Spain. These attitudes and actions created a strong bitterness between Peninsulares and Creoles and contributed to the emerging dissatisfaction between those who identified with the colony and those who identified with the Crown.

Despite being considered second class, Creoles had access to positions of respectability in the Church, the royal bureaucracy, and the local government because of the color of their skin. In particular, local *cabildos* (municipal councils that represented the interests of the local citizens) became important avenues by which the Creoles could advance in the colonial society. The failure of many Creoles to obtain the highest ranking positions created a sense of antagonism within this group toward their Spanish-born counterparts. As a result, from the Creole group emerged the first identification with New Spain rather than with Spain, a phenomenon that can be considered the precursor of a national identification. Dissatisfaction among the Creoles toward the Peninsulares manifested itself early and often during Mexico's colonial era.

Shortly after the conquest the Spanish Crown began to rein in the actions and authority of the conquistadors. As early as 1528 the Crown demonstrated its power when Charles V invited Cortés to Spain. He had to answer a series of dubious charges leveled by his political enemies ranging from theft to murder. The king greeted Cortés warmly, apparently dismissing the charges against him, and awarded him with the title of Marqués del Valle de Oaxaxa. King Charles lavished Cortés with gifts of social order and rank, allowing him to choose the lands for his *encomiendas*, but the king prohibited him from returning to his position as governor of New Spain. In 1563 a Creole uprising in Mexico City led by Alonso and Gil González de Avila conspired to place Martín Cortés at the head of the colonial government, but Martín Cortés remained on the periphery. This potential revolt represented one of the Crown's greatest fears: that distance and poor communication would allow the colonists to usurp the Crown's power in the colony. Spain acted quickly and decisively against the rebellious actions. Alonso de Avila and his brother were found guilty of treason and were publicly beheaded on the Zocalo (the main square in Mexico City). Colonial officials displayed their heads around the city as a reminder of what would happen to those who resisted the Crown.

Mestizos

This group formed the third level of colonial society. The term generally was used to identify offspring of Spanish and Indian unions. In fact, the blending of racial characteristics in a variety of permutations reflected the nearly endless forms of sexual liaisons. For example, a Castizo was an individual who had Spanish and mestizo parents, an Afrotizo had black and mestizo parents, a mulatto had Spanish and black parents, and so on. By the eighteenth century, Spanish bureaucrats officially listed sixteen racial classifications.

Indians

Indians occupied the bottom rung of Spanish colonial society. Despite the Spaniards' initial awe at the achievements of the Aztec and Inca civilizations, they soon regarded the Indians as inferior. This position remains well established into the twentieth century, as Indians continue to have second-class status.

COLONIAL ADMINISTRATION

Although it needed personnel to control the colonies, the Crown limited colonial responsibility in the operation of the colonies. As early as 1503 the Crown created the Casa de Contratación (House of Trade) to arrange explorations. Soon the Casa, directed by Juan Rodríguez de Fonseca, regulated trade, shipping, and immigration to the colonies. As Spanish colonial dominions grew, Spain created the Council of the Indies in 1524. This body governed the growing colonial policies of settlement, governance, distribution of goods, types of products that could be manufactured or grown, and the shipping schedule to and from the colonies. Soon the Council assumed responsibility to advise the Crown and, when necessary, represent the monarch.

Audiencias

In 1527 in an effort to solidify Spanish power the monarchy established an *audiencia*, or Royal Court. Originally the *audiencia* was a court of judicial review. Soon, however, it acquired authority to govern the colonies. The first president of Mexico's *audiencia* was Nuño Beltrán de Guzmán. He arrived in Mexico City with a ruthless and cruel reputation, as well as an intense dislike of Cortés. Armed with his authority he quickly limited Cortés's power. Apparently seduced by his position, Guzmán and his compatriots committed a host of crimes during what became known as one of the worst periods of corruption and injustice in Mexico's colonial experience.

Only one individual challenged the authority of Guzmán: the bishop of Mexico who was a former Franciscan friar, Juan de Zumárraga. Responding to Guzmán's criminal behavior and his attempts to limit clerical authority, Zumárraga used his position to attack Guzmán. He wrote letters to Spain denouncing Guzmán; meanwhile Guzmán had the bishop's letters intercepted. Eventually one of Zumárraga's letters reached Spain. Recognizing the end to his power, Guzmán fled Mexico City in 1529 for the western territories of Mexico.

Thereafter, Spain established a new system for governing the colony. The Crown created a new office called the Viceroyalty. The viceroy was an individual whose loyalty to the Crown was unquestionable and who served as the monarch's official representative. Don Antonio de Mendoza assumed this new position in 1535. In the colonies the viceroy wielded enormous power. As the Crown's official representative he presided over the *audiencia*, was the chief military officer, chose clerical officials and reprimanded them when necessary, and controlled the colonial treasury. Although he was president of the *audiencia*, this governing body investigated and reported on the viceroy's behavior. As a result, the Crown established a system of checks and balances ensuring Spain's dominance.

The viceroy's authority was limited in other ways. One, he did not possess the power to establish new laws. Two, each viceroy's tenure was kept short so as not to allow the time to establish allies that might threaten Spanish authority. Three, the viceroy did not determine membership on the *audiencia*; the monarchy selected all the representatives. Four, the viceroy was held in check by the *residencia* and the *visita*. These offices were designed to ensure that the viceroy served the state in a capable manner and to remind him of his subservient position.

The *visitador* examined the behavior of the viceroy during his tenure in New Spain. Theoretically the arrival of a *visitador* was supposed to be a surprise. He heard testimony from people regarding the viceroy's conduct and possessed the authority to remove him if necessary. The *residencia* was held at the end of the viceroy's tenure to determine whether he had upheld the goals of the Crown and conducted himself in an impeccable manner. In many ways this system served as a venue for colonialists to express their displeasure with the Crown's officials.

The viceroys faced challenges to their authority and had to define the nature of their rule in the colony and in relation to Spain. Mexico's viceroys were tested by the event known as the Mixtón War and by questions surrounding the implementation of the New Laws created in 1542.

In western Mexico, Indians initiated a conflict known as the Mixtón War (1540–1541). The actions were a response against the activity of Nuno de Guzmán, who had fled Mexico City to the western territories and continued his criminal behavior, only now against the Indians. The war exposed the depth of racial conflicts in Mexico. Native priests initiated the conflict when they attacked the western city of Guadalajara. Viceroy Mendoza took control of the campaign against the Indians after the Spanish were defeated in several engagements. Mendoza adopted practices to address Indian concerns, including an end to branding captured Indians as slaves, and he offered amnesty to those who would stop fighting.

Established to restrict the *encomenderos* and to protect Indians by granting them "the rights of free vassals of the Crown," the New Laws became a critical test between the goals of Spain and the needs of the colonists. At issue was the refusal of corrupt and jealous *encomenderos* to give up their privileges. When the *visitador* Francisco Tello de Sandoval arrived in Mexico in 1544 to survey the implementation of the New Laws, he found angry *encomenderos* who argued that their way of life was at risk and that the New Laws threatened colonial traditions and customs. Some hinted at the possibility of rebellion if the laws were passed. A few argued that the education and conversion of the Indians could only be attained through the *encomiendas*. However, the success of the various religious missions countered this argument. More to the point, on numerous *encomiendas* the responsibility of converting the Indians had been left to the missionaries, not the *encomenderos*.

Sandoval met with Viceroy Mendoza to discuss the proper course of action; after all, the authority of the king was at stake. A delegation of lawyers and politicians was assembled to go to the king and present the case regarding implementation of these laws. As a result, a system of exemptions was established to preserve the law, but enforcement did not occur.

With the larger colonial bureaucracy established, it was not long before the Spanish created a bureaucratic system that governed on the local level. The *Ayuntamiento* or *cabildo* (town council) oversaw and directed the community. The *cabildo* distributed town plots, directed public works, regulated the market place, and performed other duties necessary to ensure stability. In the early years following the conquest, the *cabildos* utilized the Indian *caciques* (the Spanish learned of this word for chief in the Caribbean and introduced it to Mexico) to help administer the Indian communities. Both Spanish and Indian villages were directed by the office of the Corregimiento, where officials, known as *corregidores*, operated under the control of the *audiencia*. They supervised local villages, collected tithes and duties, maintained order, and directed plans to convert the Indians. Two kinds of *corregidores* appeared: One governed Spanish towns, and the other governed Indian villages.

Corrupt practices appeared early in the Spanish colonies. In many ways the governing infrastructure institutionalized the corrupt conditions. For example, when various individuals competed for government positions a well-placed bribe could ensure an appointment. The *corregidores* gained the dubious reputation of being one of the more corrupt offices. As the Marquis of Varinas noted, "when the judge [*corregidor*] enters upon his office, his sole concern is to find means of paying off his large debts and to make a profit from his employment; and since time is short, his needs immense, the land exhausted, and his vassals poor, he must use violence and cruelty to attain what equity, moderation, and kindness will not secure."[11] The *corregidores* governing Indian villages established the *reparto de mercancías* system, which stipulated that the local population sell their products to the *corregidor*, who established artificially low prices. In turn, the Indians purchased their goods from *corregidor* at inflated prices.

Complaints about the level of corruption were directed to Spain. In a letter to Charles II, Gabriel Fernández de Villalobos explained the nature of the corruption and urged the king to reform the system or risk losing the colonies. His letter charged that corruption in the colonies began with the office of the viceroy and his decision to sell offices, licenses, or other concessions; to sell military positions including rank and posts; and to sell bureaucratic positions ranging from tax collector to inspector of mines and lands. By being part of the corruption the viceroy in essence perpetrated it. Moreover, corruption extended beyond the political arena. Even clerics found themselves having to depend on Indians for food; therefore they had to look aside as Indians participated in indigenous ceremonies involving witchcraft and sorcery.

Villalobos argued that such behavior was the "source of political offenses and scandalous crimes that cause infinite miseries."[12] The problem manifested itself as officials who bought positions faced the need to make a profit on the office to justify the expense. *Corregidores* became the principal targets of critics against corruption. The Marquis de Varinas wrote that the *corregidore's* "sole concern is to find means of paying off his large debts and to make a profit from his employment."[13] This attitude was reflected in the practice of bribery and the maxim *"obedezco pero no cumplo"* (I obey but do not comply). While expressly prohibiting unethical behavior, the Crown proved incapable of preventing these practices. This revealed the weakness of royal authority in the colony.

COLONIAL ECONOMIC ORDER

Latin American historian Murdo J. MacLeod writes, "colonies are structured by those who rule them to benefit the mother country and its ruling classes."[14] Following the conquest, New Spain witnessed the imposition of an economic system that was different from what had existed prior to the arrival of the Europeans. Pre-capitalist conditions appeared that challenged the existing feudal economic system. Prior to the Spanish arrival the Indians had operated with a barter system, but after the conquest they increasingly operated in a cash-based economy closely linked to the international market. This transition demanded a production of surplus, specifically in mineral wealth and agricultural products. In this regard the Spaniards' introduction of new agricultural tools, including the iron plow and the wheel, expanded agricultural production in New Spain. The Indians utilized the wheel in toys prior to the Spanish arrival, but the concept had never been applied in a manner that assisted in the performance of tasks.[15] The rapid adaptation of these tools by the Indians revealed that the natives were more capable than many Europeans had thought. This revelation contradicted Jerónimo de Mendieta's observations that the Indians were "monkeys who imitated everything done by the Spaniards."[16] So capable were the Indians that Spanish artisans began to resist teaching them their skills, and the artisan guilds created barriers to Indians becoming masters (the position that allowed an artisan to own and operate his own shop). As the Indians gradually learned Spanish technology and manufacturing, they moved further away from the roots of their ancient society.

A vital component of the colonial economy was the agricultural sector. Early on farms provided food for the immediate need of the colonists. As more Europeans arrived, they brought a desire to continue their own food consumption habits. In response farms added European products such as wheat, olives, grapes, and oranges; these were combined with the indigenous foodstuffs known in the New World and adopted by Europeans. Initially Spain tried to limit colonial food production to products not available in Spain, but like many other "orders" this effort was ignored.

Agricultural production geared for the international market developed in wheat cultivation, cattle ranching, textile dye products such as indigo and cochineal, and sugar. One of the driving engines behind this expansion was the hacienda. As Enrique Florescano has written, the hacienda quickly and efficiently "satisfied the domestic demands created by the urban and mining centers' markets."[17]

The formation of the hacienda resulted in land concentrated in the hands of a small number of landholders. Laws and other quasi-legal devices allowed Europeans to acquire Indian lands. Spaniards purchased land at prices far below market value if Indians did not have a record of ownership. Because proof of ownership was a Spanish legal phenomenon, it was determined that most Indians never had legal claims to their lands. Failure to prove ownership meant that anyone could purchase the land, so hacienda owners began purchasing it in record numbers. Another avenue to obtain land resulted from the Spanish policy of *congregación* that required Indians to live in communities governed by the Spanish, ostensibly for reasons of control and to ensure their conversion to Christianity. Thus when the Indians relocated, Spanish officials determined that their lands were vacant and could be purchased. All these practices resulted in a significant loss of lands previously worked by the Indians. Ironically this occurred despite laws to protect the encroachment of Spaniards on Indian lands.

Corporate Structure

Further distinctions divided the colonial society. It soon adopted a strong system of corporate stratification whereby specific social groups were able to separate and guide different colonial groups. For example, artisan guilds separated and governed artisan occupations. Each guild exercised a limited degree of political and economic autonomy and thus preserved a certain level of independence as they established guild standards and norms. The guild focused on economic concerns, principally the establishment of rules for the production and sale of products. Recruitment, training, and promotion, as well as workplace conditions and wages, were governed by the guild.

The two dominant corporate institutions in the colony were the military and the Church. Both possessed certain rights, called *fueros*, that exempted them from having to pay taxes. They also possessed judicial systems independent of the civil courts. These exemptions, and the struggle to hold them, divided Mexico well into the post-independence period.

BOURBON REFORMS

Latin American historian John Lynch writes about Spain at the end of the eighteenth century and notes that it was "a case rare in history: a colonial economy dependent upon an underdeveloped metropolis."[18] Earlier recognition of this condition led the Spanish Bourbon kings to impose broad reforms to reinforce Spanish colonial control and ensure that the colony served the mother country. Yet the Bourbon reforms exposed the weaknesses in the colonial infrastructure and actually encouraged the colonies to push for independence.

Impact of the War of the Spanish Succession

The fact that the question of royal succession was discussed revealed the weaknesses of the Spanish monarchy in the beginning of the eighteenth century. Prior to the death of Charles II, two rival empires sought to control the Spanish throne: the king of France and the Holy Roman Emperor. Each monarch had married one of the sisters of the Spanish king, Charles II; both hoped this connection would allow them to place a younger family member on the Spanish throne. Both the French and Holy Roman Empire leaders had proposed the "partition" of Spanish possessions. By dividing the territory, they argued, the balance of power in Europe would be preserved. When Charles II died in 1700, however, his will revealed that the 17-year-old grandson of Louis XIV of France was heir to the Spanish throne. But Louis XIV had to agree to these conditions; if he refused, the inheritance would pass to the son of the Hapsburg emperor in Vienna. Not surprisingly Louis XIV accepted, thus linking the thrones in Paris and Madrid.

Now the political balance in Europe was threatened in a way that Europe had not seen in centuries. As a result England, Holland, the Holy Roman Empire, and eventually Portugal and Savoy formed an alliance to resist the union of French and Spanish thrones. What followed was an eleven-year war concluding with the Peace at Utrecht in 1713. According to the treaty, the Bourbons would remain on the Spanish throne as long as no real political link was established with the French Bourbons. The war, and the subsequent treaty, revealed Spain as a second-rate power that could not determine its own political future. The treaty saw Spain lose in other ways as well: The British acquired the *Asiento* (exclusive contract) that gave them exclusive privilege to ship slaves to Spanish America and allowed one British ship per year to sell British products in the colony. As a result of these indignities and loss of authority, the Bourbon king, Philip V, began to consider how Spain could restore its glory.

In an essay written in 1742, José Campillo, former Minister of the Indies and critic of Spanish colonial policy, provided a blueprint for the Bourbon reforms. He called for abolishing the Cadiz monopoly (Cadiz was the official Spanish port for all trade between Spain and her colonies in the Western Hemisphere), reducing goods taxed in the colonies, improving communications by means of a more speedy and regular delivery, establishing intercolonial trade, and enhancing colonial agriculture production. The Bourbon kings pursued Campillo's proposals by overhauling the existing political and economic structure. The belief was that only through reform could Spain compete with other European powers. Although the proposed changes were extensive, they were also conservative; there was no call to replace the existing systems but rather to improve them.

Initial reforms addressed the colonies' administrative structure. One of the first changes was to reshape the viceroyalties because the existing ones were too large to govern effectively. These reforms were designed to enhance Spanish political control and improve the colonial economy. In 1739 and again in 1776 Spain created two new viceroyalties in New

Grenada and Rio de la Plata, in recognition of the difficulty of one vice-roy administering such large territories and growing populations. To assist the viceroys with their administrative responsibilities and address the colonial economic goals, the Ordinance of the Intendants was announced in 1786.

The intendants assisted the viceroys in administering the colonies but concentrated on economic concerns. They promoted economic growth in the mining and agricultural sectors and encouraged infrastructure improvement by building better roads, bridges, and communication systems. The intendants also pursued economic improvements by addressing problems within the office of the *corregidor*. Long known as a source of corruption and regarded as an institution that hampered economic growth, the office was replaced by *subdelegados* who were appointed by the intendants.

Soon colonists regarded these changes and regulations as interventionism on the part of Spain. As the new offices were created or reshuffled, a dangerous precedent began to emerge. Increasingly Spain filled many of the positions with Peninsulares rather than Creoles. Prior to the Bourbon reforms, Creoles had gained access to many bureaucratic offices. By 1750 as many as 51 out of 93 judges (*oidores*) on the audiencia were American-born Creoles. Yet after the implementation of the Bourbon reforms, by 1807 only 12 out of 99 were Creoles. Many Creoles found this policy insulting and began to argue that they had a closer identification with colonial concerns than the Peninsulares did, and thus Creoles should direct the colonial bureaucracy. Others saw the Crown's policy as a continuation of the long-held view that Peninsulares were inherently better than Creoles. Conservative Mexican historian Lucas Alamán speaks of the contrasting habits between these two groups and concludes, "whether it was the effect of this vicious training or the influence of a climate that conduced to laxity and effeminacy, the Creoles were generally indolent and negligent."[19] Lynch argues that in this atmosphere a sense of nationalism by colonists appeared that rejected the controlling rule of Peninsulares, but he qualifies this by calling it "a cultural rather than a political nationalism."[20]

The one institution that remained open for the Creoles was the military. As they were pushed out of administrative positions, they sought and obtained positions in the growing colonial militia. As this body grew, military responsibilities and costs were shifted away from Spain and to the colonies. In fact, Spain was following the examples of other colonial powers whereby the colonists paid for and participated in the colonial militia. By 1800 the colonial militia consisted of 6,000 Spanish-born soldiers and officers and 23,000 Creoles. This imbalance subsequently proved disadvantageous for Spain in the wars of independence in the early nineteenth century.

The reformist spirit also focused on the Church. The economic power and privileges held by the Church came to be viewed as conditions that harmed the advancement of the colony. Many Bourbon reformers saw the Church, especially the Jesuits, as a powerful and independent group. As a result, the Crown expelled the Jesuits in 1767. Although the long-term view of the expulsion was lukewarm, the initial response by many Mexicans was one of hostility, because they believed the expulsion was an arbitrary use of power by the Crown.

The issue of the privileges, or *fueros*, held by the two dominant corporate structures, the military and Church, was also viewed as limiting the hegemony of the colonial bureaucracy. In particular, the *fueros* extended to these two institutions angered many reformists. Capturing the Bourbon reform sentiment opposing the *fueros* was the Count of Campmanes, who stated, "All privileges are odious."[21] The Bourbons began to attack the privileges possessed by the corporate bodies of the Church and army. In order to have a more efficient government, it was felt that these broad privileges had to be repealed. The independence from civil courts and the exemption from taxation were regarded as detriments to the efficient functioning of the colony. Of the two corporate bodies, the Church received the greatest amount of attention, mainly because by the eighteenth century it was the most powerful financial institution in the colonies.

Economic reforms followed in at least three areas in order to improve the royal revenue. One of the more hated consequences of these reforms was the *Alcabala*, or sales tax. Under the Bourbons the tax rate rose from 4 percent to 6 percent, and more significant, perhaps, the methods of collection changed. Instead of continuing the system of tax collection by private tax collectors, the government took over direct control of the system, thereby ensuring that a rigorous collection process was observed. As a result of the rise in the tax rate and the improvements in collection, Crown revenues from Mexico rose from an average of 3 million pesos per year in the early eighteenth century to more than 14 million pesos per year by the end of the century.

Another method imposed by the Crown—and bitterly resented by Mexican colonists—was the royal monopolies granted for products ranging from tobacco to alcohol and salt. A consequence was that private citizens had limited participation in the sale and distribution of these products. Moreover, it ensured that the Crown made a substantial profit on the products. These monopolies served as visible reminders of the unequal relationship between Spain and its colony.

In order to continue making the colonies more economically efficient, the Crown pursued changes in colonial trade. Through the idea of *comercio libre* the Crown abandoned much of the restrictive governing policies that controlled Atlantic trade and intercolonial trade. The purpose of *comercio libre* was to aid Spain, not the colonies. As the literature of the day reiterated, the "colonies are useful in so far as they offer a secure market for the surplus production of the metropolis." [22] Although the Crown's economic policies sought colonial development in agriculture and mining, decrees limited what could be produced in the colonies so that there would not be competition with Spanish exported goods.

As early as 1765 complaints against the imperial system of taxation became constant and increasingly violent. The complaints against taxes set the stage for resistance, and once resistance began other complaints surfaced. The changing attitude toward the government-directed reforms was reflected in the increasingly popular cry *"Viva el rey y muera el mal gobierno"* (Long live the king, death to bad government!).

As antigovernment sentiment was evolving, two significant examples of popular discontent occurred: in the British colonies of North America in 1776, and in the onset of the French Revolution in 1789. The events in the former British colonies, now the United States, introduced the very real possibility of colonists choosing to govern themselves. The impact of Great Britain losing its colonial possessions in the Western Hemisphere, given its status as a world power, raised the question of how Spain could be expected to remain in control of its colonies. Finally, the issue of self-government exploded into the European experience with the outbreak of the French Revolution in 1789. The French attack on the institution of the monarch prompted Spanish citizens to evaluate their own monarchical form of government. Initially there emerged an element of support for the basic goals of the Revolution. The eighteenth-century ideals shaped by the Enlightenment and the Philosophes (the leading proponents of the Enlightenment) had considered the possibility of expanding the base of participation by which citizens could influence the direction of a government. Now this idea was growing, and it was reaching all areas of Spanish America. In 1794 Antonio Nariño had translated, printed, and distributed copies of the French "Declaration of the Rights of Man."

Of the eighteenth-century revolutions, the American one had greater appeal than did the French. As Francisco de Miranda noted in 1799, "We have before our eyes two great examples, the American and the French Revolutions. Let us prudently imitate the first and carefully shun the second."[23] Miranda's concern reflected the Creole fear that the French experience had taken a radical turn and that this example would threaten the Creoles' interests. As the French Revolution became more radical, especially following the execution of Louis XVI and Marie Antoinette, monarchical governments and their elite supporters became nervous. The fear that crept into the discourse was over who would direct and control the nature of change. Would the elites continue to rule, or would government be shared by all?

This fear was reinforced by a revolt in Haiti that made Spanish Creoles especially nervous. In 1804 the slave revolt on the Caribbean Island of Haiti shocked the landowners and elites. Under the leadership of Toussaint l'Ouverture and Jean Jacques Dessalines, a black-led revolt successfully overthrew the white leadership and established a black-dominated government. For many elites in Spanish America the fear was that any change in government—including independence—might lead to increased political participation by the lower classes. What people like Miranda favored was a controlled break from Spain, with the Creole interests preserved and protected by Creole leadership. If that could not be achieved, they were willing (in Miranda's words) to "remain another century under the barbarous and senseless oppression of Spain."[24]

As Spain became embroiled in the events occurring in Europe in response to the Napoleonic wars, the actions had repercussions across the Atlantic in Mexico. In 1793 Spain allied with England in the struggle against France, but three years later the Spanish shifted their allegiances and backed the French against the British. The decision was a bad one for Spain. Britain's domination of the seas allowed it to impose an embargo against Spain and nearly shut down trade between Spain and its colonies. In this economic vacuum other foreign traders began trading with the Spanish colonies. The economic policies of decreasing restrictions on trade with the colonies in order to stimulate economic growth were escalated by the increased presence of foreign merchants trading with the Spanish colonies.

In 1806 Great Britain briefly occupied Buenos Aires until local Creoles organized a militia and threw them out. The successful overthrow of the British reinforced the idea that the colonists controlled their own destiny. This sentiment was captured by the Creole leader Manuel Belgrano, who reportedly declared, "Either I am master or none at all." Not only did the victory over the British solidify the sentiment that the Creoles could control themselves, but it fostered the idea throughout Spanish America that they could both lead and protect themselves. The logic for many, if these goals could be achieved, was that there was no need for continuing the colonial arrangement with Spain.

Two years later when the French under the leadership of Napoleon Bonaparte occupied Spain, many in Mexico began to openly debate the question of independence from the mother country. Out of these debating societies emerged the first real expression of defiance toward Spain when a relatively unknown priest called for Mexico's independence. His actions propelled Mexico into a decade-long conflict before the goal of independence was actually achieved.

NOTES

1. James Lockhart and Stuart B. Schwartz, *Early Latin America: A History of Colonial Spanish America and Brazil* (New York: Cambridge University Press, 1983), 86.

2. Nigel Davies, *The Ancient Kingdoms of Mexico* (New York: Penguin Books, 1987), 249.

3. Eric Wolf, *Sons of the Shaking Earth: The People of Mexico and Guatemala—Their Land, History and Culture* (Chicago: University of Chicago Press, 1959), 171–172.

4. Charles Gibson, *The Aztecs under Spanish Rule: A History of the Indians of the Valley of Mexico* (Stanford: Stanford University Press, 1964), 100.

5. Carlos Fuentes, *The Buried Mirror: Reflections on Spain and the New World* (New York: Houghton Mifflin, 1992), 144.

6. Benjamin Keen, ed., *Latin American Civilization: History and Society, 1492 to the Present* (Boulder: Westview Press, 1996), 65–67.

7. Juan Friede and Benjamin Keen, eds., *Bartolomé de las Casas in History: Toward an Understanding of the Man and His Work* (DeKalb: Northern Illinois University Press, 1971), 146.

8. Ibid., 68.

9. Ibid., 163.

10. John Tutino, *From Insurrection to Revolution in Mexico: Social Bases of Agrarian Violence, 1750–1940* (Princeton: Princeton University Press, 1986), 58–59.

11. Ibid., 102.

12. Keen, *Latin American Civilization*, 100–101.

13. Ibid.

14. Murdo J. MacLeod, "Aspects of the Internal Economy," in *Colonial Spanish America*, ed. Leslie Bethell (Cambridge: Cambridge University Press, 1987), 315.

15. Wolf, *Sons of the Shaking Earth*, 184.

16. Ramón Eduardo Ruiz, *Triumphs and Tragedy: A History of the Mexican People* (New York: W. W. Norton, 1992), 55.

17. Enrique Florescano, "The Hacienda in New Spain," in *Colonial Spanish America*, ed. Leslie Bethell (Cambridge: Cambridge University Press, 1987), 250–284.

18. John Lynch, "The Origins of Spanish-American Independence," in *The Independence of Latin America*, ed. Leslie Bethell (Cambridge: Cambridge University Press, 1987), 1.

19. Lucas Alamán, *Historia de Méjico*, in *Latin American Civilization: History and Society, 1492 to the Present*, ed. Benjamin Keen (Boulder: Westview Press, 1996), 217–218.

20. Lynch, "The Origins of Spanish-American Independence," 40.

21. Ibid., 8.

22. Ibid., 13.

23. Ibid., 44.

24. Ibid., 46.

5

The Wars of Mexican Independence, 1808–1821

Mexico's independence from Spain, which began in the early nineteenth century, was not revolutionary. The process reflected the conservative interests of the landed elite and their response to European events rather than specific actions in Mexico; in other words, the process of breaking away from Spain was more reactionary than proactive. The royal Spanish government's enactment of the Bourbon reforms in the second half of the eighteenth century exacerbated social, economic, and political conditions within Mexico. With the French seizure of Spain in 1808, the imposition of Joseph Bonaparte on the throne, and the creation of the Cádiz junta, Mexico exploded into crisis. The instability revealed acute social divisions within Mexico. The upper classes sought to establish an autonomous government that would represent their interests, and the lower classes struggled against the dominance of the local elites.

The multiple reforms discussed in Mexico revealed the disparities between the various classes struggling to preserve their interests. Yet some common complaints were shared by the diverse groups. For example, the growing inability of Spain to effectively govern Mexico provoked widespread discontent. Also, a sense of *Mexicanidad* (an identity with things Mexican) fostered an attitude that rejected the long-established idea that somehow things European were superior. These conditions gave rise to demands for a more extensive role for Mexicans within the governing infrastructure. When French soldiers seized Spain, the discussion about independence found a willing audience.

As the Spanish Crown struggled for its own preservation, it looked to its colonies for assistance, primarily in the form of money to pay its mounting expenses. As Mexicans were asked to provide more financial support to Spain, the question of their relationship to the Crown became more intangible. Specifically, their sense of loyalty was tested as the demands from Spain increased.

At the end of the eighteenth century Mexico was the richest of Spain's colonies in the New World. Of the income generated by its colonies, more than 60 percent came from Mexico. As John Lynch has pointed out, this put Mexico in a new situation—Spain depended on the colony more than Mexico relied on Spain.[1] Of course the demands for more money heightened discontent in Mexico. Throughout its history money had been raised by "voluntary" contributions, often paid by the wealthiest within Mexico who used the contributions to ensure advancement and access to power. With the mounting instability in Europe, Spain needed more money than voluntary contributions could provide. Rising taxes affected virtually all sectors of the population, providing a device that cut across class lines—everyone could identify with this complaint, regardless of social position.

The elite grew angry when the Crown made it increasingly difficult to establish the conditions whereby the property of a family stayed intact and passed to the next generation. In Mexico this policy was institutionalized in the procedure known as the entail (*mayorazgo*). Under this system an elite family could ensure the preservation of its property as well as the obtainment of noble distinction. As the crisis grew in Europe, the Crown raised the costs for obtaining an entail. Some protested the exorbitant costs, while others simply abandoned the idea of establishing a *mayorazgo*.

Not only did the elites grow angry, but soon the Crown's demands affected artisans and the Church itself. Spain demanded loans from various guilds in Mexico. Three principal functions of the guilds were to provide funds to assist disabled workers, to support families who had lost members within the guilds, and to invest money in artisans or merchants to help expand the colonial economy. The last function was probably the most important because this money helped drive the capital-poor economy of the colony. However, the Crown saw the funds held by the guilds as a source of income.

The Crown's miscalculations continued when the monarchy introduced the Royal Law of Consolidation in the winter of 1804. The law authorized the government to seize Church lands that would then be auctioned off, as well as to seize money lent out to individuals, in order to meet the rising expenditures incurred in Europe. Just as it had with the guilds, this move against the Church threatened to weaken the colonial economy by reducing money available for internal loans. By the end of the eighteenth century the Church was the largest money lender in Mexico; in fact, in the area around Guadalajara it loaned as much as 70 percent of the funds for commercial projects. Consequently "capital rather than property was the principal wealth of the Mexican Church."[2] Opposition to the Royal Law of Consolidation was strong, but rather than invoke the established practice of ignoring royal decrees, the viceroy José de Iturrigaray, operating in the reformist spirit of the Bourbon kings, implemented the policy.

The impact of the decree reached all sectors of Mexico even though it remained in effect for only four years. Most affected were small land holders and businessmen who operated with Church loans. Faced with the immediacy of the royal decree, the Church demanded immediate payment of all loans. Those who could not make the payment had to sell their holdings at an inopportune time—it became a buyers' market, and many property holders suffered. One of the landholders affected by the decree was the father of a parish priest, Father Miguel Hidalgo y Costilla.

The Crown's colonial economic demands furthered the colonists' dissatisfaction developed toward Spain. By the nineteenth century in Mexico there emerged the sentiment that Mexicans had a nearly equal status with people from the Iberian peninsula. Increasingly there could be heard the cry favoring the monarchy but opposing the continuation of bad government. The German traveler and scientist Alexander von Humboldt visited Mexico at the beginning of the nineteenth century and noted the social disparities, concluding that conditions were ripe for an "explosion of social conflict."

The seizure of Spain by the French, and Ferdinand VII's abdication of the throne in 1808, resulted in the Creoles demanding autonomy. This was presented to Viceroy Iturrigaray in July 1808. The Creole demands were conservative, but for Peninsulares any relationship between the viceroy and Creoles suggested a sympathetic view toward Creole interests. The conservative objective of the proposal was revealed when elite Creoles asked the viceroy to assume leadership of a junta (a temporary, provisional governing body) made up of representatives of the principal cities in Mexico. Moreover, the conservative direction was underscored by the proclamation that the junta existed due to the absence of royal leadership. The implicit assumption was that the junta would step down when the king was restored to the throne. Finally, what was proposed in Mexico was being duplicated in Spain, where juntas were established during the uncertainty of foreign rule.

Although precedent existed for such a call, the proposal sparked division and outrage as the Peninsulares feared the loss of their interests under a Creole-led junta. Rather than call the junta, Viceroy Iturrigaray convoked an assembly of representatives from Mexico City. The viceroy's lack of decisiveness fed the fears of the Peninsulares that the government was poorly managed and in need of competent leadership. A contentious atmosphere dominated the meeting, and divisions developed as to who was being represented—Creoles or Peninsulares. Also, arguments arose whether Mexico would recognize the Seville junta in Spain or establish a junta in New Spain acting in the name of Ferdinand VII. Motivated by this acrimonious debate, the Peninsulares decided to act.

Early on September 16, 1808, the Peninsulares, led by Gabriel de Yermo (a wealthy plantation owner), initiated a coup by seizing Iturrigaray and replacing him with Pedro de Garibay. The Peninsulares believed they acted in a manner loyal to the Crown. For Mexico, the coup challenged any semblance of legality and marked the beginning of violent and abrupt changes in government leadership that characterized much of nineteenth-century Mexican politics. Frank Tannenbaum writes in *Mexico: The Struggle for Peace and Bread* that the Peninsulares established a dangerous precedent because they "had broken the principle of the legal succession of power and had shown that the government could be overthrown in the middle of the night by a few armed men."[3]

Garibay briefly became a pawn in the rapid series of changes. Elderly, lacking energy, and having lived more than half his life in Mexico, he was regarded by many as more Creole than Peninsulare. Soon the Peninsulares who had placed him in power replaced him with Francisco Javier de Lizana y Beaumont, whom they believed was sympathetic to their worldview. Lizana was as ineffective as their first choice. Equally indecisive, he tried to negotiate with the Creoles, but his actions placated neither camp. Lizana relinquished power in 1810 to the *audiencia* in Mexico City.

The *audiencia* proved as incapable of establishing stability as its predecessors had. In the atmosphere of weak government leadership, intrigue dominated as groups met in quasi-secrecy to discuss the colony's future. These groups hid behind the façade of debating clubs or literary discussion societies. One of the groups that emerged was the Literary and Social Club of Querétaro.

Querétaro is located in the north central region of Mexico, called the Bajío. During the colonial era, this area possessed rich mining, agricultural, and textile centers. (Today, the Bajío remains an important center of agricultural production.) Although these commercial interests generated substantial wealth for the colony, they also produced some of its greatest social dislocation. A substantial number of people had been forced off their land and found themselves dependent on the owners of land, mines, and manufacturing. Consequently they represented an important source of manpower in an armed struggle. This group had traditionally opposed the elites' political and economic policies.

Now, more clearly than ever, the colony was divided between Creoles and Peninsulares. At the core of the division was the future of the colony: Was it to remain loyal and subordinate to Spain, or would it declare independence? The sentiment expressed in the Creole "literary clubs" was for independence. In Querétaro the conspirators decided that on December 8, 1810, they would proclaim Mexico's independence, believing they would receive national support following their pronouncement.

As is often the case with conspiracies, authorities heard of their plans ahead of time. Officials in Querétaro, Guanajuato, and Mexico City's *audiencia* were alerted. But the political intrigues and divisions within the colonial government failed to produce a prompt response. Slowly, almost reluctantly, government officials made some arrests, but not before word reached one of the members of the Literary and Social Club of Querétaro—Father Miguel Hidalgo y Costilla.

FATHER MIGUEL HIDALGO Y COSTILLA

Hidalgo was from a Creole family who found themselves battling entrenched discrimination at the hands of the Peninsulares. Paintings and woodcuts portray a tall man with brilliant white hair set around an impressive face with a stern visage. Noted as a defender of the downtrodden, well read, and with a capacity to forcibly express his ideas, he emerged as an important participant in the literary club in Querétaro. Father Hidalgo was the parish priest in Dolores in 1810 who soon found himself leading a revolution. In his capacity as leader of this revolt he became an icon of Mexicans who resisted tyrannical rule, and today he is regarded as the father of Mexican independence. National heroes are difficult to evaluate in the best of circumstances, and Hidalgo is no exception. Initial examination tends to lead to the conclusion that like other revolutionary figures, he suddenly found himself in front of a revolutionary movement. But evidence suggests that while his leadership of Mexico's independence may appear to have been accidental, much of his past influenced his actions.

Trained as a priest initially under Jesuit teachers, Hidalgo changed his religious education when the Spanish decree, influenced by the Bourbon reformist movement, expelled the Jesuits in 1767. His education for the priesthood comprised traditional work in Latin, rhetoric, and logic. Like many priests, Hidalgo also learned some Indian dialects. Although he was steeped in the typical clerical education, Hidalgo did not advocate or live the traditional lifestyle expected of many eighteenth-century Mexican priests. Instead, influenced by the ideas of the Enlightenment, he challenged traditional political and religious ideas. He questioned the absolute authority of the Spanish king and challenged numerous ideas presented by the Church, including the absolute power of the Pope, the virgin birth, and clerical celibacy. He enjoyed behavior regarded as outside the parameters of priests, including dancing and gambling. He even openly lived with a woman named María Manuela Herrera. His defiance resulted in his appearance before the Court of the Inquisition, although the Court did not find him guilty.

At age 57 in 1810, Father Hidalgo had served as parish priest in Dolores for seven years. He obtained his parish in 1803 despite his hearing before the Inquisition, which did not stop his secular practices. He continued to read censored works from North America and France, he violated colonial agricultural practices by raising grapes and making wine, and he nurtured a growing resentment of the behavior and exemptions of Peninsulares. In Dolores, Hidalgo observed his parishioners' impoverished condition and taught them manufacturing techniques in pottery and textiles and how to plant olives, grapes, and mulberries for silkworms. Hidalgo's policy was to make the Indians more self-reliant and less dependent on Spanish economic policies. These goals, however noble, violated Spanish mercantilist policies that protected Spanish agriculture and industry. As a result, Spanish officials ordered the elimination of these practices.

When the government began arresting suspected conspirators, word reached Hidalgo early on September 16, 1810. Whether one accepts Hidalgo's subsequent actions as heroic or as cold, calculated, and bloodthirsty, the events that followed cemented his status as a historical figure. Fearing his arrest, Hidalgo called his parishioners by ringing the church bell, where they heard his call for independence. The Grito de Dolores, or shout from Dolores, has become part of Mexico's historical icons. His speech captured the discontent felt throughout Mexico and articulated the distinction between the role of the monarchy and that of the bureaucracy. The Grito de Dolores was conservative; it did not condemn the monarchy. Instead the statement "Long live Ferdinand VII" called for its continuation, but the concern about bad government was reflected in the proclamation "Death to bad government." Both Creoles and Peninsulares could understand the issues expressed by these phrases; however, the Peninsulares in all likelihood reacted with horror at the strong anti-Spanish cry "Death to the Gachupines." (Gachupines was a name also given to individuals born in Spain.) The Grito also emphasized religion with the cry "Long live religion." In fact, Hidalgo used the Virgin of Guadalupe, one of Mexico's more holy symbols, at the head of the insurgent army.

At this moment the movement's leadership shifted in a dangerous direction. An important participant in the rebellion, military captain Don Ignacio Allende, was not capable of exercising authority because Hidalgo was now regarded as the leader. Allende had risen to a position of authority and respect, and he had acquired military training when Mexico established a colonial militia. With the outpouring of support that followed the Grito de Dolores the mob was led by Hidalgo, who did not have military training. Consequently little discipline existed to control the mob. Allende opposed the mob's destruction of property, rape, and murder. Hidalgo agreed but responded that he understood the historical patterns that shaped such responses. The events that followed—first at Guanajuato and later in Guadalajara caused many Creoles, who had earlier advocated independence, to fear that the masses would threaten their position. As a result, a strange alliance developed between Creoles and Peninsulares that lasted for more than a decade.

Regardless of the alliance, the masses frightened the elites. The differences between Creole and Peninsulare may have been obvious to the Europeans, but for the Indians and the *castas* (the offspring of Europeans, Indians, and/or Africans) the distinction was not as clear. Both acted in a superior manner, expected subservient behavior, handed out harsh forms of punishment, and regarded the lower classes as a source of labor and economic gain, either through tribute payment or as consumers of colonial goods. The populace's fear grew after the mob, estimated at

60,000 and armed with virtually every type of weapon, descended on Guanajuato. Conservative Mexican historian Lucas Alamán, who witnessed the events at Guanajuato, wrote in 1850 about Hidalgo's army. He wrote, "when the insurgents had taken the Alhóndiga they gave rein to their vengeance. In vain those who had surrendered begged on their knees for mercy. Most of the soldiers of the battalion were killed; others escaped by taking off their uniforms and mixing with the crowd. . . . the populace gave itself up to the pillaging everything that had been stored in the Alhóndiga, and it was scattered in a few minutes."[4] It was at Guanajuato that the mob's actions reinforced the elite's fear of the masses. When Hidalgo's forces reached the city, residents fled to the *Alhóndiga* (the granary) for safety, but in two days the mob entered the granary and killed an estimated 400 to 600 men, women, and children. The fury of the people also manifested itself at San Luis Potosí and Zacatecas.

Hidalgo's uncertainty as a leader revealed itself outside Mexico City. On the way to the city, royalist forces defeated Hidalgo's mob. Responding to the losses incurred by his troops, and perhaps concerned that the mob would repeat its actions from Guanajuato, Hidalgo decided not to attack Mexico City. Numerically his forces outnumbered the royal army, but they lacked the discipline of trained soldiers. This lack of control was repeatedly demonstrated. When Hidalgo's troops fought trained soldiers, they suffered heavy losses.

When Hidalgo decided not to attack Mexico City, the rebels retreated to Guadalajara. Initially they occupied Guadalajara with lower-class support. Workers in Jalisco lived in difficult conditions and had watched their income drop over the past decade. This made them a receptive audience for Hidalgo's promises. Following his arrival he promised to end slavery, tribute payments, and taxes on alcohol and tobacco products. These rather conservative promises attracted further support for his army.

In Guadalajara the rebel violence mounted. Hidalgo's forces seized suspected loyalist citizens and executed an undetermined number. Although the mob did not loot the city as it had in Guanajuato, it did target the property of those it thought were responsible for decades of poor treatment. These actions, like those in Guanajuato, set the stage for similar reprisals by the loyalist forces, who had managed to regroup from earlier losses.

The tide turned quickly at the end of 1810 and early 1811. Various insurgents accepted government pardons. On the battlefield, rebel forces

suffered setbacks. First at Guanajuato, royalist soldiers defeated the remaining rebel army and punished those suspected of sympathizing with
Hidalgo. Once royalist control had been reasserted, the soldiers marched
to Guadalajara, arriving in January 1811 with nearly 6,000 men. Although Hidalgo had an estimated 80,000 men, the disciplined royalist
army decimated the untrained mob and the rebel army fled toward
Aguascalientes. Along the way Hidalgo's officers seized control, reducing the priest to a mere figurehead.

Two months later, on March 21, 1811, Hidalgo was captured and arrested. Excommunicated by an ecclesiastical court, he was then found
guilty of treason. He and his compatriots were beheaded and their heads
were placed on pikes on the granary walls in Guanajuato, where they
remained for ten years until independence to serve as a reminder of the
consequences of treasonous behavior. Such grisly warnings, however,
did not deter those who were committed to independence.

Hidalgo's death in 1811 resulted in a political vacuum until 1812. The
royalist military commander, General Félix Calleja, continued to pursue
rebel troops. During this period of uncertainty another priest, José María
Morelos y Pavón, who had led rebel movements with Hidalgo since
1810, assumed control.

JOSÉ MARÍA MORELOS Y PAVÓN

Like his predecessor, Morelos had trained as a priest, was well read,
and was appreciated by members of his church. Unlike Hidalgo, he surrounded himself with capable military men. Two of these, Guadalupe
Victoria and Vicente Guerrero, survived Hidalgo and Morelos and continued to fight until Mexico achieved independence in 1821. Morelos also
demanded from his soldiers discipline and respect for property. As a
result, the armies under Morelos did not acquire the reputation for in-
discriminate looting and murder that Hidalgo's had acquired.

Morelos continued fighting in the rugged part of the country south
and west of Mexico City, where his troops repeatedly escaped the royalist army. In September 1813 Morelos and sympathizers met at Chilpancingo to outline their goals. At the congress Morelos called for the
creation of an independent Mexico and a broad participatory government. The last part upset both Creoles and Peninsulares because such
language threatened their interests. Chased out of Chilpancingo by the
royalist army, Morelos fled to the mountains to continue guerrilla campaigns. A year later, in October 1814, Morelos and his supporters met to

create a constitution for an independent Mexico. Modeled after Spain's 1812 constitution, it appealed to conservatives. But the reality of the constitution and the precarious situation of Morelos and his followers did not draw sustained support from either elites or peasants.

As before, events in Europe influenced the direction of events in New Spain. In May 1814, Ferdinand VII was restored to the throne and quickly reasserted his power. First he eliminated the Cortes (a parliamentary body created to establish a constitution in the absence of monarchical rule when the French occupied Spain), while in Mexico he named General Calleja the new viceroy. Calleja aggressively campaigned against insurgent sympathizers. Moreover, with stability reestablished in Spain, the Crown sent more troops to Mexico. As more soldiers arrived there and assumed control over various regions, they lent Mexico the air of an occupied territory. As has been the case with other occupying armies in other times and places, resentment developed among those being occupied. In Mexico the actions by the viceroy and Spanish soldiers created dissension toward Spain. The government's repression validated the insurgents' call for home rule.

Now Morelos and his small band were relentlessly pursued by the Spanish. Late in 1815 Morelos was caught and suffered the same fate as Hidalgo. Following an ecclesiastical trial for heresy, Morelos was tried for treason. He was executed on December 22, 1815, and his head joined Hidalgo's at Guanajuato to act as a deterrent for potential traitors. (Among the royalist forces credited with the capture of the rebel leader was Augustín Iturbide, who would rise to such a position of prominence over the next few years that ultimately he was selected leader of the conservative-dominated independence movement in 1821.)

With the two prominent leaders dead, the insurgent movement degenerated into regional skirmishes led by lower-ranking rebel commanders. Prominent among these were Vicente Guerrero and Guadalupe Victoria. Although they were committed to the ideals expressed since 1810, both men used the instability as an opportunity to wage a guerrilla war whose goals remained poorly delineated. As a result, Mexico faced another six years of uncertainty as the royalist forces unsuccessfully tried to defeat the guerrilla bands. Their failure prolonged the presence of Spanish soldiers operating throughout the country. As occupying armies have learned, the uncertainty of the enemy's identity often results in widespread abuses against many elements of the population. Not surprisingly, the viceroyalty was targeted for its failure to provide safety to the population. At this juncture the Spanish government faced hostility not only from rebels but also from formerly supportive citizens who grew increasingly discontented with the arbitrary rule. The actions of the Spanish government in Mexico, coupled with (1) the political instability since the days of the Bourbon reforms, (2) the French occupation, and (3) the insurgent movement reawakened the attitude that the colony was poorly governed. Thus the dual cry favoring the king and "Death to bad government" resurfaced.

As the second decade of the nineteenth century came to an end, events in Spain again influenced the colony. Liberals had grown disenchanted with Ferdinand's failure to abide by the 1812 constitution, which had been a stipulation of his restoration to the Spanish throne in 1814. In 1820, as the Crown enacted plans to send more troops to Mexico, liberal Spanish officers led by Rafael de Riego refused to follow the king's orders unless he accepted the 1812 constitution. With another threat to stability in Spain, questions again appeared concerning the direction of the colony and its relationship with Spain. In particular, conservatives feared the liberal policies being implemented in Spain. Among these were a more free press, an atmosphere conducive to frank and open discussion of policy, anticlerical policies, and the release of political prisoners who had participated in the insurgency movement in Mexico.

While conservatives grew nervous, royalist forces continued to pursue rebel leaders still operating in the countryside. Vicente Guerrero remained the primary target. Chasing after him was Agustín Iturbide, the royalist officer who had assisted in the arrest and execution of Morelos in 1815. Iturbide had managed to fall from grace with the viceroy due to his corrupt practices in the areas he controlled, but conservatives convinced the viceroy to place him at the head of the royal army so he could put down the rebel forces. In an impressive series of moves of deception and thievery, Iturbide acquired military control and the necessary funds to pursue Guerrero. But Iturbide learned he faced a daunting task in trying to capture the guerrilla leader, who had lived and fought for nearly a decade against the very soldiers trying to capture him. Rather than attempt to defeat him, Iturbide sought to have Guerrero join him. Following a series of negotiations and demonstrations of his real intentions, Iturbide convinced Guerrero to put down his arms and join in the movement declaring independence for Mexico.

AUGUSTÍN ITURBIDE

In his position as head of the army, with the support of Guerrero, and together with other insurgents including Guadalaupe Victoria, Iturbide announced the Plan de Iguala on February 24, 1821. Iturbide's pronouncement initiated a precedent for political change that dominated Mexico until the twentieth century; all change followed pronunciation of a plan that outlined the change of government and the new direction being considered. Iturbide's plan consisted of three planks: (1) Mexico would declare independence from Spain, (2) Creoles and Peninsulares would receive equal treatment, and (3) the Catholic Church would remain the central form of religion (at the expense of religious intolerance for other religions). Another disturbing trend surfaced with Iturbide's plan—the role of the army in obtaining these goals. The army, which promised to uphold the Plan de Iguala, became known as the Army of the Three Guarantees. Creoles and Peninsulares now joined the flood of support for the Plan de Iguala. For the next six months the Spanish government, following the lead of the viceroy, attempted to stem the tide favoring independence, but the momentum was too great. Accompanied by the rebel leaders Vicente Guerrero and Guadalupe Victoria, Iturbide at the head of the Army of the Three Guarantees marched into Mexico City on September 27, 1821.

Mexico's independence came at a terribly high price. The political arena became a stage for great farce, scandal, assassination, deception, and thievery. In many ways it marked the condition of Mexico until the Reforma (the period from 1855 to 1876 during which the exponents of liberalism challenged the conservative traditions of the Church and military and sought to implement capitalism in Mexico) forced Mexico to examine its political and social organization and recognize the need for genuine change. Moreover, Iturbide's emergence as a political leader also marked the beginning of the era of the caudillo (further explained in Chapter 6) in Mexico's political arena. As elsewhere in Latin America, the country found itself repeatedly led by charismatic military leaders.

One can only speculate, but the independence achieved under the leadership of Iturbide would probably have surprised both Hidalgo and Morelos. It was a conservative movement more concerned about the preservation of elite status than the implementation of policies to advance equality to the masses. As a consequence, much of Hidalgo's social concerns were abandoned. The conservative social stratification, although gradually breaking down by the influence of capitalism in some areas, was still preserved, as people's status remained strongly influenced by race and skin color. In reality the nature of change in 1821 resulted in Mexico's independence from Spain, but at the cost of little variation in the quality of leadership. Very little changed, except that Creoles obtained what they had sought for centuries; replacement of Peninsulares in positions of leadership and influence.

Soon Iturbide fell under the sway of his limited political power and at the same time demonstrated a lack of political savvy that ultimately killed him. As Mexico attempted to create a nation, those politicians capable of engineering a movement for independence did not have the talent to engineer a viable government. Initially governed by a junta with Iturbide controlling both membership and the issues considered by the junta, Mexico floundered. This weakness revealed itself when divisions undermined the meeting in February 1822 of a constitutional congress. Congress considered lowering military pay and decreasing the size of the army. The farce reached absurd levels in May 1822 when Iturbide's loyalists, in a carefully orchestrated manner, marched through the streets of Mexico City shouting "Long live Iturbide" and demanding that he take control of the government. On the balcony of his home Iturbide repeatedly refused to do so, but he was not sincere. Iturbide went to the Congress the next day with his supporters filling the balconies overlooking the floor. Under this pressure the Congress capitulated and named him emperor Augustín I. In July 1822 an elaborate ceremony was held in the cathedral in Mexico City where Iturbide accepted the crown of the nation. His rise to the throne of Mexico's empire was matched by an equally dizzying descent from the same seat.

The empire lasted less than a year. The exuberant waste of money and the creation of new titles and outrageous new rules of etiquette angered many. Moreover, the treasury had no money, the wars of independence had devastated Mexico's economy, and—more important for the immediate needs of the new empire—the government could not pay the army, which numbered around 80,000. As a result people grew so angry that the press began to voice its discontent. Iturbide then demonstrated his political inability when he censured the press, which only fueled more expressions of disapproval. His policies contributed to the formation of a political opposition forged out of groups that overlooked their differences because of their hostility toward the emperor.

In what was becoming a pattern in Mexico, the military dictated the nation's political future. It was from the military that one of the more destructive players in Mexico's history emerged—the chameleon caudillo Antonio López de Santa Anna. In 1822 he commanded the port at Veracruz. As Lesley Bird Simpson wrote, Santa Anna's "greatest gift was to smell out a popular cause and put himself at the head of it."[5] Such was the case when Santa Anna announced his opposition to Iturbide in December 1822. The emperor, also capable of detecting the changing political winds, tried to stop Santa Anna by inviting him to Mexico City. Recognizing the danger of such an invitation, in early spring 1823 Santa

Anna responded with his Plan de Casa Mata, which called for Iturbide to abdicate the throne, for the end of the empire, and for the formation of a republic governed by a written constitution.

Iturbide fled into exile, supported by a government pension with the understanding that if he returned to Mexico he would be killed. But responding to his own false sense of need and at the urging of monarchists, Iturbide came back to Mexico in July 1824, landing on the east coast at Tamaulipas. He was shot within five days. With the Plan de Casa Mata and Iturbide's execution, Mexico's experimentation with an empire came to an ignominious end. For the next half-century Mexico struggled to create a stable national government. In some ways the actions of Iturbide, the acts of deception, the use of the military, the *pronunciamientos* (pronouncements), the bombastic declarations, and the reliance on personal charisma set the stage for Mexico's dual struggle to ruin itself while at the same time attempting to forge a nation. These actions were practiced and perfected in the character of Santa Anna, who dominated Mexico until 1855.

NOTES

1. John Lynch, "The Origins of Spanish-American Independence," in *The Independence of Latin America*, ed. Leslie Bethell (Cambridge: Cambridge University Press, 1987), 1.

2. Ibid., 12.

3. Frank Tannenbaum, *Mexico: The Struggle for Peace and Bread* (New York: Alfred A. Knopf, 1954), 37.

4. Lesley Bird Simpson, *Many Mexicos* (Berkeley: University of California Press, 1941), 213.

5. Ibid., 228.

6

The Aftermath of Independence, 1821–1876

Events after 1821 revealed that creating a government presented unanticipated problems that the enthusiasm of independence failed to anticipate. Economic and political problems made Mexico vulnerable to domestic quarrels and threats from international powers. Also, the nation faced the daunting task of recovering from the devastation of nearly a decade of fighting. Some historians have called this period of nation building unstable, farcical, or even like theater of the absurd.

From 1821 to 1857 no less than fifty different governments proclaimed control over the nation. All sorts of governments—from dictatorships, to constitutional republican governments, to monarchies—experimented with different methods to placate the divisions among the elites, and nearly all the governments struggled to ensure elite dominance over the masses.

Perhaps nothing better established a system of control over the masses than did the institution of the caudillo and the multiple relationships that governed this system. Latin American historian Frank Safford traces the origins of the caudillo to the era when the Bourbon reforms were imposed on Mexico. Safford defines the caudillo as one"who used violence or the threat of violence for political ends." The caudillo needed supporters to fight for him and his efforts, but the supporters also needed him to carry out their goals. Safford calls the relationship one of "mutual dependence."[1] Obviously the caudillo rewards those who serve him and follow him, but others make it possible for the caudillo to operate in a manner that ensures the preservation of their political and economic interests.

In the post-independence period, economic problems created instability. However, it appears that certain areas, such as agricultural and mining centers in the Bajío, suffered more than others; in fact, agricultural and mining centers were targeted by the competing armies.

Other economic factors made the transition from colony to independent nation difficult. Not the least was Mexico's rising national debt resulting from more than ten years of fighting. From 1808 to 1822 the national debt more than doubled, from 20 million pesos to 45 million pesos.[2] This debt gave foreign powers a reason to intervene in Mexico's internal affairs, either by demanding repayment or by dictating Mexico's economic policy. Mexico's indebtedness revealed other problems as the nation's leaders tried to write a constitution.

Some Mexicans, notably Mariano Otero, protested against the activity and presence of foreign interests in Mexico. Otero wrote in 1842 that "trade is no more than the passive instrument of foreign industry and commerce . . . and today those cabinets, in everything submissive to the mercantile spirit, are profoundly interested in keeping us in a state of misery or backwardness from which foreign commerce draws all the advantages."[3]

Following Augustín Iturbide's flight into exile, three military officers—Nicolás Bravo, Guadalupe Victoria, and Pedro Celestine Negrete—controlled Mexico through their positions in a junta. They called for a constituent assembly to meet and write a constitution. Following elections for assembly deputies, the constituent assembly met in November 1823. It culminated with the Constitution of 1824. The delegates used the U.S. Constitution as a model, although they abandoned the separation of church and state clause, stating that only Catholicism would be practiced in Mexico. The creation of a federal republic with executive, legislative, and judicial branches upset those who favored a monarchical government, preferably with a European monarch.

The new constitutional government was flawed from the start and exposed the acute divisions among Mexico's ruling elites. Political divisions contributed to a sense of distrust, personal jealousies, and an atmosphere that made it nearly impossible to allow serious governmental debate. Instead of having established political parties, divisions manifested themselves within the masonic movement. Two rival masonic groups divided Mexico's political atmosphere; the York Rites and the Scottish Rites. Masonic groups, or Freemasons, emerged in the late colonial period as secret societies that advocated the ideas of economic liberalism gaining popularity. Initially concerned with economic issues, these groups soon debated political ideologies and provided the base for the liberal and conservative political factions that evolved in Mexico. Conservative centralists aligned with the Scottish Rites faction; meanwhile federalist supporters were identified with the York Rites freemasons. The secrecy of these masonic groups allowed them the freedom to engage in political machinations free from public exposure.

At times the distance between these two ideological camps was almost impossible to ascertain. Conservatives, or members of the Scottish Rites, favored a strong centralized government and frequently hoped for the restoration of a European monarch. Their dream manifested itself in the 1860s with the imposition of the Austrian prince Maximilian on the throne. Conservatives protected the *fueros*, or privileges, possessed by the Church and military that had origins reaching well back into the colonial experience. Liberals favored the creation of a federalist republic that would limit military and Church *fueros*. In fact, liberal opposition to the Church originated in economic issues more than political ones. As the Church had long been one of the larger landowners in Mexico, it loaned out considerable monies for investment purposes and was exempt from taxation on investments and land holdings. Beyond those differences, however, the two political ideologies reflected greater social divisions than genuine differences on political or economic issues. For example, both conservative and liberal elites saw the state as an institution that existed to protect their interests by keeping rural peasants and the urban workers under control. Members of each political camp switched back and forth according to their individual political needs at the moment. Regardless of the differences between liberals and conservatives, one precedent had been established early on—the interventionist role of the charismatic caudillo.

In the atmosphere of uncertainty, the old insurgent generals Guadalupe Victoria and Nicolás Bravo became president and vice-president respectively in the 1824 election. Chosen under the rules established by the Constitution of 1824, Victoria and Bravo represented the divisiveness of Mexican politics in the early days of independence. Victoria was a liberal, whereas Bravo identified with the conservative centralist viewpoint. Their divergent positions contained a seed of pragmatism in that each political camp was represented and thus neither felt excluded from national politics. A degree of stability resulted, with Victoria serving out his four-year term. He outlasted his vice-president, Bravo, who, with conservative support, attempted to end the secret political societies and establish a powerful central government. Recognizing his inability to achieve these goals, Bravo fled into exile.

The Victoria government did more than simply survive and keep at bay the divergent political factions clamoring for political influence. Led by the conservative cabinet member Lucas Alamán, Mexico achieved some important foreign objectives: diplomatic recognition by the United States, limits on U.S. citizens colonizing in Mexican territories, and commercial treaties with Great Britain. The latter revealed a double-edged sword for Mexico. As an independent nation it could now import manufactured goods from England, but these products soon outperformed goods manufactured in Mexico.

Political stability ended with Victoria's term in 1828. In that year's elections Manuel Gómez Pedraza ran as a conservative against former insurgent general Vicente Guerrero representing the federalist position. The election was so close that Guerrero protested the election results and "pronounced" against Gómez Pedraza. Backed by federalists and General Santa Anna, Guerrero denounced the 1828 electoral vote. His actions established the precedent whereby elections would be held, but in actuality charismatic caudillos determined who would assume the office of the presidency. As a result of Guerrero's opposition, the 1824 constitution existed only on paper.

THE ERA OF THE CAUDILLO

To say precisely when the era of the caudillo began would be speculative. In many ways Agustín Iturbide was Mexico's first caudillo insofar as his assumption of power rested on his popularity and the underlying threat of violence to those who resisted his control. Moreover, the military played a paramount role in his ascension to power and short-lived tenure. In what became a pattern, the military determined who came to power and, oftentimes, how long they remained in power.

Mexico's undisputed claimant to the title of the classic caudillo is Santa Anna. Frank Tannenbaum called him "the evil genius of Mexican destiny. No other character in that turbulent and chaotic period embodied in his own person so much evil and charm."[4] His political actions were directed by his pathological sense of detecting which way the political winds blew. If Santa Anna believed that his goals required switching political ideologies, then he did so, apparently without a second thought. He surrounded himself with sycophants, wore conspicuous uniforms, created bombastic titles, and retained amazing popular support. Even after he lost Texas, and then nearly half of Mexico, he was still invited back to lead the nation, only to finally be turned out in the Revolution de Ayutla in 1854. For an individual who craved the limelight, in his latter years he suffered an ignominious end: Instead of dying for the glory of Mexico, he was simply ignored.

The Struggle over Texas

Being located on the frontier, Texas remained outside Mexico's mainstream colonial orbit. Missionaries had little success in penetrating the territory, and other settlers failed to populate it. By 1800 less than ten thousand people resided in the area. To increase the population, Mexico encouraged settlement by allowing U.S. citizens to settle there. Under Moses Austin, Catholic families began moving there. Mexico's struggle for independence lent a degree of uncertainty to the project until Moses Austin's son, Stephen, acquired permission to continue his father's development. Under his direction citizens could move into the region if they were Catholics, recognized the sovereignty of Mexican law, and were considered of good moral character.

Cheap land and the presence of slavery encouraged dramatic colonization by U.S. citizens in Texas. Mexico's government established regulations to ensure assimilation into the Mexican legal, social, political, and religious orbit. But problems arose for a variety of reasons. Some had merit, whereas others simply led to mounting dissension in the far distant territory. For example, only Spanish was used for legal transactions, Catholicism was the only accepted religion, legal issues had to be resolved in the capital, and there were growing differences between the small Mexican population and the increasing number of U.S. immigrants.

Mexico correctly feared that the United States wanted to annex Texas, and actions by private U.S. citizens caused additional concern. On at least one occasion private military forces tried to proclaim independence for the territory. At the beginning of the nineteenth century Aaron Burr informed Spain that the United States would challenge the borders between the United States and Mexico.

While the situation in Texas festered and grew tenuous, events in Mexico City added to the nation's instability. By 1829 President Guerrero had managed to anger the conservative centralists. But the political infighting was temporarily shelved when the Spanish threatened to regain control over Mexico. Led by Santa Anna, the Mexican military defeated the Spanish at Veracruz. Guerrero claimed that his government had preserved Mexican national sovereignty.

But politicians and citizens can be a fickle bunch, and within months of defeating the Spanish, the Guerrero government fell to a revolt in December 1829 led by Vice-President Anastasio Bustamante. Guerrero struggled for more than a year against Bustamante, but he was captured and shot in January 1831. With Guerrero out of the way, Bustamante began implementing a conservative political program. For example, state authority was limited, property was protected, and the power of the Church was ensured. While the conservative agenda was pursued, Bustamante addressed the nation's indebtedness and encouraged growth in the textile industry. As a result, British and U.S. investors came to Mexico. The first mills opened in 1833 with machines imported from the United States.

The experimentation with a strong central government failed in the face of growing pressure from the periphery, in particular from Zacatecas. Valentín Gómez Farías, leader of the federalist movement, challenged Bustamante. At almost the same time, theologian José María Luis Mora outlined the basic liberal position that stipulated the nation's right to seize and sell Church lands. As Gómez Farías organized an opposition force, Santa Anna joined him. He also opposed Bustamante, primarily because he opposed Guerrero's execution (Santa Anna had befriended him in 1828). The Bustamante government now found itself facing a two-front war: the charismatic and popular Santa Anna from the east, and Gómez Farías's organized military force from the north. Unable to stem the tide against him, Bustamante stepped down in late 1832. A mere formality of an election took place in March 1833, resulting in Santa Anna's assumption of the presidency; Gómez Farías joined him as vice-president. In an action that underscored his pathology, Santa Anna retired to his hacienda in Veracruz when he became bored with national politics. Thereafter his vice-president assumed all responsibility.

With Santa Anna "retired," Gómez Farías began to implement the liberal program. The government initiated anti-clerical reforms that included ending the legal requirement of paying tithes. They tried to limit the Church's landholding rights, but the Church aggressively opposed this policy and ultimately retained these rights. Then the Church found a friend in the military. When the liberals tried to limit the size of the military, these two institutions allied against their common enemy. In 1834 the military led a revolt against Gómez Farías and looked to Santa Anna for leadership who returned to the capital and resumed his presidency. All of Mexico's military supported the revolt except factions in Zacatecas, which suffered for their indiscretion. Gómez Farías followed a well-traveled path into exile, fleeing to New Orleans, and the liberal measures were repealed.

The political pendulum in Mexico, which had swung dramatically to the left with the liberals in office, now swung equally hard to the right with the conservatives restored to office and Santa Anna deciding at this time that he was a conservative. In this conservative atmosphere the Congress repealed the 1824 federalist constitution and established a centralist government. The rejection of the 1824 constitution caused the discontented citizenry of Texas to announce their break from Mexico.

War with Texas

When Texas announced the formation of the Lone Star Republic, Santa Anna decided he had to defend Mexico's sovereignty. In the winter of 1835–1836 he assembled an army and marched north to Texas, arriving at San Antonio in early March 1836. In what has become a well known story, the Mexican army surrounded the rebellious Texans in the mission known as the Alamo. On March 6, 1836, the Alamo fell to the Mexican army following several days of siege. Santa Anna had specifically given orders that no quarter was to be given to the rebellious soldiers. His order, and the subsequent death of all the Texans at the Alamo, as well as heavy losses in the Mexican army, made future relations between these two factions almost impossible.

While Texans sympathetic to the rebellion reeled from the events at the Alamo, another event made it even more difficult to remain neutral. As the Mexican army searched for remaining rebel forces, Colonel Nicolás de la Portilla captured a group of Texans and inquired how the prisoners should be treated. Santa Anna instructed him to execute all captured prisoners. Although he was morally opposed to the orders, Portilla had 365 Texans shot. The Goliad Massacre, as it became known, furthered the push by Texas for independence from Mexico.

In the days that followed, the Texans strengthened their remaining army forces and moved against Santa Anna and his troops. The Mexicans in the meantime relaxed their guard to the extent that at San Jacinto on April 21, 1836, the Texans destroyed Santa Anna's army in revenge for the events at the Alamo and the Goliad Massacre. Santa Anna disguised himself in a recruit's uniform and escaped, only to be captured when his soldiers automatically saluted him. Threatened with execution, he capitulated to his captor's demands and signed an agreement with Sam Houston, commander of the Texas forces, granting independence for Texas in exchange for his freedom.

However, Mexico's Congress refused to recognize the agreement negotiated with the Texans. Santa Anna now validated the congressional position, arguing that in signing the document he had acted as a private citizen and therefore the treaty should not be accepted. For Mexico, the loss of Texas revealed weaknesses that haunted the nation and its relations with the United States for decades. The Mexican government had repeatedly demonstrated an inability to exercise political power; now in 1836 it revealed an inability to protect the nation. Mexico did not grant diplomatic recognition to Texas, but the United States recognized its independence in 1837, supporting the claim made by many Mexicans that the United States had long sought this region.

Despite the loss of Texas, the year 1836 was not a complete disaster for Mexico. It finally achieved diplomatic recognition from Spain, and its Congress created a new centralist constitution. Meanwhile Santa Anna had retired in disgrace to his hacienda, where he awaited an opportunity to redeem his reputation. In Mexico City, Bustamante had returned to the presidency, but he remained a federalist and called for the restoration of the 1824 constitution. Santa Anna was never far from the presidential chair, however, and from Veracruz he waited for the opportunity to reclaim leadership of Mexico. The chance to regain his lost prestige came in the Pastry War with France.

The Pastry War

The Pastry War in 1838 revealed again the role of foreign nations in Mexico's affairs. The conflict was named after claims made for damages suffered by a French pastry shop owner when Mexican soldiers nearly destroyed the shop. The war gave Santa Anna the chance to redeem himself from the debacle with Texas, but his redemption had a price. During the struggle with the French at Veracruz, Santa Anna was struck by a cannon ball and his left leg had to be amputated from the knee down. Thereafter, according to Fanny Calderon, the wife of Spain's first minister to Mexico and witty observer of Mexico, Santa Anna never tired of talking about his leg. In fact, for Mexico the leg lived several lives depending on whether Mexicans wished to honor or despoil the image of Santa Anna. In 1842 in an elaborate ceremony with parades, speeches, diplomats, and cabinet members in attendance, Santa Anna's leg was reburied in Mexico City. Two years later, when he again fell from favor, the "leg" was disinterred and dragged through the streets of the capital until it was destroyed. The leg's treatment could serve as a metaphor for Santa Anna's career: While he was popular and victorious the populace endured most of his behavior, but when he failed the people rejected him.

For Bustamante, the restoration of Santa Anna's status as hero spelled trouble. From 1839 to 1842 the president faced a nation divided by attacks from both political camps. The nation was rocked by a series of political alterations that defy the imagination: At one point Bustamante named Santa Anna interim president, and at another time federalists struggling against the centralist government captured Bustamante only to release him later. In this atmosphere of political instability Bustamante angered the extreme elements in both political camps.

The U.S.–Mexican War

Following the Louisiana Purchase in 1803 and the doubling of U.S. territory, many Americans had looked at the region controlled first by Spain and, after 1821, by Mexico as a logical area for U.S. expansion. After the territory's experimentation with independence, the United States annexed Texas in 1845. In the previous year James Polk had run as the Democratic nominee for the U.S. presidency espousing expansion. When he was inaugurated in 1845 Polk reiterated his goals of territorial acquisition, specifically mentioning California. He was not alone in expressing the idea of the United States acquiring more territory. The editor of the *Democratic Review*, John O'Sullivan, in 1845 wrote that it was "our manifest destiny to overspread the continent."

To acquire this territory the United States needed to provoke a crisis that would necessitate military intervention. In the late spring 1845 the U.S. army under General Zachary Taylor received orders to establish a camp on the eastern border of the Rio Grande River. This action deliberately challenged the traditionally recognized border between Mexico and Texas—the Nueces River, which flowed into the Gulf of Mexico about 150 miles north of where the Rio Grande entered the Gulf. Now the U.S. military encampment openly challenged Mexico's border claim. As Colonel Ethan Allen Hitchcock noted in his diary, "it looks as if the government sent a small force on purpose to bring on a war."[5] On April 25, 1846, the Mexican army clashed with U.S. troops, killing sixteen. General Taylor requested militias from Texas and Louisiana, and in a separate note to President Polk he stated that the hostilities had "commenced."[6]

U.S. citizens were less than enthusiastic. Individuals such as Henry David Thoreau and Abraham Lincoln spoke out against the U.S. declaration of war. Meanwhile in Mexico, conservatives and liberals united as never before. In characteristic hyperbole, Santa Anna responded that the action would lead to war with the United States.

Santa Anna, however, was in exile when he made this bold statement. Once again the caudillo had angered politicians and military officials, and a series of military revolts had forced him to flee Mexico for Cuba. However, the military revolts could not preserve stability. When war broke out in 1846, the government of José J. Herrera pursued negotiations with the United States. When others opposed this course of action, Herrera was overthrown. In this atmosphere of political instability, and facing an attack from the United States, Mexicans looked again to Santa Anna.

Seeking out his former vice-president, Gómez Farías, Santa Anna tried to return to Mexico. Gómez Farías arrived in Mexico City first, where he governed through the restored 1824 constitution. The United States allowed Santa Anna to enter Mexico at Veracruz, hoping that his presence would create instability or that he would seek peace with the United States. Thus on September 16, 1846, Gómez Farías and Santa Anna arrived in Mexico City, and Congress made them vice-president and president respectively in December.

Thereafter Santa Anna left to fight, while Gómez Farías remained in Mexico City to hold together the government and raise funds to support the military effort. Meanwhile, in March 1847 U.S. forces under General Winfield Scott landed at Veracruz. From April to September the Mexican forces commanded by Santa Anna gradually retreated to the capital. Even when the capital was surrounded the Mexican soldiers fought on, causing increased losses on both sides. The courage of Mexico's soldiers was dramatized by the actions of young boys who attended the military college located at Chapultepec castle. There the *niños heroes* (the young heroes) became icons in Mexico's pantheon of heroes. Rather than surrender to the U.S. army, some military cadets leaped from the castle walls. An unknown cadet named Juan Escutia wrapped himself in the Mexican flag and jumped to his death. As a consequence of his action,

Escutia became a national hero. Despite the bravery and heroism of the *niños heroes* and many other Mexican soldiers, Mexico City fell to the United States. Displaying much less bravery than the *niños heroes*, Santa Anna resigned as president and fled the country.

The response of many Mexicans was open hostility toward the United States. Outside of Mexico City the people did not want to surrender, and Melchor Ocampo, governor of Michoacán, argued that the U.S. forces would not be victorious in the countryside. He was not alone in his call, but the majority of Creoles (perhaps fearing what would happen if they did not dictate the outcome) agreed to stop the fighting. Their decision to lay down weapons meant more than acceptance of defeat at the hands of the United States; it meant acceptance of the Treaty of Guadalupe-Hidalgo, which demanded that Mexico relinquish more than half its territory from Texas to California—for $15 million.

In the aftermath of defeat, as Mexicans searched for explanations for their loss, many blamed Santa Anna. Others harshly turned the lenses of introspection on themselves and concluded that Mexico might have gotten what it deserved. Still others adopted a position that grew in popularity following the defeat—that Mexico suffered the injustice of being a neighbor with the United States. Strong criticisms were also leveled at the Church and the military, corporate bodies viewed as incapable of responding to the changes needed to stabilize Mexico's economic and political sectors.

Two prominent liberals represented the breadth of liberal participants. Melchor Ocampo was well educated, had translated French intellectual writings into Spanish, had traveled to Europe, engaged in scientific farming, and was trained in law. He entered politics, serving as governor of Michoacán and later as representative in the national assembly. Ocampo and others represented the intellectual wing of the liberal movement influenced more by European political ideology than by intellectual ideas in Mexico.

Also an intellectual thinker, but perhaps more a pragmatic realist, was Benito Juárez. He was a Zapotec Indian born in 1806 in a remote area of Oaxaca and orphaned at the age of 3. At age 12 Juárez traveled to Oaxaca City, where with the assistance of one of his sisters he secured work as a book-binding apprentice to a Franciscan lay brother. At first Juárez spoke little Spanish, but through his work and classes Spanish became his second language. Influenced by the Franciscans, Juárez attended the seminary but grew bored and entered law school, receiving his degree in 1831. Juárez also entered politics, first in Oaxaca City and then in the state legislature. In his capacity as a lawyer and government official Juárez learned, as Ocampo had in Michoacán, about the unfair treatment of the poor by the practices employed by the Church or the arbitrary behavior handed down by the landed elite.

During the U.S.–Mexican War, Juárez served as provincial governor of Oaxaca and introduced components of his political reformist ideas. Even during the wartime instability he built schools to expand educational opportunity, rehabilitated the port facility at the present-day Puerto Angel, reduced the size of the state bureaucracy, and even lowered Oaxaca's state debt.

In March 1848 Santa Anna fled to exile in Venezuela and did not return for five years. In March 1853 he came back to again resume the presidency, having been asked to help Mexico recover from the instability following the war with the United States. Pronouncements, civil wars, corruption, and failure to respond to the financial crises facing Mexico (the $15 million paid to Mexico as part of the Treaty of Guadalupe-Hidalgo was quickly consumed) had caused conservatives to reconsider his authoritarianism and grant him even more extensive authority. Now Santa Anna forced many liberals into exile, lavished rewards and promotions on loyal officers, and created titles such as "Perpetual Dictator" to be shouted in his presence. But not all liberals fled the country. Some, such as Juan Alvarez, began to revolt against Santa Anna. Thus in August 1855 Santa Anna fled into exile for the last time. Allowed to return in 1872, he died in 1876 a forgotten man.

REFORMA (1855–1876)

For liberals, two institutions—the Church and military—had long been viewed as a threat to liberty and the preservation of private property. Criticism of these institutions' privileges, or *fueros*, had roots in the colonial past. The military's failure in the U.S.–Mexican War, and the harsh treaty imposed on Mexico, led to calls for reform of the existing infrastructure. Miguel Lerdo de Tejada had written in 1848 that the Church and military had been responsible for much of Mexico's problems since independence. [7]

Unification of the *puros* (radical liberals) and *moderados* (moderate liberals) occurred in 1854 when Juárez and Ocampo met in New Orleans, Louisiana, while in exile. There they announced support for the guerrilla actions of Juan Alvarez and hammered out a set of principles known as the Plan de Ayutla. Following Santa Anna's departure the liberal opposition forces now occupied Mexico City, and Alvarez was elected president. But at age 65 he was a reluctant president. He followed a radical liberal, or *puro*, policy in appointing *puros* to important cabinet posts, among them Benito Juárez as minister of Justice, Miguel Lerdo de Tejada as minister of Development, and Melchor Ocampo to the office of Foreign Affairs. Having been born during Mexico's struggle for independence, they had grown up with personal experience of two distinct phenomena: All had come of age in a period of terrific political and economic instability, and all had been persecuted by Santa Anna.

Juan Alvarez was president when the first of the two classic liberal laws was passed. In November 1855 Minister of Justice Juárez pushed through Ley Juárez, a law restricting clerical *fueros*—specifically the authority of church courts. The attack on corporate *fueros* spread to Mexico's military—not an insignificant move, given the role of the military in determining Mexican governments since the days of Iturbide. A month later Alvarez named Ignacio Comonfort temporary president and announced his own resignation.

Comonfort directed a more aggressive liberal policy against the traditional privileges of the Church. Conservatives struck against the Comonfort government, but not before the passage of Ley Lerdo. Believing conservatives had used the Church to finance their military campaigns, the government confiscated Church land. Under Minister of Finance Miguel Lerdo de Tejada, all urban and rural property owned by the Church had to be sold at reduced prices. If the Church could not sell this property, the government would hold public auctions. Ley Lerdo also stipulated that the Church could not own property in the future. Essentially Ley Lerdo meant that no corporate body could own land; broadly defined, this meant that communal land owned by Indian villages, or *ejidos*, could be disentailed. Initially the *ejidos* were exempt from having their lands seized; soon, however, the goals of Ley Lerdo were extended to the *ejidos*, resulting in extensive loss of land held by Indians.

While the liberal laws attacked corporate privileges of the Church and military, Congress debated a new constitution. To no one's surprise, the delegates were concerned with the precedent established by Ley Juárez and Ley Lerdo and the issue of whether Mexico would create a centralist or federalist government. In the end, the Constitution of 1857 established a centralist component. The anti-clerical attacks continued under the liberal Comonfort government. In April 1857 more power was stripped from the Church with the passage of the Iglesias Law (named after Minister of Justice José María Iglesias). This additional anti-clerical legislation regulated the collection of clerical fees from the poor and prohibited clerics from charging for baptisms, marriages, or funeral services. As with Ley Lerdo, the Church condemned this legislation.

Now Mexico was bitterly divided between conservatives and liberals over the more radical elements of the constitution. Despite the division, Comonfort won the presidential election held in September 1857. He soon found himself the target of both camps; he was either too liberal or too conservative. Conservatives pronounced against the constitution and rebelled against Comonfort. They captured Mexico City and forced the president to accept their demands and then resign. Thereafter another Mexican army general, Félix Zuloaga, occupied the office of the presidency. Political stability had eluded Mexico again.

The War of the Reform (1858–1861)

The three-year War of the Reform, or Reforma, represented a continuation of divisions that had fractured Mexico since independence. Characterized by intense divisions, hostility, and violence, the war bitterly divided Mexico. When conservative general Zuloaga pronounced against the liberal government, he received support from the Church and the military—the two corporate elements criticized by liberals during the Reforma.

After arriving in Mexico City, Zuloaga's supporters closed Congress and arrested liberal politicians—not the least of whom was Benito Juárez, the Chief Justice of the Mexican Supreme Court. According to the 1857 constitution, he was second in line to be president should anything happen to the sitting president.

With Comonfort's ouster, Mexico collapsed into another period of war. Although traditionally it had been easy to recognize divisions between conservatives and liberals, now the makeup within these two camps was not so easily determined. The years of fighting and instability since independence had blurred the lines between the two political ideologies. The Church and military tended to support the conservative side, but there were exceptions. Some clerics favored the liberal reforms for the Church, and in rural areas many landholders also adopted the liberal position because Ley Lerdo represented greater opportunities for them to acquire more land.

Benito Juárez was the leader of the liberal faction until his death in 1872. When Zuloaga assumed the presidency, Juárez fled the capital and became the de facto leader of the movement defending the 1857 constitution. The conservatives controlled Mexico City, but not the important city of Veracruz—from which Juárez directed the opposition movement, and from which the liberals obtained supplies and money through duties received in the port city.

As the war struggled on for more than two years, violence committed by both sides rose to horrifying levels. Church property became the target of liberal forces' destructive appetites. Clerics who resisted actions carried out by the liberal armies faced the firing squads. Conservatives were no less guilty. Following a battle for Mexico City, General Leonardo Márquez ordered his soldiers to execute the medical staff who assisted liberal soldiers.

From their position at Veracruz, liberals under Juárez passed more anti-clerical laws designed to ensure the power of the state over the Catholic Church. These actions included ending the collection of tithes, limiting the number of convents and their membership, and restricting the number of religious holidays and the practice of religious processions. All these laws had the overarching goal of separating church and state. Meanwhile, from Mexico City, the Zuloaga conservative faction denounced the Reforma laws and openly defied liberals by publicly taking communion.

In this hostile political atmosphere the war dragged on, with the number of dead on both sides mounting and property destruction also rising. As the fighting continued, troops and officers in the liberal army acquired experience and talent that enabled them to compete with the conservative army. During the early stages of the war the conservatives had been the most experienced forces, but by 1860 the liberals had acquired significant military expertise that saw increasing victories for the liberal army. Twice in 1860 the conservative forces led by General Miguel Miramón failed to seize Veracruz. By late summer the conservatives were defeated at Oaxaca and Guadalajara, and on December 22, 1860, Miramón surrendered outside the capital. Liberal forces reoccupied Mexico City on January 1, 1861, and Juárez joined them a week later.

Aftermath

The liberal celebration in Mexico City hid an ugly reality. The liberals won the War of the Reform but now needed to direct the recovery from years of fighting. In this atmosphere foreign governments made claims on debts, and conservatives continued to dream of establishing a monarchy in Mexico.

Enormous problems faced the Juárez government elected in March 1861. The nation's infrastructure of roads, bridges, and port facilities bore the scars of marauding armies. Textile mills, haciendas, villages, and agricultural fields had suffered similar damage. Soldiers, failing to find jobs, turned to banditry that became even more pervasive on the nation's roads.

Facing the daunting task of recovering from the wartime damage, the Juárez government had to overcome infighting and respond to growing pressure from the conservatives. The liberal wing divided over how to treat conservative supporters. Juárez granted amnesty to those facing execution, even when conservative soldiers failed to extend the same opportunity to liberals. In 1861 conservative guerrillas still operating in Mexico caught and executed three liberal leaders, among them Melchor Ocampo. More radical elements in the liberal camp called for retribution, but Juárez refused to let revenge dictate his policy. His actions almost cost him the presidency when Congress considered his resignation, but the legislative body failed to obtain the necessary votes.

Economic issues threatened the Juárez government and ultimately paved the way for the establishment of a monarchy. In 1861 Spain, Great Britain, and France signed an agreement to seek payment for debts owed their citizens and compensation for property damaged during the War of the Reform. Their claims could not have come at a worse time, considering that Mexico was wracked from the damage of war, facing enormous costs to rebuild, working with a weakened commercial system, experiencing hostility from within and outside the governing party, and completely lacking finances. Despite these problems, Juárez did not dispute the three nations' claims. But he needed time; as a result he called for a two-year delay before repaying the debts, which Congress rejected (Congress opposed repayment at any time). The position taken by Congress revealed the internal divisions in Mexico and the difficulty Juárez had in governing.

Meanwhile the three signatory powers decided to "teach Mexico a lesson," but as Mexican historian Victor Alba has pointed out, these actions reflected different agendas. Ostensibly the Europeans entered Mexico in January 1862 "to preside over the country's regeneration."[8] For France, however, Mexico's "regeneration" meant more than debt collection, it meant establishing a Catholic monarchy and taking control of Mexico. The plan represented the long-held dream of many conservatives, who either remained in Mexico or had fled to Europe, of creating a European-style monarchy.

Recognizing their different goals, Britain and Spain withdrew. But France continued to send troops into Mexico, confident that the United States would not invoke the language of the Monroe Doctrine of 1823, (which restricted European colonial efforts in the Western Hemisphere) because of the distraction of its own civil war. Moreover, conservative Mexicans had informed the French that the Mexican people eagerly awaited the arrival of a European monarch and would assist the French army in defeating Juárez. Perhaps both the French and their Mexican conservative allies questioned the validity of these beliefs when outside the city of Puebla, on May 5, 1862, the Mexican military—led by General Ignacio Zaragoza, and assisted by Brigadier General Porfirio Díaz—defeated the French. This did not thwart the French occupation of Mexico or the ultimate goal of taking Mexico City; it merely delayed the fruition of conservative dreams. But May 5—Cinco de Mayo—became one of Mexico's more enduring national holidays.

The French intervention marked Mexico's second experiment with an emperor, this time the Austrian archduke Maximilian. The experiment lasted less than five years. Napoleon III gambled that if the intervention was successful, the French would acquire valuable raw materials for their growing industrial infrastructure while at the same time obtaining a new market for their products.

For the conservatives the French intervention turned out to be a mistake as well—so much so that the foreign presence helped bridge differences between liberals and conservatives. To the surprise of many conservatives, Maximilian's policies were fairly liberal in the areas of education, land and property reform, free press, and commercial goals. The conservative camp became even more embittered when it was apparent that the liberals' anti-foreign position caused them to be viewed as defenders of Mexico's nationalism. As a consequence, some conservatives joined liberals in opposition to Maximilian.

The arrival of the Hapsburg prince Ferdinand Maximilian was not solely the result of French imposition, but the consequence of Mexican conservatives' invitations as well. Conservative representatives had traveled to Maximilian's palace in Austria in the fall of 1863 to offer him the throne. Before he accepted, however, Maximilian insisted on a show of support for his rule from the Mexican people. Thus the conservative government held a plebiscite that fraudulently demonstrated Mexican support for a monarchy and Maximilian. Armed with these results, Maximilian also received from the French emperor Napoleon III assurances of French troops in Mexico as long as Maximilian assumed the costs to maintain their presence. The agreement, known as the Convention of Miramar, significantly increased Mexico's foreign debt—all before Maximilian left Europe.

Having received the appropriate invitation, and backed by French soldiers, Maximilian and his wife, Charlotte, departed for Mexico. They arrived at Veracruz in May 1864. To a careful observer, aspects of their arrival might have offered insight into the problems and divisions in Mexico. The citizens of Veracruz offered their new emperor a chilling greeting—a suggestion of hostility. In addition, the roads to Mexico City offered no improvements for the new king's reception. His ornate coach, designed for the relatively well maintained roads of Europe, was no match for the bad roads in Mexico; the coach broke down so often they soon transferred to a more sturdy stagecoach. The couple received a more welcoming response the closer they came to the capital. They arrived on June 12, 1864, and established themselves in Chapultepec castle—the former residence of viceroys and the scene of bravery by the *niños heroes.*

Once in place in Mexico City, Maximilian soon learned that the conservative plebiscite did not recognize the depth of opposition toward a monarchy. In the countryside, Juárez's liberal faction moved its opposition government to San Luis Potosí and finally to Ciudad Juárez. Meanwhile, other liberal supporters including Porfirio Díaz in Oaxaca and Juan Alvarez in Guerrero operated against Maximilian. This level of opposition across Mexico revealed nonexistent control of the countryside by the conservatives and a clear discontent with any foreign presence. Such hostility to a foreign presence fostered a spirit of Mexican nationalism.

In 1865 foreign intervention again played a critical role in Mexico's history. During the years of the U.S. civil war, the United States focused so little attention on Mexico that the language of the Monroe Doctrine remained dormant. The United States had not recognized Maximilian's government but had not assisted the Juárez government either. With the U.S. civil war over in April 1865, policy toward Mexico changed. Freed from its domestic instability, the U.S. government interpreted the French actions as a violation of the Monroe Doctrine and thereby revealed its traditional distrust of monarchy. First under President Abraham Lincoln and then under President Andrew Johnson, the United States allowed arms and ammunition to reach Juárez. President Johnson then applied diplomatic pressure against the French government to abandon its support in Mexico. Furthermore, the U.S. government allowed veteran soldiers of the U.S. civil war to enlist in the Juárez military, where they were offered employment and the promise of land for their efforts. Approximately 3,000 veterans from the U.S. Union Army joined Juárez's army in 1865–1866. Meanwhile the second component of foreign influence in Mexico occurred in 1866 when Napoleon III, facing pressure from rising Prussian militarism in Europe, pulled troops out of Mexico, in essence abandoning Maximilian.

With increasing conservative discontent coupled with U.S. aid to the liberals, Maximilian found himself in a difficult position. He contemplated abdicating but reconsidered after conservatives asked him to stay. In fairly short order, the Juárez government assumed the offensive. Maximilian in a vain effort assumed command of the armed forces and was defeated at Querétaro after a prolonged siege of the city.

For a moment Maximilian's fate was uncertain. Eschewing plans for his escape, the emperor surrendered his sword and was placed under the command of General Mariano Escobedo. He faced a military court-martial in which the outcome was understood, but his punishment was not immediately determined. International pressure rained on the Juárez government to allow Maximilian to leave for Europe. Juárez stood his ground, probably recalling Maximilian's order of October 1865 that called for the immediate execution of all Juárez supporters within twenty-four hours of their capture. Along with other captured conservative leaders, including General Miramón, Maximilian fell before the firing squad on June 19, 1867.

With Maximilian's execution the conservative dreams of a monarchy for Mexico also died. It is significant that the conservative elements who hoped for a more powerful presence of the Church in Mexico also abandoned this position. But these were costly victories for Mexico. The nation faced the daunting task of rebuilding its commercial infrastructure, which had suffered from nearly a decade of internal warfare. Under these conditions Mexico began to create a more stable political and economic infrastructure than it had ever had since achieving independence in 1821.

From 1867 to 1876 and the emergence of Porfirio Díaz, Mexico established the foundation for economic recovery and experienced a degree of political stability that contrasted with the events of the previous decade. When elections were held in October 1867, Juárez won a third term as president. Some people complained that he violated liberal principles by running for a third term, but Juárez and his defenders responded that his previous two terms had been consumed by internal war and foreign interventions.

Now Juárez embarked on a program of economic recovery, and the model affected Mexico well into the twentieth century. The pattern paralleled practices employed among other Latin American nations. Mexico, directed by a powerful caudillo, followed a program of development identified as the import/export model of economic growth. A key element called for distribution of primary materials—first from the mining sector, then from the agricultural sector, and by the turn of the century from the petroleum-producing sector for the international market. To achieve this goal, Mexico had to overcome a reputation based on decades of political instability represented by *pronunciamientos* (pronouncements), civil wars, foreign interventions, and bandits operating in the countryside. Furthermore, Mexico had to create an infrastructure that facilitated the exportation of its products—this required improvements in the nation's internal transportation network and in its Atlantic and Pacific port facilities.

Led by Secretary of the Treasury Matías Romero, Mexico adopted tax reforms to induce foreign investment; tariff reforms also helped encourage recovery in the mining sector. One significant result of restructuring the nation's fiscal system was the presence of British investment in railroad construction projects. Because an improvement in the transportation system was expected to attract investment, construction moved ahead on the Mexico City–Veracruz railroad line. British capital and technology helped overcome the construction difficulties of crossing steep ravines and traveling from sea level to an elevation of more than 9,000 feet en route to Mexico City. Completed with government subsidization in 1872, the new line spurred construction on other railroads. Symbolically the railroad linked more than the capital to the coast: The completion of the line received official support from the Church, demonstrating an improved relation between church and state that had not existed for years.

To further facilitate foreign and domestic capital investment, the Juárez government initiated a campaign to thwart the actions of bandits operating with almost complete freedom in the countryside. In 1869 Congress provided money to fund the rural police force called the Rurales. Men with military experience in the War of the Reform and the civil war—and, if one is to believe common perceptions, former bandits—joined the Rurales to patrol the nation's roads. Although critics opposed the aggressive practices of this police force, stability improved along Mexico's highways.

Perhaps seduced by these successes and intoxicated by his access to power, Juárez made the unpopular decision to run for office a fourth time. Now he could not claim that his previous tenure had been interrupted by either domestic or foreign instability. The election revealed how far Mexico's political system had advanced and how far it needed to go. Two other candidates opposed him: Porfirio Díaz, hero at Cinco de Mayo and the Battle of Puebla; and Juárez's secretary of Foreign Relations, Sebastián Lerdo de Tejada, brother of Miguel Lerdo de Tejada and author of Ley Lerdo. As a result of the three-way division, none of the candidates received a majority of votes. Thus the decision fell to the Congress, which, with a large number of Juárez supporters, gave the office to Juárez. Subsequent actions by Díaz revealed how the political arena had still not changed. In November 1871 Díaz "pronounced" against Juárez on the ironic (as it would turn out) charge that Juárez's assumption of office for a fourth term violated the principle of no reelection, the position liberals had espoused when they overthrew Santa Anna in 1855. Díaz, in this case, erred in his read on public opinion. Support for his plan did not manifest itself, and he found himself a spokesman for a revolt lacking military support. He was defeated. Díaz had been beaten, but scattered elements of his supporters were still in the field when the nation received the news that Juárez had died on July 19, 1872. Much like Juárez had done earlier, Sebastián Lerdo de Tejada, as Chief Justice of Mexico's Supreme Court, assumed the presidency on a temporary basis until elections could be held in October 1872. At that time Díaz and Lerdo campaigned for the presidency, which Lerdo won handily. With Juárez's death essentially eliminating the need for Díaz to revolt, and Lerdo winning easily, Díaz accepted the results and retired to the political sidelines to await the 1876 election.

Having buried the hero of the reform movement and the civil war, and seeing Díaz accept the 1872 political result, Lerdo set goals for Mexico that continued much of what Juárez had begun. To ensure amicable relations with Díaz and his supporters, Lerdo offered amnesty to the former rebels. Lerdo looked to the Rurales to provide stability in the countryside, and he increasingly viewed the federal government as the power to resolve conflicts within or between states. Mexico's liberalism was coming full circle to the position that had begun in 1857 in the debates over the constitution; that is, liberals increasingly favored a more centralist government, a position long favored by the conservatives.

Lerdo pursued more railroad construction, overseeing the building of more than 16,000 kilometers of lines in his four-year tenure. Construction of a railroad connecting Mexico City with the U.S. border began under a joint contract between Mexico and Great Britain. As with the construction of the route from Veracruz to the capital, the British played an increasingly prominent role in Mexico's transportation development. With the creation of a reliable internal transportation network, other British capitalists moved in.

Not all funds went to the development of Mexico's infrastructure, however. As had been initiated under Juárez, more schools were built in hopes that the construction and hiring of more teachers would attract more students. Even though Lerdo boasted that his government more than doubled the number of schools, the number of students increased only by about 5 percent per year. Of those students eligible to attend school, only 22 percent were female.

Given the direction of political change in Mexico, particularly with Lerdo's drift toward the centralist camp and the growing presence of foreign capitalists, Lerdo faced criticism from both liberals and conservatives. When it became clear that he was going to ignore the idea of "no reelection" and seek a second term, the position that Díaz had raised against Juárez (a president who enjoyed greater popularity than Lerdo), Díaz pronounced against Lerdo with the Plan de Tuxtepec in March 1876. What began as a political move to defend the liberal goals enunciated in the 1857 constitution was, in reality, the return of a caudillo to Mexico.

NOTES

1. Frank Safford, "Politics, Ideology and Society," in *Spanish America after Independence, c. 1820–c. 1870*, ed. Leslie Bethell (Cambridge: Cambridge University Press, 1987), 72–76.

2. Jan Bazant, "The Aftermath of Independence," in *Mexico Since Independence*, ed. Leslie Bethell (Cambridge: Cambridge University Press, 1987), 4.

3. James D. Cockcroft, *Mexico: Class Formation, Capital Accumulation, and the State* (New York: Monthly Review Press, 1990), 65.

4. Frank Tannenbaum, *The Struggle for Peace and Bread* (New York: Alfred A. Knopf, 1954), 43.

5. Howard Zinn, *The People's History of the United States, 1492–Present* (New York: Harper Perennial, 1995), 149.

6. Ibid.

7. Bazant, "The Aftermath of Independence," 28.

8. Victor Alba, "Reforms," in *Mexico: From Independence to Revolution, 1810–1910*, ed. W. Dirk Raat (Lincoln: University of Nebraska Press, 1982), 146.

7

The Porfiriato, 1876–1911

> It is one of the many charming inconsistencies of Mexico that
> Porfirio Díaz, the military caudillo and bitter enemy of Juárez,
> should have succeeded the lawgiver of Mexico for a third of
> a century as an irresponsible despot, under the cloak of the
> liberal constitution that Juárez and his devoted company had
> fought so long to establish.[1]

In 1876, in an action reminiscent of the methodology frequently used to
acquire power, Porfirio Díaz pronounced the Plan de Tuxtepec against
the Lerdo government and seized power. One of the many ironies was
Díaz's insistence that the liberal constitution of 1857 serve as the legal
foundation for his almost 35-year rule. Porfirio Díaz chose to govern as
an authoritarian dictator rather than adhere to a liberal democracy.

Díaz was born in 1830 into a mestizo family in Oaxaca, the same state
where Juárez was born. As with Juárez and Ocampo, Díaz identified
with the liberal faction that opposed Santa Anna. When the French in-
vaded in 1862, he was one of the youngest generals who fought the
French at the Battle of Puebla. By the 1870s he had become a national
hero; urban and rural workers viewed him as a man who represented

the people. Díaz's popularity was so great that he personally escaped blame for the problems in Mexico; instead, his handlers and bureaucracy were routinely criticized.

The pattern followed by Díaz paralleled similar ones in other Latin American nations. In Mexico the institution of the caudillo continued with Díaz, but now power was not the only goal. In Latin America, and Mexico, stability was being achieved with the new caudillos. But gaining stability meant establishing "order and progress," with the larger goal of achieving national economic growth and political strength. These gains were symbolized in the construction of railroads, the currying of favor with foreign governments and capital, the addition of more modern technology to industry, and the ending of the political uncertainty that had characterized Mexico previously.

While Díaz helped achieve the political transformation in Mexico, he also continued the economic transition. Initiated by Juárez, the modernization of Mexico's economic infrastructure had been continued by Lerdo. Both men directed railroad construction and promoted internal stability with the creation of Rurales, the police force assembled to end rural banditry. As did his predecessors, Díaz acquired a nation that had been mired in political and economic instability for more than fifty years. Consequently Mexico had benefited little from the scientific, technological, and industrial changes being experienced in other nations.

The economic crises facing Mexico in 1876 reflected these failures and the recurring governmental instability. Foreign debts (some decades old) remained outstanding, bureaucratic salaries had not been met, Mexico's credit within the international financial community was nil, and the Treasury had no funds.

The failure to implement scientific, technological, and industrial changes was evident in virtually every sector. Mechanical farm implements had only begun to appear on the haciendas, underscoring a complaint of Andrés Molina Enríquez (an ardent proponent of agrarian reform in Mexico) that the large haciendas thwarted agricultural innovations rather than encouraged them. With the growing, landless rural population, Mexico's agricultural sector could still rely on human labor.

Much of the mining sector, especially extractive techniques, remained mired in the practices of the eighteenth century. At the beginning of the nineteenth century, the German scientist and explorer Alexander von Humboldt noted that little of Europe's modern mining techniques were employed in Mexico. Von Humboldt's complaint still echoed in 1876.

Given the nature of Mexico's political struggles, civil wars, and coups, little money or incentive existed for investment in infrastructure. As a result the nation's roads, bridges, and port facilities were in disrepair, and a communications system hardly existed. On many roads vehicular traffic was nearly impossible. Like centuries earlier, people and goods moved via human or animal power.

Under these conditions Díaz established an authoritarian dictatorship that lasted until 1911. During his first term he silenced the opposition by announcing that he would not seek the presidency in 1880. He thereby made clear his support of the concept of no reelection, the position he cited to pronounce against Sebastian Lerdo in 1876. As a result, Díaz's opponents could wait and position themselves for the upcoming election.

Meanwhile, Díaz also structured a network that ensured his return to power in 1884. He claimed that he followed the letter of the law by not running for the presidency in 1880. In that eight-year period, however, both in and out of the presidency he laid the groundwork for a 35-year period of tyrannical rule called the Porfiriato. Díaz operated by instigating political factions to fight among themselves and then positioning himself as the mediator. Two dominant groups emerged during the Porfiriato; the Científicos, an upwardly mobile professional and political group identified with José Yves Limantour, secretary of the Treasury under Díaz, and the Jacobins, represented by General Bernardo Reyes. By all appearances, Díaz favored the Científicos and their economic plans to modernize Mexico.

INTERNATIONAL DIPLOMATIC RECOGNITION

Recognition from various countries came slowly to Mexico following Díaz's ascension to power. U.S. president Rutherford B. Hayes granted diplomatic recognition in 1876; in exchange Mexico agreed to pay 4 million pesos of U.S. claims in Mexico. At the same time Mexico stabilized conditions along the border with the United States. For years the United States had complained that outlaws from Mexico were crossing the border to attack settlements in the United States and then retreating across the border. On different occasions the United States had threatened to send military forces into Mexico to hunt down these outlaws. Díaz, however, insisted this was a Mexican problem and that his government would resolve the issue. Keeping his promise, he increased Mexican forces along the U.S.–Mexican border and stopped some of the outlaws. As a result, complaints from the United States and threats to intervene in Mexico decreased. European nations also extended diplomatic recognition to the Díaz government. Even France re-opened diplomatic relations by the end of Díaz's first administration. Other nations from Latin America also followed suit.

Díaz followed the viewpoint promoted by the Científicos that a stable Mexico would attract foreign capitalists to invest in Mexico's development. But more than diplomatic recognition was needed. To achieve stability Díaz employed a time-tested method of reward or repression known in Mexico as *"pan* or *palo"*—bread or the stick. Those who supported Díaz received bread; those who did not received the stick. He employed these tactics with virtually anyone at any social level. For example, when peasants seized control of haciendas in Hidalgo, Puebla, and San Luis Potosí, he duped them into meeting for negotiations; then once they laid down their weapons as a further stipulation for their meeting, Díaz had them shot. As another example, when Veracruz governor Luis Mier y Terán captured some elite landholders who had initiated plans to move against the president, he inquired what to do with the suspected rebels; Díaz responded with the grisly telegram *"matalos en caliente"*—kill them at once. The governor's acquiescence to Díaz's orders committed him to the president and delivered a powerful message to those who considered future rebellious action in Mexico.

With stability returning to Mexico, more foreign capital flowed into the nation. Former Juárez representative Matías Romero traveled in the United States and spoke about investment opportunities in Mexico. These campaigns brought construction contracts to build railroads connecting Mexico's industrial centers with the U.S. border. Soon other U.S. capitalists viewed Mexico as an opportunity for investment in land, industry, and commerce.

As the 1880 election neared, Díaz reiterated his pledge not to run for the presidency. After all, the slogans from the Plan de Tuxtepec were still too fresh in the memories of many for Díaz to break that promise. Instead he established a precedent for twentieth-century Mexican politics: The sitting president chooses his successor. Díaz named Secretary of War Manuel González to run for the presidency. This put other presidential hopefuls in a dangerous position because to seek the presidency would brand them as an opponent, to be dealt with accordingly. Few stepped forward to contest the election, and with Díaz's approval González won easily in 1880. Although he was handpicked and assumed to represent all the policies initiated by Díaz, González tried to govern on his own. His efforts resulted in charges of corruption and incompetence that reminded many people of political practices prior to the liberal reform movement.

González continued to promote stability and encouraged foreign investors to assist in construction of the nation's infrastructure, particularly the railroads. His administration created incentive packages, including tax abatements, to induce foreign capital to Mexico. One consequence was that it became easier for private citizens (domestic or foreign) to acquire public lands. Private companies that conducted surveys of Mexico's countryside could determine if any land was "vacant" (i.e., determine if there was no legal claim to the land). If no one could claim ownership the private survey companies could keep one-third of the land, while the rest was sold in government-directed auctions. Many small landholders who had farmed for years often did not possess a legal deed to their land. Under the new interpretation they did not legally own it, and therefore it could be seized. In this way sharp-eyed legal professionals and land-hungry speculators forced many people off their lands. Those who lost their land faced two alternatives: Remain in the countryside and work for the new landholders at low wages, or, as many began to do, move to the industrial centers springing up around some of Mexico's older communities or seek work in the new industrial centers such as the textile mills at Río Blanco or the copper mining center at Cananea.

González continued supporting the construction of railroad lines, granting government subsidies to construction companies to complete the task. Other funds were used to assist in the development of Mexico's communication system, beginning with a telegraph system whose lines followed the railroad. The telephone appeared in many of Mexico's cities by the mid-1880s.

The costs of this modernizing campaign continued to mount, forcing the González administration to portray Mexico as an even more attractive arena for foreign investment. For example, in 1884 the mining laws dating from the colonial era were revised. These had stipulated that land ownership did not automatically convey subsoil, specifically mineral, ownership. But in 1884 Congress changed this law, granting subsoil rights to landowners. As another example, the discovery of oil at the end of the century led to an increase in foreign investment in oil. With the value of land increasing owing to the change in the laws, and the railroad system expanding more people invested in land and thereby drove up its value and forced even more people off the land.

The harsh reality of many small farmers losing their land, the concessions to foreign investors, and the charges of corruption caused many people to view González's four-year tenure negatively. Yet he achieved much that has been erroneously credited to subsequent Díaz administrations. Many projects, such as railroad and communications construction, were achieved under González. He also improved diplomatic relations, which resulted in an increased flow of foreign capital, and continued to battle the rural bandits.

REELECTION OF DÍAZ IN 1884

For the most part, Díaz remained on the political sidelines while González ruled. Díaz briefly reigned as director of the Department of Development, assisting more investors in considering Mexico. He reappeared at the end of Gonzalez's term to criticize his successor and position himself to regain the presidency. But he did not remain uninvolved in shaping his political future. In 1881 his marriage to Carmen Romero Rubio symbolized two important points in his attempts to promote stability. Carmen was 18 years old at the time, born to a family of wealth and prestige, and devoutly Catholic; with this background she did much to polish Díaz's language and etiquette. She was also the daughter of Manuel Romero Rubio, who had supported Sebastian Lerdo de Tejada and served in his cabinet. Thus, the first important point, the marriage helped Díaz bridge hostilities with Lerdo's former supporters. Romero Rubio accepted Díaz's program (perhaps he was as much a political opportunist as Díaz) and even served in his cabinet as minister of the Interior. Second, Carmen's devotion to Catholicism and connections to the Catholic hierarchy helped Díaz assuage concerns among conservatives and Catholics as to whether the government would uphold the anti-clerical components of the 1857 constitution. The significance of the couple's wedding in the National Cathedral in Mexico City was not lost on Catholic observers. The anti-clerical components of the 1857 constitution remained law, but Díaz never strictly enforced these laws. In exchange, at least for a while, the Church was a tacit supporter of the government.

In 1891 the Church's tolerance toward the Díaz government began to wane. In that year Pope Leo XIII issued the papal bull *Rerum Novarum*, stating that workers deserved a "just material and spiritual reward."

Soon some elements in the Catholic Church established what became known as Christian Socialism, a two-tiered program of protection for the workers and preservation of their spiritual needs. These two responses by the Catholic Church marked the beginning of moderate opposition to the government.

With his victory in 1884, Díaz began implementing the political mechanisms that ensured his political dominance into the twentieth century. He eliminated political rivals in the Congress by acquiring de facto power through which he determined congressional candidates. With a malleable Congress in place, constitutional reforms followed. Díaz altered the constitution so that he could legitimately run for the presidency in 1888, arguing that he needed to recognize the will of the people who wanted him to lead. As the dictatorship was fully implemented, a constitutional revision extended the term of the presidency from a four- to a six-year term.

Díaz continued to address the issues of violence and opposition that threatened stability in the country. Along with suppressing groups that caused violence (e.g., frontier Indians or peasant movements), he eliminated other threats to the government. His methods can be characterized as conciliation with certain forces and co-option of other groups. For example, he positioned regional strongmen, or *caciques*, so that they could benefit from the wealth coming into the country. He placed his supporters close to those preparing to purchase land or invest in Mexico. Consequently many *caciques* profited from this access and thus had a reason to be supportive of Díaz and ensure that their region of the country remained stable. He also kept these individuals and factions suspicious of each other in a classic divide-and-conquer approach to domestic politics.

The method of co-option worked for other groups as well. Through the increased government bureaucracy Díaz brought in potential or real opponents to the state apparatus to buy off their discontent. As a result, a sense of loyalty for Díaz existed within the government.

Where conciliation and co-option failed, Díaz resorted to outright repression. From 1884 to 1900 he faced numerous threats to the nation's stability. For example, on the northern frontier various Indian groups raided settlements in Mexico and occasionally made forays into the United States. More than once the U.S. government threatened military intervention to suppress these raids. As another example, in the agricultural centers throughout Mexico peasants periodically rose up in protest against their treatment by the landed elite. Many of the complaints centered around the peasant farmers' loss of land and the contract labor systems that were crudely disguised methods of tying the rural workers to the estates.

With the expanding military—carefully controlled by Díaz through salary dispensations, promotions, and favored postings—the government put down or isolated some of these threats. Moreover, with the growing railroad system by 1900 encompassing more than 16,000 kilometers of rail lines, the army could be quickly positioned. Díaz also continued to utilize the Rurales, the paramilitary forces implemented by Juárez. The institution of the Rurales served two important purposes: It assisted in quelling Indian, peasant, or bandit activity; and it served as a device to balance the power of the regular army.

Banditry revealed a larger issue in Mexico. What factors made crime an option, and why were some criminals viewed as popular figures or heroes? Paul Vanderwood, in his book *Disorder and Progress*, argues that for many people crime offered a "means of social mobility."[2] Although economic opportunity was such a means for some people, others advanced socially in terms of how the public viewed them. Bandits thus were portrayed in popular songs called *corridos* that romanticized their independence, civility, and Robin Hood imagery. Jesús Arriaga, also known as Chucho el Roto (Broken Dog), embodied all these characteristics. His stealing from the wealthy and the Church made him very popular, and his defiance of authorities underscored one level of discontent by the masses. When a local official placed a bounty on his head for 2,000 pesos, Arriaga responded with a bounty on this official of 4,000 pesos.[3]

The stability that Díaz introduced to Mexico would prove false. It is significant that the power of the national state promoted this situation in multiple areas. Perhaps nothing revealed the expansion of the centralized state more than fiscal affairs. Again, the process had begun before Díaz with the Juárez government. But under Díaz Mexico's finances dramatically improved. Led by finance minister José Yves Limantour, Mexico balanced its budget in 1896. This did not represent some sleight of hand performed by state accountants; rather, it represented the flow of foreign money into Mexico and the nation's substantial industrial growth averaging more than 8 percent per year in the last two decades of the nineteenth century. To ensure the continuation of foreign capital, but also to raise revenues, the government imposed low taxes on foreign corporations (in some cases taxes were delayed for several years), levied custom revenues on imported products, and taxed precious minerals obtained in Mexico.[4]

Economic growth benefited the political situation as well. To assist their citizens' investments, foreign governments granted diplomatic recognition to Mexico and pursued measures to support the Díaz government. Although this provided a degree of stability, it revealed how dependent Mexico was on foreign capital and governments, as well as the vagaries of the international market. Two nations exerted the greatest influence on Mexico by the end of the nineteenth century—the United States and Great Britain. By 1900 the U.S. capitalists matched British investment, and soon U.S. capital surpassed the British. By the early twentieth century, as much as 50 to 60 percent of foreign investment in Mexico came from the United States.[5] U.S. capital poured into the nation's mining centers, such as William Greene's copper mining conglomerate located at Cananea in the state of Sonora. The restructuring of Mexico's mining laws granting subsoil rights to landowners also attracted more foreign investment. U.S. dollars flowed into Mexico's agricultural sector, creating what John Kenneth Turner described as "the typical Mexican farm . . . the million acre farm."[6] Such large farms were not limited to foreign owners. The governor of Chihuahua, Luis Terrazas, owned or controlled through family connections upwards of 15 million acres.

Since the early days following independence the British had pumped money into the mining sector, often with dismal returns but in the belief that economic and political stability would ultimately bring a positive return. During the Reforma and the modernization campaign that followed, British capital branched out into railroads, port facility improvements, and large industry development such as steel. One of the more visible and publicized British successes was the construction of canals and a tunnel system that for the first time protected Mexico City from the threat of floods.

While mining grew substantially, the oil industry became a choice area of foreign investment led by Britain and the United States. Initially oil companies purchased land where oil appeared on the surface. Soon more vigorous exploration began. Edward Doheny, a U.S. citizen, bought nearly 600,000 acres of land along the east coast near Veracruz. The British, led by Sir W. D. Pearson (who had led several engineering projects in Mexico, including the Mexico City drainage project), moved into the oil sector. The Pearson family became so important that its members bragged they could obtain any concession they wanted from the Díaz government. Out of his early investments Sir Pearson soon established the El Aguila Oil Company, which became the largest oil-producing company in Mexico.

Other foreign investors sought opportunities in Mexico's industrial growth. For example, the French moved into the textile sector, and established facilities in Mexico City, Puebla, Guadalajara, and Monterrey.

CONSEQUENCES OF THE PORFIRIATO

From 1876 to 1900 the Díaz government stabilized Indian and peasant activities, controlled labor, and eliminated any real political opposition. As a result, domestic and foreign observers praised Díaz. Investor growth led to the government's restructuring of the legal system in an effort to modify laws governing mining, textiles, and agriculture. Although the 1880s were relatively slow years for economic growth, foreigners still represented 67 to 73 percent of all capital invested in Mexico. The 1890s, however, saw a reversal in the trend from the previous decade. From 1890 to 1894 investors obtained a 10 to 15 percent return on their money, whereas during the last six years of the decade their return rose to between 20 and 25 percent.[7] This success imbued foreigners with a mistaken sense of haughty complacency.

Those sycophants who praised Díaz and gained influence and wealth because of their connection to the caudillo failed to see—or chose to ignore—the groundswell of discontent being expressed in Mexico, from the *campesinos* (rural agricultural workers) in Morelos and San Luis Potosí to the industrial workers at Río Blanco and Cananea. Soon intellectuals such as the Flores Magón brothers (liberal proponents who protested the inequality of growth during the Porfiriato), or individuals such as Pancho Villa, Emiliano Zapata, and Francisco Madero, or thousands of common folk in Mexico, were making their discontent known.

The defenders of the Porfiriato pointed to the nation's progress. One of the measuring sticks of Mexico's development was the railroad system. Statistically it was hard to argue against its progress: In 1876 the nation had had less than 800 kilometers of railroads, but by 1910 more than 19,000 kilometers of lines knitted the nation together. Admittedly the primary direction of the lines was to the U.S. border or to port cities where products grown or produced in Mexico entered the international market. The Porfirian sycophants cited improved literacy and increased newspaper publications to support their argument that Mexico had become a modern nation.

Rural Population

For the rural population, the Porfiriato escalated the devastating land reform policies associated with the Ley Lerdo. With the move to limit corporate landholding privileges, many village *ejidos* lost their lands as well. Under the González administration, private companies surveyed Mexico armed with the proviso that one-third of the land they declared vacant was theirs.

As Mexico's land became more valuable with the actions of land speculators, the arrival of the railroads, and the impact of commercial agriculture, the rural population felt the brunt of these changes. Increasingly the rural population lost its lands; by 1910 an estimated 90 percent had lost land. In Morelos, the state that produced Emiliano Zapata, the acquisition of lands by the haciendas led one newspaper editor to compare the growth of haciendas and the subsequent loss of village lands to the "daily enclosing the city . . . as in a ring of iron." So little land remained that the villagers had to bury their dead more than a mile away.[8] Whole villages were consumed by the powerful haciendas or, in some cases, surrounded by the haciendas and denied access to water or enough land to support the village. As John Womack noted, in Morelos in 1876 there were 118 pueblos (rural villages); eleven years later the number had declined to 105.[9] As a result, many villagers were forced into a dependent relationship with the new landed elite whereby they worked for pitifully low wages; some even worked in a condition of underemployment whereby they were hired only for seasonal work. The insult of their low wages was worsened by the fact that many were paid in scrip only accepted at the hated *tiendas de rayas* (company stores), where owners inflated prices and even went so far as to charge for the privilege to shop at the store. If a worker found himself in debt to the *tienda de raya*, he was bound to continue working for the owner until his debt was paid. Moreover, increased indebtedness could be passed on to one's children and was upheld by the Mexican legal system.

Mexico's industrial growth and export-oriented model placed great demands on the people and land. As the textile industry grew, the consumption of domestically produced cotton increased. Consequently more landowners planted more acres in cotton and fewer acres in foodstuffs. This raised the value of land for growing cotton and caused food prices to escalate. From the 1870s to the outbreak of the revolution, agricultural exports rose dramatically. In the Yucatán, exports in henequen (a fiber plant) increased "from 11,000 to 123,000 tons, tropical fruits from 1,000 to 10,000; caucho and guayule, the principal forms of rubber, increased from nothing to 8,000 and 5,000 tons respectively."[10]

Water rights became a critical issue for many small landholders and defined their relation to the landed elites. As the encirclement of haciendas continued, those left with land often did not have access to water for irrigation. When the villagers of Tequesquitengo in Morelos repeatedly petitioned for water, the nearby *hacendado* unleashed his irrigation ditches, flooding the town until only the steeple was visible.[11] As Alan Knight has pointed out, such failed petitions were sources of discontent. But the contemptuous action at Tequesquitengo, or the viewpoint of one of Morelos's hacienda managers who stated "let them farm in a flower pot" in response to the *campesinos'* demands for access to land, demonstrate the growth of what Knight calls "moral outrage."[12] Once this spirit is repeatedly tapped, people break into what appears to be spontaneous violence; but in truth the violence has evolved from a long history of poor treatment.

The economic impact of commercial agriculture had other consequences beyond the loss of land for the rural population and their subsequent displacement. Export agriculture required less labor, and as a result rural unemployment or underemployment rose. Declining employment opportunities also made it difficult for the domestic market to absorb goods produced in Mexico.

Emergence of Factory Systems

Because investors in the industrial sector came on the scene late, they purchased the most advanced technology of the time. Thus the purchase of foreign technology further tied Mexico to foreign interests. These expenditures were costly, but the way to maximize profits was to utilize Mexico's cheap and growing labor pool. The flight of the rural population to the urban areas fulfilled a classic component of liberal economic theory: Small agricultural producers lose their land and thus become available to work in the growing factories. The labor pool expands, and supply outstrips demand. The outcome for labor was an unequal relationship with a management who could pay low wages and demand long hours, knowing there were plenty of people willing to accept these conditions.

The dependent relationship with foreign capital manifested itself in a variety of ways in Mexico, not the least of which was the need for foreign technicians to set up the technology and to train the machine operators. In many workplaces the result was a work force of Mexicans in positions of low skill being directed by foreigners. In 1909 on Mexico's railroads, "68 percent of the engineers and 8 percent of the conductors were foreigners."[13]

Owners strictly regulated workers. Indeed, workers were required to carry employment records documenting their work record and indicating why they had left their last job. Those who had been involved in unions or suspected of activities to benefit workers were blacklisted. Some workplaces arbitrarily fined workers for union activity. Other methods of repression involved arbitrary fines for stipulated and unsubstantiated problems that occurred on the job. Workers were struck, sworn at, and forced to labor in dangerous conditions; women laborers also faced the threat or realities of sexual harassment.

Mexican workers also saw their wages weakened when they were paid in silver, whereas oftentimes their foreign bosses were paid in gold. Companies, as well as haciendas, routinely used the *tiendas de rayo* that served to thwart worker mobility and keep them indebted to their bosses. When the strike broke out at the textile facility in Río Blanco, the first target of the strikers was the *tienda de rayo*. It was burned on the first day of the strike.

It is likely that working conditions in most all-rural and urban settings were unsatisfactory and deplorable. Workers routinely faced long hours, at low pay, and labored in hazardous conditions. In the textile centers such as Río Blanco, workers averaged a 72-hour workweek. Inadequate wages increasingly became a divisive issue between workers and management. In the 1890s compensation kept some pace with the rise in the cost of living, yet by 1900 wages and the price of goods fluctuated wildly. As Rodney Anderson has demonstrated, wages failed to match the rise in the cost of foodstuffs—at the turn of the century workers spent nearly 70 percent of their wages on food.[14]

In this atmosphere workers looked for change. Initially they would appeal to local *caciques* or, if that failed, seek an audience with Díaz. Their goals reflected the viewpoint of nineteenth-century liberalism, citing the language of the 1857 constitution and the liberal policies represented in the figure of Benito Juárez. In other words, they wished to preserve capitalism and reform the existing structure.

As early as 1850 workers' organizations had appeared to address the inequities that existed in the workplace. For the most part, these were mutualist societies that provided assistance to their members in the form of payments for medical problems, unemployment, and some compensation for the elderly. The 1870s witnessed a substantial increase in these groups, although these organizations tended to fall along craft lines rather than within a particular industry. The mutualist societies' ideological goals focused on ensuring workers' economic and social protection; in other words, these groups were not actively criticizing capitalism but rather demanding what they perceived as a sense of equality.

Tangential to, and occasionally associated with, the mutualist societies were groups, such as the anarchists, that viewed capitalism and the state as detrimental to their status. Anarchist groups influenced by similar movements in Europe urged workers to protest, usually through the device of the strike. Mexican labor historian John Hart argues that the anarchists directed the nation's first industrial strikes. For the most part the workers affiliated with the mutualist societies had not favored the strike, but beginning in 1865 they nonetheless resorted to this tactic. The majority of strikes that followed took place in the larger industrial complexes in the textile or mining sectors. The prevailing demand, which would remain well into the twentieth century, was for better wages.

The Catholic Church reinforced workers' activism when, in 1891, Pope Leo XIII issued his papal bull entitled *Rerum Novarum*. From this call Catholic associations sprang up, but the Church became more concerned with controlling the ideological direction occurring in the country. By the turn of the century, anarchist labor associations began adopting a position that was decidedly anti-clerical. By 1905 the Partido Liberal Mexicano (PLM) argued against the conciliatory position adopted by the government toward the Church. Preceding the formation of the PLM, Catholic congresses first met in 1903. They continued to meet until 1919, advocating improved wages for urban workers and better workplace conditions, speaking against the practices that contributed to rural indebtedness and opposing the calls for secular education.

In this atmosphere of labor discontent, a theme of social reform could be detected. From the actions of the PLM to the complaints addressed by the Catholic congresses, workers and their leaders revealed the abuses of Mexico's workers. The belief was that Díaz tacitly supported these conditions. Nothing substantiated this belief more than the events of June 1906 at the Cananea copper mine (located in the northern state of Sonora, and owned by U.S. citizen William Greene) and the events of January 1907 at the Río Blanco textile mill in Veracruz. In both places, conditions for workers were deplorable. Foreign workers dominated the management and technical positions, whereas Mexicans labored in the lower ranking positions at long hours and poor wages. At Río Blanco workers experienced regular deductions in their pay to cover costs to maintain the machines. Moreover, children as young as age 8 and 9 were employed in the mills. In June 1906 workers at Cananea struck and sought negotiations with William Greene, who refused to meet with them. The situation soon became violent when workers attempted to make their way into the facility and were greeted by water cannons and gunfire. Quickly the workers armed themselves, and gunshots from both sides were exchanged. Greene appealed to the governor of Sonora for aid, specifically from the Rurales. When it became apparent that they could not arrive in time, Greene contacted officials in Arizona to make troops available to him. The Sonoran governor allowed U.S. volunteers to enter Mexico, where, in an attempt at preserving a sense of legality, they were sworn in as Mexican volunteers. These soldiers arrived at Cananea, where more violence followed with victims from both sides being killed. Mexican Rurales soon arrived at Cananea and brutally suppressed the strike. The suspected leaders of the strike were captured, summarily tried, and hung. But the damage was done. The government now was viewed as willing to use foreign military forces to suppress Mexican workers.

The theme of government protection for industrialists at the expense of Mexican workers was reinforced months later at Río Blanco. The violence at the French-owned textile mill began following a strike in January 1907. When relatives of the strikers attempted to purchase goods at the *tienda de raya*, they were denied. Soon a riot ensued with fights, gunfire, and destruction of the *tienda de raya* when someone set it on fire. Both Rurales and the federal army were called in. When they arrived they opened fire, killing women and children. The government's use of foreign troops and the national military to suppress striking Mexican workers validated the complaint long heard in Mexico—"Mexico is the mother of foreigners and the stepmother of Mexicans."

By the end of the Porfiriato the working people—both rural and urban—reacted to the new order by forming local, regional, and national workers' associations. These organizations, together with others dissatisfied with the Díaz regime, joined rebel armies late in 1910, convinced that the removal of Díaz would cause conditions in Mexico to improve. Although the revolutionary coalition experienced divisions within its ranks, by May 1911 it had defeated federal forces at Ciudad Juárez and forced Díaz to resign. During the revolutionary struggle that followed the fall of Díaz, industrial workers and peasants organized to improve their position in society.

In spite of the complaints being heard and increasingly substantiated by government action, many people believed that the problems facing Mexico remained primarily political. If problems in this arena could be addressed, it was thought, then other issues could be adequately resolved. Although a political crisis surrounding the 1910 presidential election ultimately supported this viewpoint, revolutionary change is rarely so orderly. As a result, from the political crisis that began with an apparently innocent interview by Díaz in 1908, there emerged an explosion of issues revealing that problems in Mexico went well beyond the political sector.

NOTES

1. Lesley Bird Simpson, *Many Mexicos* (Berkeley: University of California Press, 1941), 287.

2. Paul Vanderwood, *Disorder and Progress: Bandits, Police, and Mexican Development* (Wilmington, DE: Scholarly Resources, 1992), 90.

3. Ibid.

4. Friedrich Katz, "The Liberal Republic and the Porfiriato, 1867–1910," in *Mexico since Independence*, ed. Leslie Bethell (Cambridge: Cambridge University Press, 1991), 82.

5. Rodney D. Anderson, *Outcasts in Their Own Land: Mexican Industrial Workers, 1906–1911* (DeKalb: Northern Illinois University Press, 1976), 19–20.

6. John Kenneth Turner, "The Díaz System," in *Mexico: From Independence to Revolution, 1810–1910*, ed. W. Dirk Raat (Lincoln: University of Nebraska Press, 1982), 212.

7. Anderson, *Outcasts in Their Own Land*, 27.

8. John Womack, *Zapata and the Mexican Revolution* (New York: Vintage Books, 1968), 45.

9. Ibid., 45.

10. Alan Knight, *The Mexican Revolution: Porfirians, Liberals and Peasants*, Vol. 1 (Lincoln: University of Nebraska Press, 1986), 80–81.

11. Womack, *Zapata and the Mexican Revolution*, 45.

12. Ibid., 63, Knight, *The Mexican Revolution*, 162, 167.

13. Anderson, *Outcasts in Their Own Land*, 89.

14. Ibid., 64.

8

The Mexican Revolution, 1910–1920

Illuminated by car headlights on the night of May 21, 1911, Francisco Madero and the leaders of the federal army signed the treaty of Ciudad Juárez ending the dictatorship of Porfirio Díaz. Although the treaty marked a significant victory for the forces seeking to overthrow Díaz, it did not lead to radical changes in the political system. What followed was an intense period of struggle characterized by political infighting among various rebel factions. At the heart of this tumultuous period was the divisive nature of the revolutionary process. More than a victory for those who opposed Díaz, the 1911 treaty epitomized a revolution that forced individuals to choose sides, shattering any sense of national unity. Subsequently the country endured nearly a decade more of bloody civil war as revolutionary movements struggled for dominance. Throughout this divisive and violent period Mexico's working people sought to exercise their influence and thereby became important players in the revolutionary struggle.

The reverberations of the revolutionary military struggles from 1910 to 1920 reached all areas of Mexico, although with different results. As Alan Knight portrays in his commanding work *The Mexican Revolution*, the struggle was not a singular national experience. Different groups of Mexican society experienced it in different ways. For some, the revolution proved an inconvenience; for others, the revolution caused great upheaval and radical changes in their homes and work environment.

BACKGROUND

Initially a response to the uncertainty created by Díaz's comments in an interview with an American journalist, the revolution began as a political event but soon developed into a social movement. During the chaotic and violent years of the second decade of the twentieth century, many different elements in Mexico's society began to make their demands known.

The economic progress of Porfirian Mexico excluded most citizens. Nonetheless, the Mexican Revolution was not simply a revolt against economic deprivation. Changes in the social order and political uncertainty also provided the opportunity for people to protest and demand improvements.

In the first decade of the twentieth century, cracks began to appear in the façade of the Díaz government. As dissatisfaction with the regime grew, the caudillo became increasingly repressive. Unpopular local leaders (*jefe políticos*) fostered unrest and resentment toward the government through their arbitrary and exploitative rule. This affected all levels of society, most particularly the common people, who were already disaffected by the economic changes of the past twenty years of the Porfiriato.

At the end of the nineteenth century, Mexico had experienced significant economic growth and stability. From the mid-1880s onward the Mexican government had pursued domestic and foreign investment in Mexico for railroad construction, textile mills, and mines. German, British, U.S., and French representatives imported, sold, rented, and repaired machinery for the growing industry and agriculture. In Mexico's cities, foreign capitalists invested heavily in municipal economic infrastructures, rapidly assuming a significant role in the nation's industrial growth: Foreign capital controlled an estimated 67 to 73 percent of all capital invested in Mexico. The investors were well rewarded; in the 1890s investments returned between 10 and 25 percent.[1]

Despite this significant economic growth, the benefits of industrialization failed to reach many of the nation's workers. Instead, industrial growth reinforced and exacerbated longstanding problems. Poor compensation had not always been a problem for workers, because during the boom years of the 1890s wages had risen for agricultural and industrial labor. But this trend failed to continue. By 1900 Mexico's economy displayed economic instability paralleling problems in Europe and the United States. In Mexico wages exhibited a similar instability, with wide fluctuations during the last years of the Porfiriato. Declining wages and rising food prices caused workers to spend more than half their income on food alone. As the price of other basic goods also increased, the standard of living fell for many people.

In February 1908, with the presidential election two years away, Mexico's 78-year-old dictator, Porfirio Díaz, held an interview with American journalist James Creelman. Díaz informed Creelman of his plans to retire in 1910. He explained that Mexico was capable of democratic action and that "if an opposition party were to arise in the Republic, I would regard it as a blessing and not an evil." Díaz's meaning was not clear, although perhaps his intentions have been best captured by John Womack's phrase that "he was sincere, but not serious."? Regardless, Díaz's statement led to political maneuvering and intrigue as politicians evaluated how best to advance their own interests.

Ambitious politicians had to decide between supporting their choice for a vice-president or the incumbent and thus appearing not to oppose Díaz's choice if and when that choice was made. The president still retained significant popularity and influence. In announcing its support for Díaz, the Partido Político Independiente stated that "Díaz should continue for a longer period of time in office . . . because there is no one who has the prestige equal to his."

Most politicians chose to stay out of the presidential race because a direct challenge to Díaz carried too much risk. Yet discontent was expressed against the president nonetheless. For example, the Catholic newspapers *El País* and *El Tiempo* voiced disapproval of a Díaz-led ticket. Other groups were formed, not to campaign against Díaz but to advance new vice-presidential candidates: specifically, Bernardo Reyes and Ramón Corral. Given the fact that Díaz would be 80 years old if elected in 1910, many believed the vice-president-elect would be Mexico's next president. Following the Creelman interview, two individuals emerged seeking the vice-presidency: Díaz's minister of War, Bernardo Reyes; and incumbent vice-president Ramón Corral, supported by the Científicos.

By early 1909 Bernardo Reyes, governor of the state of Nuevo León, became the popular choice for vice-president. Having risen to power in Porfirian Mexico through the military and having served as minister of War, he was popular with army officers and some workers groups. Indeed, workers responded favorably to Reyes's promise of schools for their children and compensation for job-related accidents. Support for

Reyes grew so quickly that by the summer of 1909 numerous groups advocated his candidacy. Formed in May 1909, the Partido Político Independiente supported Reyes for vice-president, believing him the "most prestigious of his [Díaz's] collaborators."

Initially, Díaz allowed Reyes considerable freedom. Soon, however, as more people pronounced for Reyes, the president's patience grew short. Then Díaz asked Reyes to go to Europe on a government mission. Either through genuine fear from challenging Díaz or his political weakness, Reyes accepted, effectively ending his candidacy. With Reyes gone, Díaz announced that Corral would be his vice-president in 1910.

Reyes's withdrawal forced his supporters to look elsewhere, and they soon backed Francisco Madero. The son of a wealthy and influential family from Coahuila, Madero was well educated, having studied agricultural technology at the University of California at Berkeley. After completing school he operated his family's haciendas and thereby became interested in the condition of the workers. Observing the fraudulent nature of local elections, Madero decided political reform was essential to address problems in Mexico. Following the Creelman interview, Madero discussed Mexico's political problems in a 1909 publication, *The Presidential Succession in 1910*. The book marked the beginning of Madero's political career and the formation of the Anti-Re-electionista Party, which ironically used Díaz's old political slogan "Effective Suffrage—No Re-election."

Madero made an extended national political tour in 1909–1910, campaigning in almost all states. By 1910 many workers supported him. Despite his upper-class origins, his moderate political platform, and the traditional perception that elites were not interested in workers' issues, nonetheless workers believed that, unlike other politicians, he actually *heard* their complaints. In a now well-known speech at Orizaba on May 22, 1910, Madero pointed out that workers wanted liberty to form associations in order to exercise their rights. He concluded with the famous statement, "Gentlemen, you do not want bread, you want only freedom because freedom will enable you to win your bread."[3] In response to Madero's increasing popularity, as the elections approached the Díaz regime stepped up its repressive actions. The government silenced the opposition press, arrested Madero "for insulting the president and fomenting rebellion," and apprehended thousands of people. The outcome of the elections surprised no one: Mexico again elected Díaz.

With his successful reelection Díaz initiated plans to celebrate his victory and the anniversary of Mexico's independence, both scheduled for

September 6, 1910. It was an ostentatious celebration. Foreign representatives attended, expensive champagne was imported, and in the capital
the urban poor were herded out of the downtown areas. These events
epitomized everything wrong with Mexico and the Díaz machine.

After the election, in the disguise of a mechanic, Madero escaped to
the United States. On October 5, 1910, he presented the Plan de San Luis
Potosí declaring that the election had been fraudulent and that he was
assuming the presidency. However, his call for an uprising and the Plan
de San Luis Potosí were not well received. Despite the illegality of Díaz's
election, many people simply accepted the results. Guadalajara's municipal government even praised Díaz for preserving the peace. The newspaper *La Gaceta de Jalisco* captured the prevailing sentiment when it wrote
that the people "did not want to live in . . . uncertainty."

But revolutionary forces ultimately grew and moved with increasing
success against Díaz. By May 1911 rebel forces surrounded the federal
army at Ciudad Juárez, resulting in their surrender. Negotiations ended
in Díaz's resignation and his subsequent exile to France. León de la Barra
was appointed provisional president. Throughout the country people
gathered in the streets to celebrate the peace signed in Ciudad Juárez.

While citizens danced in the streets celebrating the end of the Porfiriato, other signs indicated serious problems for Madero and the interim
presidency of de la Barra. Various regional rebels demanded recognition
of their earlier demands. One of the earliest to voice this position was
the revolutionary figure Emiliano Zapata, whose reputation still has tremendous cachet in Mexico today.

Zapata was from Morelos. Unlike many rural *campesinos*, he owned a
small piece of land and supplemented his income as a horse trainer. His
reputation was so good that at one time he was employed by a wealthy
family in Mexico City. But he tired of the job and returned to Morelos
when he noticed that the horses lived better than some people did in
Mexico. Initially Zapata did not support the Plan de San Luis Potosí, but
soon he did when he believed Madero favored a land reform program.

However, before long Zapata split from Madero. Tension developed
between the two men when de la Barra sent troops to Morelos to enforce
rebel disarmament. Madero had personally asked Zapata to ensure that
his men disarm, but de la Barra instructed General Victoriano Huerta to
do the same thing. Soon contacts between the Mexican army and rebel
troops led to violence. Like the interim president, Madero also called for
complete surrender of rebel forces in Morelos. Consequently, Zapata assumed Madero and de la Barra were in agreement regarding the ag-

gressive treatment meted out by Huerta. As a result, prior to the election in October 1911, Zapata had abandoned Madero.

THE PRESIDENTIAL ELECTION OF 1911

The agreement worked out at Ciudad Juárez in May 1911 named de la Barra as interim president until general elections could be held in October 1911. Now the initial euphoria following Díaz's downfall was tempered by the presidential campaign. Madero received the nomination from his party in August 1911. He soon faced a short-lived opposition from Bernardo Reyes, who had recently returned to Mexico. Initially Reyes supported Madero but then he changed his mind and decided to run himself. In 1909 Reyes had represented popular disenchantment with Díaz; now in 1911 he symbolized the stability of the former Díaz regime. U.S. ambassador Henry Lane Wilson reported that Reyes appeared as the "nominal savior of the old Díaz regime," but in fact Wilson did not think he was up to the task. In a critical attack on Reyes's character, Wilson compared him to "a lath painted to look like iron." The ambassador's description of Reyes's weak character proved accurate when Reyes, believing he did not have the support to win the national election, withdrew from the presidential campaign and fled to Texas. Thereafter, as in the 1910 campaign, few people disputed who would win the presidency. Madero's electoral victory validated Wilson's prediction "that Madero will triumph over all of his enemies."[4] Madero won in a landslide with 98 percent of the vote.

Francisco Madero

Supposedly when Díaz was being escorted into exile, he commented that Madero had "unleashed a tiger, now let's see if he can control it." Like revolutionaries at other times in other places, Madero learned that the acquisition of power and the implementation of reforms often disappoint as many people as they satisfy. Imbued with an enthusiastic faith in democracy, he believed that political reform would bring about substantial and beneficial change for Mexico. But Mexico was not a homogenous entity. There were many factions who wanted many different things from the government, and Madero soon learned that he either moved too slow or too fast. In the end, his attempted reforms failed to satisfy.

Madero's regime faced problems from the outset. Prophetically, U.S.

ambassador Wilson noted a week before Madero won the election that there was strong opposition against him. Wilson wrote, "people believe his policies to be impractical, his intelligence dubious, and his character lacking in firmness, vigor and consistency."[5] Although this statement may have captured the popular sentiment in Mexico, it also revealed the ambassador's contradictory views toward the new president. Following Madero's victory Wilson had high praise for him. Yet by 1912 he had reversed his position, primarily because critical divisions threatened Mexico and the ambassador blamed Madero. His criticisms, found primarily in State Department memos, increasingly challenged the president's ability to govern. Wilson's observations were supported by the British vice-consul in Guadalajara, who reported that "the feeling of want of confidence [regarding Madero] is universal from the highest to lowest in this state." The vice-consul concluded that discussion of presidential substitutes had already been considered.[6]

Although he has often been criticized for failing to do enough for either *campesinos* or urban workers, Madero did initiate policies to address the enormous and divisive issues between the owners of the haciendas and the factories and their workers. To deal with the rural problems he established a National Agrarian Commission to examine the issue of land ownership, and the group recommended that the government acquire some land that would be sold to small farmers. But very little money was available and the landowners asked high prices, so ultimately not much land was distributed.

In the area of labor reform the government implemented a two-prong approach to provide increased benefits for workers while at the same time controlling the formation of workers' associations. But as with land reform, little was actually achieved. In 1911 strikes increased (particularly in the textile industry) as workers demanded higher wages, shorter workdays, and improved working conditions. Responding to conflicts between workers and owners, the government created the Department of Labor on December 13, 1911.

The Department attempted to stabilize owner-worker relations by preventing strikes and improving workplace conditions. These initial efforts introduced a trend of increased government intervention in the workplace that began in 1912. That year, textile industry strikes and owner-initiated work stoppages grew increasingly violent. To address these problems the government called a meeting between textile workers and employers in July 1912 in Mexico City.

Although the owners' representatives outnumbered the workers, the outcome was an improved salary structure and better working conditions. Owners accepted the government-directed plan establishing a daily minimum wage, a ten-hour workday, limitations on owners' power to summarily dismiss workers, and the elimination of arbitrarily imposed workplace fines. However, ultimately the owners rescinded their agreement to support the decrees, and the conflicts remained unresolved.

In the end, Madero did not carry out his liberal goals with the vigor many people had envisioned. Wanting to preserve economic stability and ensure foreign investment, as well as facing growing rebel activity against his regime, Madero discovered that the revolution consumed him. The fact that he failed to achieve much of what the liberals favored is somewhat understandable in light of the enormous drains on energy and money facing his government.

When Madero became president in October 1911, the revolution had assumed different meanings for different places and regions within Mexico. People responded to key issues ranging from anti-clericalism to agrarian reform to educational goals and policies. The revolution was never a homogenous phenomenon, but rather a series of multiple demands for fairly specific issues. And those who seek change are rarely patient.

From late 1911 until his murder in February 1913, Madero faced continuous attacks on his government. The revolutionary process became more radicalized as different factions presented their demands for a new Mexico.

Revolutionary Factions

The first serious break came when Emiliano Zapata pronounced against Madero with the Plan de Ayala on November 20, 1911. Zapata blamed Madero for failing to address the issue of land distribution for rural *campesinos*, and Madero defended his administration by saying he had not promised as radical a position as Zapata demanded. Nevertheless Zapata's pronouncement and his call for land reform became a prominent source of opposition against Madero.

Zapata's action opened a floodgate of pronouncements against Madero. In December 1911, Bernardo Reyes returned from the United States. Because of his former connections with the military he was perceived as a viable threat, but he soon learned he did not have substantial following within the military. Now his association with the Porfiriato was no longer an advantage. Recognizing this, he surrendered to Madero's government and was imprisoned in Mexico City (a locale that would have deadly consequences in 1913; see subsequent discussion).

From the northern state of Chihuahua, Emilio Vásquez Gómez pronounced against Madero because Madero had abandoned his brother, Francisco Vásquez Gómez, as vice-president on the eve of the presidential elections. Although this revolt lacked a substantial agenda Ciudad Juárez was captured, which elevated the seriousness with which Madero regarded the Vásquez Gómez faction. With the city in rebel hands, Madero turned to Pascual Orozco, a former ally against Díaz. Orozco, who was from Chihuahua, convinced Vásquez Gómez to abandon the revolt and thus avoided the possibility of men from the same state firing on each other.

In an action that would be repeated in early February 1913, Pascual Orozco, financed by the Terraza clan from Chihuahua, pronounced against Madero in March 1912 with the Plan de Orozquista. Because Orozco's plan matched the serious charges put forth earlier by Zapata, it appealed to a wide sector of Mexico's population, especially urban workers. Recognizing the issues that emerged from the strikes at Cananea and Río Blanco, and the textile strikes in 1911 and early 1912, the plan called for a ten-hour workday, better wages, improved working conditions, and an end to the *tienda de rayas*. With a nod to the issues raised by Zapata, the plan also called for the return of illegally seized land. It also accused Madero of failing to achieve his stated goals in the Plan de San Luis Potosí and of practicing nepotism (several family members occupied prestigious government posts), and corruption.

The bold language of the Plan de Orozquista was matched by the rapid speed with which its proponents put an army in the field. Untrained and poorly armed, Orozco's forces nevertheless achieved rapid victories, even against the better trained and better equipped national army. Not until Madero placed Victoriano Huerta in the field were the rebel forces suppressed—as it turned out, only for a short time.

Meanwhile another revolt was led by the nephew of Porfirio Díaz, Félix Díaz. Unlike the other movements, which were revolutionary, the Felicista rebellion sought to restore the old order. Yet in some ways the revolution had already bypassed the old order. When Félix Díaz issued an appeal from Veracruz for men to join his movement, few responded— so few, in fact, that Díaz was captured by the army and charged with treason and found guilty. Facing execution, he was saved by Madero's humanitarian side and was sentenced to a prison term instead. He joined fellow rebel, and now prisoner, Bernardo Reyes in jail in Mexico City.

The irony was that Díaz returned Madero's humanitarian favor by re-
belling against him in early 1913.

Beginning in February 1913 Madero's revolution consumed him. For
ten days, starting on February 9, Mexico City suffered from intense fighting known as the Decena Tragica. It was led by General Manuel Mon-
dragón and joined by former political prisoners Félix Díaz and Bernardo
Reyes, who revolted against Madero. Disregarding his advisors' advice,
Madero turned to Victoriano Huerta to suppress the rebellion. But
Huerta joined the rebels, arrested Madero and his vice-president, and
forced them to resign.

The Decena Tragica was compounded by the interventionist role
played by U.S. ambassador Henry Lane Wilson. Fearing the direction of
the Decena Tragica and Madero's inability to control the situation might
threaten American lives and property, and having already begun to
abandon any pretense of support for Madero, Wilson began negotiations
with Félix Díaz and Huerta. The three men worked out an agreement
legitimizing seizure of power from Madero at the U.S. embassy in Mexico City. The gist of this agreement, known as the Pact of the Embassy,
blamed Madero for the instability and credited Díaz and Huerta with
the foresight to intervene to restore stability. On February 18, 1913, General Aureliano Blanquet placed Madero under arrest. In a series of
pseudo-legal machinations, guided by the Constitution of 1857 and
designed to preserve an air of legality, Huerta assumed the office of the
presidency on February 18, 1913. The travesty of these events was
matched only by the murder of Madero and his vice-president on the
evening of February 21, 1913—supposedly while they tried to escape.
Most people believe the president was murdered; it has never been satisfactorily proven who was responsible for the order.

Victoriano Huerta

Huerta's assumption of power fulfilled the hope that a strong leader
would return peace to Mexico. Thus he escaped serious criticism despite
the nature of the coup and the murder of Madero and his vice-president,
Pino Suárez. Many newspapers remained silent about Huerta's violent
acquisition of control. The Catholic paper *El País* expressed sorrow at
Madero's death and suggested an investigation into the deaths but rejected the view that government officials had killed Madero.[7]

Initially, at least, Huerta appeared to be in control. Granted, Emiliano
Zapata's forces operated in the state of Morelos, but they seemed a small

and isolated problem. Soon, however, Huerta's government faced rebel activity on numerous fronts. On March 26, 1913, Venustiano Carranza announced the Plan de Guadalupe, refusing to recognize Huerta's government and proclaiming adherence to the 1857 constitution. Carranza and his supporters became known as the Constitutionalists.

With this announcement, Mexico split among three armies. Huerta controlled the federal army and Mexico City. To the south of Mexico City, Emiliano Zapata and his forces did not condemn Huerta's overthrow of Madero but criticized him for failing to restore lands in Morelos to the *campesinos*. In the north the Constitutionalist armies formed, denouncing Huerta's government and raising the stakes in May 1913 when Carranza declared that his forces would summarily execute all captured federal soldiers.

Despite the activity of Ambassador Wilson, the U.S. government in the waning days of the Taft administration had declined granting diplomatic recognition to the Huerta government. Instead Taft left the decision to incoming president Woodrow Wilson. Ambassador Wilson had repeatedly sought U.S. diplomatic recognition from the Wilson administration, but it was not forthcoming. Disapproving of the way in which Madero had been removed, President Wilson decided to force Huerta from office. In a document that Wilson sent to selected nations dated November 13, 1913, he made his position toward Huerta clear: "If General Huerta does not retire by force of circumstances, it will become the duty of the United States to use less peaceful means to put him out."[8] Despite his hostility toward Huerta, Wilson believed that the revolution, with its goals to benefit the people, was a noble cause.

As events turned out, the United States did resort to "less peaceful means" to oust Huerta and ultimately influence the direction of the Mexican Revolution. President Wilson favored the Carranza faction in Mexico; his administration maintained contact with representatives of Carranza in Mexico, while Carranza had officials operating in Washington. In February 1914 the United States abandoned its arms embargo against Mexico, allowing Constitutionalists to obtain weaponry in the United States. Two months later, in April 1914, U.S. naval forces visited the port of Tampico. While some men were ashore, an incident occurred that the U.S. naval commander, Admiral Henry T. Mayo, determined was an insult to the United States. President Wilson supported Admiral Mayo and used the offense and the suspected arrival of weapons for the Huerta faction as a pretext to occupy Veracruz. Now Huerta faced growing forces in Mexico and direct military pressure from the United States.

Believing his situation to be irreversible, he stepped down as president and went into exile in July 1914. U.S. troops, however, remained in Veracruz until November 1914. Although Carranza benefitted from the U.S. occupation in Veracruz as well as the relaxation of policies concerning arms acquisitions from the United States, he openly criticized the intervention. On more than one occasion Carranza requested that the United States withdraw its troops. As a result he appeared to be a defender of Mexican territorial sovereignty yet continued to receive delivery of weapons for the Constitutionalists.

VENUSTIANO CARRANZA AND THE CONVENTION AT AGUASCALIENTES

Following Huerta's flight into exile, various revolutionary factions struggled to establish their power. In this atmosphere of political instability Venustiano Carranza emerged as the dominant political leader. Being able to obtain arms from the United States and exercising control over the vital port facilities at Veracruz, Carranza claimed control. Conscious of the tentative legal position that he possessed, on September 13, 1914, Carranza called for a meeting of rebel leaders to determine a provisional president until national elections could be held. In an unexpected move for the Constitutionalists, but one that revealed how the revolutionary process had become more radicalized, the representatives viewed the assembly as more than an electoral body. Instead, many representatives demanded that the forum discuss a multitude of issues relating to social, political, and economic reform.

On October 10, 1914, delegates arrived at Aguascalientes, a neutral site. The delegates negotiated between the desires of Carranza, the land reform issues enunciated by Emiliano Zapata, and the conservative goals of Pancho Villa, who desired to restructure the status quo as outlined by Madero. The delegates represented the diversity of participants in the revolutionary fighting; many wore military uniforms, and a few wore civilian clothes—almost all carried weapons. The opening of the convention witnessed an impressive display of confraternity among the delegates, but cooperation soon gave way to open hostility. The rift that developed exemplified the divergence of opinion concerning the direction the revolution should take.

Despite the divisions at the convention, which Charles Cumberland described as a "snarling and quarrelling mass of humanity, which at times lost all sense of a deliberative body,"[9] by late October 1914 the representatives had approved labor and agrarian reform measures. These provided the foundation for labor and land reform elements that were incorporated into the 1917 Constitutional Convention. Of particular importance, the delegates committed to Zapata's Plan de Ayala. For the first time in Mexico's history government representatives committed themselves to support the welfare of the rural population.

However, these achievements marked the end of the cooperative relationship among the rebel factions. Because internal fighting among the rebel groups continued, the provisions were never implemented. Although the achievements at Aguascalientes suggested a spirit of harmony, the infighting revealed divisions among the revolutionary factions. These divisions came to a head on October 30, 1914, when the delegates dismissed Carranza as head of the revolutionary movement and named Eulalio Gutiérrez as interim president until elections could be held. Carranza denounced the decision and withdrew to Veracruz, recently abandoned by the United States. In the meantime the convention, aided by Villa, installed Gutiérrez in Mexico City. Consequently, Mexico was divided between those who identified with Villa and Zapata and those who viewed Carranza as the leader.

When the Constitutionalists fled Mexico City, Villa and Zapata claimed the capital. Zapata and his men viewed the city as a strange and uncomfortable place; moreover, they were not certain as to their role there. Much was new to these men, and their discomfort manifested itself in a variety of ways. According to John Womack, one evening when a fire engine responded to a fire with its bells clanging the hurried movements through the city alarmed the Zapatistas so much that they opened fire and killed twelve people.[10] In the end Zapata and his men retreated to the relative comfort of Morelos, where they received pleas from Villa and his representatives to meet. The meeting took place, but at a site selected by Zapata on the outskirts of the city.

The meeting of these two men represented the differences that existed in Mexico at that time. In his dress and distrust for the city, Zapata represented the *campesinos* and their views. Villa, dressed in the outfit being worn by contemporary U.S. and European calvary officers and obviously feeling more comfortable in the capital, portrayed the viewpoint of the northern sector of Mexico. The one issue they did agree on was their mutual distrust and dislike of Carranza. Both men spoke of him disparagingly, which seemed to break the ice between them. They hammered out a series of agreements as to how they would defeat Carranza, which ultimately proved to be a weak position on which to establish an alliance. By the end of December 1914 the two factions had split. Constitutionalists took advantage of this division and targeted Villa, who posed a greater threat because of his broad national appeal.

Villa's demise occurred at the Battle of Celaya in April 1915. Alvaro Obregón, a Constitutionalist general, used military techniques employed on the battlefields in Europe with devastating consequences against Villa's forces. The loss severely undermined Villa's power and limited his activities to northern Mexico. With Villa's defeat, the forces under Zapata retreated to the hills around Morelos. Zapata wisely believed that Carranza could focus his forces on Zapata if he desired, and such a military encounter could be potentially disastrous. With the leaders divided and somewhat neutralized after April 1915, Carranza directed his attention to maintaining power and pursuing constitutional reforms.

Carranza continued to enhance his position through the absorption of political rivals. To attract as many opponents as possible, the Constitutionalists initiated arrangements with labor and the agrarian population. Carranza's actions represented his "vague recognition of the social dimension of the revolution."[11] Although the March 1913 Plan de Guadalupe omitted reforms for workers, by 1914–1915 the Constitutionalists sought support from the Casa del Obrero Mundial, the leading labor institution established under Madero. Carranza appealed to urban and rural workers when he amended the Plan de Guadalupe on December 12, 1914, calling for "improvements for the condition of the rural peon, the worker, the miner and in general all the classes of workers." He pointed to the Constitution of 1857, saying that it had been established to "uphold the rights of man, freedom of labor . . . and that it promised the enactment of laws for the betterment of the condition of industrious Mexicans."[12]

Previously the Casa had resisted any involvement in the revolution, believing identification with one group would cause aggressive acts by one of the other factions. Despite this concern, on February 9, 1915, the Casa announced its support for Carranza. This decision was not terribly difficult or brazen; it recognized the growing success of the Constitutionalists, hoped to capitalize on their success, and viewed favorably the proworker positions adopted by them. For example, Jalisco's interim Constitutionalist governor, Manuel Adjure Berlanga, had implemented a minimum wage and reduced the workday to nine hours in 1914. As a result of the Constitutionalists' rhetoric and actions, the Casa and the Constitutionalists cemented an alliance on February 20, 1915, following a series of secret meetings.

Now Casa-affiliated workers joined the Constitutionalist military in divisions known as the Rojas Batallones (Red Battalions). The workers' military participation reflected their stake in the Constitutionalist government. The number of troops the Casa committed to defeat Villa and Zapata, and the effect of their contributions, long have been debated. The numbers vary widely, as do most statistics provided by the workers associations. The workers participated in a few conflicts but most likely did not influence the outcome. After all, given the short period between the agreement of February 1915 and when the workers actually fought, they had little time to organize, equip, and train for combat. Nevertheless at the Battle of Celaya, Red battalion forces composed of painters, tailors, and carpenters under the command of Alvaro Obregón contributed to defeating Villa. In Guadalajara, streetcar workers joined provisional Constitutionalist governor Manuel Diéguez in the fighting against Villa. Regardless of the number of workers or their battlefield value, their presence with the military had important symbolic value.

To attract those in the countryside to his revolution, Carranza promised a series of measures to benefit the rural population—not the least of which were restoration of illegally seized lands and protection of small property. The political intent was to steal thunder from Zapata's demand for land reform. Significantly, Carranza's declarations set the precedent for the land reform measures contained in Article 27 of the 1917 constitution (see subsequent discussion).

As Carranza attempted to broaden his base of support, the nation collapsed into near anarchy. Interim president Gutiérrez abandoned Mexico City, opening the way for Obregón and his troops to take the city. The Constitutionalists now controlled the capital but continued to rule from Veracruz. Gutiérrez moved to Nuevo Leon, where he claimed he was still president. In Morelos, Zapata called for a new president.

On October 19, 1915, the United States granted recognition to the Carranza government. Although there was the requisite celebration among those allied with the Constitutionalists, others reacted less favorably to the news. Leocardío Parra, commander of the Villista soldiers, refused to accept the Constitutionalists' promises of amnesty. The U.S. State Department reported that Parra believed that "they [he and his soldiers] had no faith whatever in the promises of the Carrancistas." He and his soldiers believed that should he and his forces decide to accept the amnesty and turn in their guns, they would soon all be shot.

U.S. businessman Daniel E. Lowery noted in an interview with U.S. consular officials that "everywhere I have been I find the Carrancista forces are dreaded by all classes alike." In repeated dispatches throughout the last half of 1915, the U.S. consul in Guadalajara reported that the Constitutionalists received little support from the citizens of Guadalajara, noting in October 1915 that "a large majority of them . . . seemed very much disappointed."

THE CONSTITUTIONAL CONVENTION AT QUERÉTARO

After Venustiano Carranza and the Constitutionalists consolidated their hold over political and military rivals on the battlefields, they moved to legitimize their goals for the revolution. Carranza concluded that a new constitution would provide the legal mechanisms to justify Constitutionalist rule. Although he possessed the power to dictate the constitution, other elements were poised as well to influence the outcome—including Mexican workers and those who wanted to lay the groundwork for land distribution as sought by Zapata.

In September 1916 Carranza called for elections to be held in the following month to select delegates to the Constitutional Convention. The balloting excluded members from Villa's or Zapata's forces. Meanwhile, Carranza drafted his plan for a constitution. Unknown to Carranza, many convention delegates opposed key provisions of his draft constitution, including his provisions on labor.

On December 1, 1916, Carranza addressed the Constitutional Convention gathered at Querétaro, where he presented his draft of the Constitution. The convention was held in Querétaro because this city had become headquarters for Carranza and the Constitutionalists since early 1916. Other than the strengthened position of the executive branch, the document differed little from the 1857 constitution. It contained only limited reforms for labor. Following Carranza's address, radical representatives pushed for more aggressive social reforms. They argued that Carranza's proposals failed to respond to problems of the proletariat. A substantial number of delegates wanted an amendment that addressed labor issues.

The constitution provided a dramatic change in the way in which things would be done in Mexico. Three articles—Article 123, Article 27, and Article 130—were significant.

The Constitutional Convention and the proposals contained in Article 123 represented potential gains for the workers. The promises of Article 123 improved the workers' subservient condition within Mexican society but also protected the economic elites. In any case, Article 123 marked the beginning of the process of co-optation whereby the workers were incorporated into the capitalist-oriented political system. This revealed the full strength of the emerging nationalist state: Not only did it create Article 123, but it placed itself as the principal arbitrator between the workers and owners with capital. By calling for the creation of Boards of Conciliation and Arbitration to review workers' complaints, and by assuming the right to determine if strikes were legal, the federal and state governments acquired key roles in mediating conflicts and in determining the future of Mexico's working class.

Article 27 attacked the principles established under Ley Lerdo that allowed claims to be made against communally held land and was later bastardized to allow land speculators to acquire land from the rural population. The article contained a significant nationalist feature in restoring subsoil rights to the Mexican state rather than to those who owned the land. Moreover, land and the subsoil minerals, including oil, had to be owned by Mexican nationals or at least by foreigners who would subscribe to Mexican law. This article was an attempt to thwart the exploitative relationship that foreign capitalists had for so long possessed in Mexico. Not surprisingly, it did not please the *hacendados* and foreign mineral and oil investors.

Article 130 strengthened and enforced the anti-clerical language enunciated in the 1857 constitution, but which was rarely enforced. The atmosphere of de facto tolerance of Catholicism and the unwillingness to enforce these provisions had been a cornerstone of the relationship between church and state during the Porfiriato. Now that all changed. The proviso furnished the government the means to control matters of worship, establish rules for clerical officials, limit the Church's right to property and its involvement in political affairs, and exclude the Church from participating in the nation's educational system. In essence the article, according to Jean Meyer, author of *The Cristero Rebellion*, "had the effect of denying the Church any legal personality."[13] Article 130 allowed state governments to determine the number of clerics based on the state's population, abolish religious orders, prohibit the Church and clerics from owning property, and restrict voting rights and the Church's teaching privileges.

Soon thereafter Mexico's high-ranking clerical leadership denounced the attempt to regulate the Church. Many of Mexico's Catholic leaders had fled to the United States to escape Constitutionalist anti-clericalism. From exile in San Antonio, Texas, Catholic clerics protested the constitution and Article 130 in February 1917. The depth of the Catholics' anger was evident in their acceptance of the decision by the Catholic hierarchy in Guadalajara to close the churches rather than condone an increased role of the federal government in Church affairs. The church in Jalisco went on strike and suspended normal services, baptisms, marriages, funerals, and saints' celebrations.

The extent of the protest caught both state and national officials by surprise. By February the governor and the state legislature recognized that the decisions of the state to regulate the Church had failed because the Church would not observe the regulations. Recognizing a political setback, Jalisco governor Diéguez repealed the anti-clerical legislation. Catholics celebrated what they believed to be their victory against the state. It was, instead, the first skirmish in a long and bloody war.

On February 5, 1917, the Constitutionalists announced the creation of the national constitution. When the delegates left Querétaro in early 1917 with a national constitution, the Mexican Revolution entered a new and decisive phase. Regional caudillos still struggled against the newly energized nationalist state; after nearly seven years of conflict they did not easily give up. Famous rebel leaders, including Emiliano Zapata, continued to seek ways in which to impose their goals on Mexico.

In March 1917 Carranza won the presidential election, and he assumed office on May 1, 1917. Numerous problems faced the nation in the early days of his presidency. Rebel factions, such as those led by Villa and Zapata, retained their regional strength and sought to pressure the new administration. Various rebel troops carried out violent acts such as attacking and burning trains, resulting in a lack of certain goods and escalating prices. Given this violence, the U.S. State Department advised Americans not to come to Mexico unless they had established interests in the country.

It has been traditionally thought that Mexico's economic problems were caused by the instability of so many years of fighting. Certainly the banking infrastructure was weakened by different currencies circulated by rebel factions. Some industrial centers were damaged, either directly by the actions of military factions or indirectly by the uncertain economy. Despite these problems, the economy did not suffer as badly as has been argued. John Womack maintains that the years of revolutionary fighting from 1910 to 1917 actually saw economic growth in certain businesses, most notably in the oil industry.[14] The most pressing and frustrating problems facing the nation were the continued violence and Carranza's reluctance to enforce the 1917 constitution.

One problem outside the control of President Carranza served as a significant distraction for his administration. Europe had been embroiled in war since 1914, but events in early 1917 expanded the involvement of both Mexico and the United States. In March 1917 Carranza received a proposal from the German foreign secretary, Arthur Zimmerman, that Mexico and Germany align together. When the war concluded, Zimmerman proposed, Germany would assist Mexico in obtaining territory lost to the United States during the U.S.-Mexican War of the nineteenth century. The note was widely publicized in the United States to promote hostility against Germany, but the Mexican government rejected the proposal. Although the Wilson administration put serious pressure on Mexico to align with the United States, the Carranza administration adopted a policy of neutrality.

ESTABLISHMENT OF CROM, A NATIONAL LABOR UNION

The decision to create the Confederation Regional Obreros de Mexico (CROM) demonstrated the national revolutionary leaders' concern with the emerging working-class movements. In 1918 the minister of Industry, Commerce, and Labor and future president of Mexico, Plutarco Elias Calles, called for a national labor union. He and other government officials had grown concerned over the expanding number of labor unions.

Responding to these fears, the Carranza government decided to create a national labor union. Coahuila's governor, Gustavo Espinosa Mireles, closely connected with Carranza, issued invitations to the nation's unions for workers' representatives to meet in the state capital of Saltillo to establish a national union. To increase its influence, the federal government paid the expenses of the delegates traveling to the conference. From May 1 to May 12, 1918, meetings took place that gave rise to the CROM.

The three major ideological groups represented at Saltillo were the Anarcho-Syndicalists, the Socialists, and the "Unionists," the latter being essentially pro-government delegates. Luis N. Morones spoke for the Unionist camp. Morones evolved into the dominant figure of the nation's labor movement for the next decade. During the ensuing debates most of the radical Anarcho-Syndicalist and Socialist delegates withdrew, leaving conservative Unionist delegates free to establish the CROM. One reason for the walkout was ideological—the expressed desire of the former groups to oppose the government, and their concern with the Unionists' close relationship with the American Federation of Labor. The delegates aligned with Morones favored a cooperative arrangement with the national government.

The delegates maintained that CROM's constituents were the nation's industrial workers. Initial debates considered incorporating agricultural workers into the CROM, but that idea never evolved beyond the discussion stage because of the perception that agricultural workers were relatively powerless. Thus a potentially important relationship between rural and industrial workers was not established.

CROM's official goal was to bring together all factions of labor and free it from domination by the political sector. However, the obvious relationship of this national labor organization with Carranza's government, as well as other national figures such as Alvaro Obregón, pointed out the hypocrisy of that goal. Other workers groups, such as the Confederación General de Trabajadores (CGT) formed in 1921, viewed the conservative direction of the government as reason enough for a more independent and more militant workers movement.

Despite the existence of alternative union groups such as the CGT and those connected with the Catholic unions, the CROM established and maintained a dominant position throughout the 1920s by its alliances with the "Sonoran dynasty" of Presidents Alvaro Obregón (1920–1924) and Plutarco Calles (1924–1928). The close relationship between CROM and the national government empowered CROM to eliminate competing workers organizations, thereby extending its dominance over the labor movement.

With CROM bought and paid for after Saltillo, the national labor organization became increasingly dependent on the government. The idea of an active government in workers' issues was not new. Historically, workers often had looked to the government to address their problems.

Despite the promises obtained for the workers with the enunciation of the constitution, Article 123, and the formation of the CROM during his presidency, Carranza resisted the union movement and made very little effort to advance legislation beneficial to the workers. His begrudging support of the rights of labor to unionize and to strike was lost in the reality of his actions. In early May 1917 strikes broke out in Mexico City, Orizaba, Puebla, Tlaxcala, and Jalisco. In all cases workers demanded increased salaries and greater recognition from the owners and the government. The majority of decisions saw the government siding with the owners. Actions taken by the Carranza government rode roughshod over strikers or unions that sought a measure of independence. The few incidents in which Carranza responded favorably revealed more about his arbitrary frame of mind than a real concern for the workers.

In the area of land reform Carranza continued a conservative policy, much as he did with labor. Responding to his belief that the president had not fulfilled the land distribution aspects of Article 27, Emiliano Zapata issued an open letter to Carranza in March 1919. He charged that the goal of the revolution—to benefit the masses—had been violated by Carranza and his immediate associates. Zapata accused Carranza of manipulating the revolutionary process to benefit himself and his friends, leaving the people with nothing. Zapata concluded by maintaining that the distribution of land alluded to by Carranza in 1915 with his amendments to the Plan de Guadalupe and stipulated in Article 27 had been ignored. Zapata's charges were sweeping and insulting. Offended, but cognizant of the power that Zapata possessed not only as the leader of a military force but also as the embodiment of an important aspect of the revolutionary struggle, Carranza made the decision to eliminate Zapata.

A series of negotiations followed between Carranza and General Pablo González (who had fought in Morelos) over how to eliminate Zapata. An elaborate plan evolved whereby one of González's lieutenants, Jesus Guajardo, would abandon Carranza for Zapata. Following a series of maneuvers to demonstrate his feigned new loyalty, including the execution of former Zapata deserters, a meeting was held between Guajardo and Zapata. En route to the meeting some of Zapata's men urged caution, being uncertain of Guajardo's sincerity. But the normally cautious Zapata dismissed their worries. On the afternoon of April 10, 1919, as he entered a hacienda, Zapata was killed in a hail of bullets fired by Guajardo's men. His white horse escaped the gunfire; people would speak for years thereafter of sighting the horse on the nearby hilltops—occasionally with Zapata riding it.

The Plan de Agua Prieta

The death of Zapata did not mark an end to the revolutionary violence. In 1919 Carranza named Ignacio Bonilla as his successor. The response against Carranza occurred quickly. Led by Alvaro Obregón, and supported by Plutarco Elias Calles and Adolfo de la Huerta, the Plan de Agua Prieta was presented to the nation in April 1920 denouncing Carranza's intentions and demanding his immediate resignation. Opposed to Carranza's plans to name the next president, Obregón sought the presidency through the political slogan "Effective Suffrage—No Re-election," which had emerged from the revolutionary process during the previous nine years. Soon elements from the agrarian sector, the military, and the urban industrial workers sided with the Plan de Agua Prieta.

By the early spring of 1920, following Obregón's flight out of Mexico City and Carranza's attempt to suppress political opposition in Sonora, the movement against Carranza commenced. The break was official with the enunciation of the Plan de Agua Prieta on April 23, 1920. The plan accused Carranza of ignoring popular suffrage, transgressing on the sovereign rights of the states, and threatening the principles of the revolution. With the enunciation of the plan, the supporters of Obregón denied recognition of Carranza's government and any states suspected of supporting Carranza. Soon Obregón and his followers came to dominate the political situation, marking the beginning of what Mexican historian Jaime Tamayo has called the first phase of modernization for postrevolutionary Mexico.[15] But modernization carried a heavy price tag. Political instability followed the announcement of the Plan de Agua Prieta. State governors who were aligned with Carranza forfeited their authority. Meanwhile local recent elections were declared invalid in the belief that Carranza loyalists had fraudulently determined the outcome.

The Pact with Obregón

On the national level the CROM leadership sided with Obregón and his Sonoran followers against Carranza. Backing from CROM was critical for two reasons. First, the national labor union provided Obregón with a base of support from a key emerging economic and political force. Second, and perhaps more important, CROM's declaration for Obregón marked a significant break with Carranza, who had been president when the union was formed. CROM's abandonment of Carranza revealed the level of dissatisfaction workers felt toward his administration and its failed attempts to advance their cause.

The new pact completed a three-pronged base of institutional support for Obregón in which he obtained the support of the unions, the military, and the agrarian associations. Yet each organization competed against one another, preventing one from becoming dominant and ultimately preserving Obregón's authority. In ensuing conflicts the mediation performed by the government elevated its position against the competing factions. The practice of government playing the role of mediator, although not new to Mexican politics, became an important component of politics following the revolution.

Recognizing that he no longer possessed control, Carranza seized as much gold as he could and fled to Veracruz by train in an attempt at exile. En route he learned that the governor of Veracruz had joined the

Agua Prieta movement. Carranza abandoned the train for horseback and continued his flight to the coast and exile, but he was caught and executed by a member of his entourage whose loyalty was actually with Obregón. Thereafter Obregón and his immediate supporters called for an investigation into Carranza's death, but in the end no concrete evidence connected Obregón to the murder. In the absence of a president and in need of elections, Mexico was governed from June until December 1920 by interim president Adolfo de la Huerta.

NOTES

1. Rodney D. Anderson, *Outcasts in Their Own Land: Mexican Industrial Workers, 1906–1911* (DeKalb: Northern Illinois University Press, 1976), 19–26.

2. John Womack, *Zapata and the Mexican Revolution* (New York: Vintage Books, 1968), 11–12.

3. Anderson, *Outcasts in Their Own Land*, 260–262.

4. U.S. Department of State, Records Relating to the Internal Affairs of Mexico, 1910–1929, 812.00/2384 (September 11, 1911).

5. Ibid. (September 22, 1911).

6. Ibid., 812.00/3070 (March 1, 1912).

7. Robert E. Quirk, *The Mexican Revolution and the Catholic Church* (Bloomington: Indiana University Press, 1973), 36.

8. Arthur Link, *Wilson: The New Freedom* (Princeton: Princeton University Press, 1956), 387.

9. Charles C. Cumberland, *Mexican Revolution: The Constitutionalist Years* (Austin: University of Texas Press, 1974), 204.

10. John Womack, *Zapata and the Mexican Revolution* (New York: Vintage Books, 1968), 219.

11. Alan Knight, *The Mexican Revolution*, Vol. 2 (Lincoln: University of Nebraska Press, 1986), 313–314.

12. Berta Ulloa, *Historia de la Revolución Mexicana, 1914–1917: La Constitución de 1917* (Mexico City: El Colegio de México, 1983), 271; U.S. Department of State, Records Relating to the Internal Affairs of Mexico, 1910–1929, 812.504/4 (February 3, 1915).

13. Jean Meyer, *The Cristero Rebellion: The Mexican People between Church and State, 1926–1929* (Cambridge: Cambridge University Press, 1976), 12–13.

14. John Womack, "The Mexican Revolution, 1910–1920," *Mexico since Independence* (Cambridge: Cambridge University Press, 1991), 198–200.

15. Jaime Tamayo, *En el Interinato de Adolfo de la Huerta y el Gobierno de Alvaro Obregón, 1920–1924* (Mexico City: Siglo Veintiuno Editores, 1987), 18.

9

Consolidation of the Revolution

The Constitution of 1917 outlined the rules governing relationships among the national and regional governments, the Catholic Church, and *campesinos* and workers. It remains the ruling tool in Mexico today. The 1920s witnessed the struggle among these factions as they established their identities and pursued what they believed the revolution promised. Although the Constitution provided the mechanism to protect these different factions, it did not instruct the people as to how they should incorporate these new changes. As a result, beginning in the 1920s the nation struggled to define this reorganization which continued to evolve with new demands and problems. Old practices died hard. Venustiano Carranza's assassination on the eve of the decade and Pancho Villa's violent death in 1923 reminded many of Mexico's previous methods of government.

THE PRESIDENTIAL ELECTION OF 1920 AND ALAVARO OBREGÓN

The practices of popular politics and corrupt political behavior clashed in the 1920 presidential campaign. Arrangements negotiated between Alavaro Obregón and the national labor movement smacked of Porfirian practices. But Obregón was not alone. His actions paralleled Carranza's previous attempt to name his choice for the presidency and to oppose Obregón's candidacy. Out of this corrupt behavior, which disregarded the ideals of the constitution, emerged some semblance of a new political direction.

The campaign for the presidency began in 1919. Obregón received support from a variety of emerging national parties as well as the national labor union. Finally the *agraristas* (those who demanded redistribution of land to the *campesiños*) and the military broke with Carranza in 1920 and supported Obregón.

Now Obregón tried to improve his poor relationship with the Catholic Church, which distrusted him because of his previous actions as Constitutionalist revolutionary general. While serving as an officer in the Constitutionalist army Obregón had targeted the Church, calling the clergy a "malignant tumor" and the Church part of "the reaction." He had held clerical officials for ransom and confiscated Church property. Not surprisingly, the Catholic Church opposed Obregón's candidacy.

In reality his goal, on the national level, was to prevent political opposition from weakening the authority of the new regime. The Catholic Church was a threat to the state's authority and its ability to carry out revolutionary plans, because it created rival institutions, such as labor organizations, that competed with the national government. As Alan Knight has written, the national government viewed the Church's utilization of "new forms of mass mobilization" as an infringement on the national government's monopoly, something the "state would not suffer gladly."[1]

Following the pronouncement of the Plan de Agua Prieta and the death of Carranza, Obregón won the 1920 presidential election. His victory signaled more than his ascension to the presidency, it marked a new change in Mexico: For the first time since 1910, it appeared that stability had returned. The price had been astonishingly high, with more than 1.5 to 2 million dead as a result of the violence of the past decade. Assassins' bullets had felled the significant leaders of the era—Madero, Zapata, and Carranza. Even Pancho Villa, repeatedly a thorn in the side of administrations in Mexico City and the United States, had put down his guns and retired to his hacienda.

While the nation mourned the loss of those who died in the revolution, Obregón faced the immediate task of rebuilding Mexico. The nation's domestic economy was in shambles, and the international economy had been weakened by the world's economic powers making the transition from war to peace as World War I ended. At this time Mexico's dependency on the international market revealed the problems inherent in such a relationship. As the U.S. economy slowed down it failed to absorb goods produced in Mexico, a situation that had further consequences as employment opportunities for Mexicans decreased. The one product that remained in demand was oil. In the postwar era, Mexico was the world's third largest producer of oil.

The role of oil had a profound effect on Mexico's relations with the United States following the enunciation of the 1917 constitution. U.S. oil interests opposed Article 27 and its limitations on land ownership to Mexican nationals or to foreigners who agreed to abide by Mexican law. The nationalist language of the article caused oil executives to fear that their oil interests in Mexico would be jeopardized, especially if Article 27 was applied retroactively, because then all foreign property would be affected. Protecting American property rights in Mexico became a key issue between Obregón's government and that of the newly elected U.S. president, Warren G. Harding. The United States, first under Woodrow Wilson and then under Harding, bowed to pressure from property interests and refused to grant diplomatic recognition to the Obregón government.

U.S. diplomatic recognition was essential for Mexico, but the conditions stipulated by the United States proved onerous. Obregón's response to these demands was closely observed—especially by the Mexicans, who believed the United States was placing excessive pressure on Mexico. Negotiations lasted for nearly three years as both sides debated implementation procedures for Article 27 and the makeup of the claims commission established to determine property damage that occurred during the revolutionary fighting. Mexico wanted recognition to ensure the continuation of U.S. investments in the country. Furthermore, the lack of recognition deterred other nations from investing in Mexico. And economic pressure could be applied in one other manner as well. U.S. oil corporations understood that denying Mexican oil access to the U.S. market would weaken Mexico's economy. Obregón refused to bow to such pressure; instead he argued that to restrictively apply the language of the constitution would weaken the device. Finally the Mexican Supreme Court resolved the impasse between the two nations over the status of foreign oil corporations in Mexico. Beginning in September 1921 the Supreme Court heard a series of cases in which the judges ruled that Article 27 could not be used to acquire property retroactively. The Court based its decision on the determination that if foreign property had performed in a beneficial manner prior to May 1, 1917, when the constitution went into effect, then the property would not be seized.

As a result, the Obregón administration initiated negotiations without thinking it had bowed to U.S. pressure. The negotiations culminated in what became known as the Bucareli Agreements. The two countries agreed to respect the decision by the Mexican Supreme Court and to establish a commission to determine the value of U.S. citizens' property losses that had occurred during the revolutionary struggle. In exchange, the United States granted Mexico diplomatic recognition. Not surprisingly, Obregón faced criticism that his government had sold out to the United States.

While facing pressure from the U.S. government and private investors, Mexico implemented several key components of the revolutionary constitution. Leading the way, and perhaps the most successful, was educational reform. The success, however, was limited. Despite significant school construction, illiteracy levels revealed that the educational programs left much to be desired. In 1921 illiteracy levels hovered at 71 percent; by 1934 they had been reduced to only 62 percent.[2]

The driving influence behind educational reform was José Vasconcelos, Obregón's minister of Education. Trained as a lawyer and self-educated in a wide range of intellectual works, Vasconcelos believed in making educational opportunities available to everyone. Under his direction the government built a number of public schools. He then hired individuals and inculcated them with a missionary zeal to reach out and educate the youth in Mexico, including Indians. He sent teachers into the more remote areas, some places two to three days' travel from a main highway or railroad line. The government's insistence on educating the Indians was in keeping with the postrevolutionary reawakening of *indigenismo* that was popularized through the mural works of artists Diego Rivera, José Clement Orozco, and David Alfaro Siquieros.

Later, under President Calles (1924–1928), educational reforms continued, but Moisés Sáenz's goals as minister of Education departed from those of his predecessor. The government continued to extend educational programs in rural areas and to challenge the Church's educational goals. In the rural communities, educational goals emphasized vocational training rather than academic pursuits. Still later, under President Cárdenas (1934–1940), educational reform included sex education and a socialist agenda. Both approaches caused an outburst of opposition. As John Sherman notes in *The Revolutionary Right*, Mexico's conservatives rallied against these programs. Moreover, as Sherman suggests, the debate put in sharp contrast the goals of the Cárdenas administration as opposed to the more mainstream concerns in Mexico.[3]

Land Reform

The Constitution of 1917 provided limited direction for the implementation of land reform to assist those who had lost lands during the Porfiriato. But the process advanced slowly. The complexity of Mexico's agricultural sector demanded caution rather than wholesale adoption of the language of Article 27 and its goals of returning land to the rural population.

The moderate response by Obregón manifested itself in a multitude of ways. Although he was willing to distribute land to the peasants, he continued to protect the large estates out of concern that Mexico would face a potential food shortage. Despite all the problems within the haciendas, they still produced enough surplus food to feed those outside the agrarian sector. Obregón was unwilling to risk a transfer of land that might reduce Mexico's agricultural production, and during his tenure the nation continued to import food. Ultimately, during his administration only 3 million acres were returned to *ejidos*; in comparison, the large estates still controlled 320 million acres.

Labor Issues

The government looked to Article 123 to improve conditions for labor, but achievement of these goals came at a high price. Lacking a national labor code, individual states established their own codes. Within the states, local municipalities established their own regulations for conditions in the workplace. As a result, government on the local and state level was omnipresent in the workplace.

On the national level the government established a close relationship with the Confederación Regional de Obreros Mexicano (CROM), led by Luis Morones. Created in 1918, CROM became the official government labor union and routinely trumpeted government policy. Morones established an important relationship with Obregón and placed the union in close proximity with the government. Rather than openly challenge the government's labor policy, CROM and Morones hammered out a relationship whereby the government took care of labor and labor supported government policy. The quid pro quo arrangement became the cornerstone of labor relations with the government for the better part of the twentieth century. From this relationship workers' wages rose, but rarely enough to offset the devaluation of the Mexican peso and, most telling, never enough to annoy the capitalists. With this relationship labor leaders consistently supported the government, and in exchange the workers' representatives received access to government officials and, often, financial payoffs. Luis Morones earned a well-deserved reputation as a corrupt official, more concerned with lining his pockets than advancing positions for the workers.

The policy of co-option reached ordinary workers as well. On local levels, municipal governments created Boards of Conciliation and Arbitration that decided issues between working people and their employers. During Obregón's four-year tenure these boards consistently ruled in favor of workers, causing business leaders to complain. In this prolabor atmosphere, other labor organizations challenged CROM's dominance. The government, however, opposed radical labor elements in Mexico, principally the Communist Federation of the Mexican Proletariat and Industrial Workers of the World. Obregón's government followed an equally aggressive policy against Catholic-associated unions.

The government established procedures to make it difficult to create opposition unions. For example, new unions were required to register with local officials. The government also determined if strikes were legal, frequently ruling that strikes led by opposition unions were not. If these actions did not work, the government was not above more draconian measures, including deportation of radical labor organizers.

The government measures negated attempts to advance more radical workers' initiatives. Capitalism remained sacrosanct. The majority of workers associations supported it, but this is not to suggest that workers accepted their status quietly. As concern grew about the relationship that labor leaders, particularly Morones, had with the government, a rival union, the Confederación General de Trabajadores (CGT), formed in 1921. At the same time Catholic-associated unions grew dramatically during the early 1920s. Catholic unions were the clearest example of union formation that grew out of opposition to government labor policies. Although they operated on the periphery of union activity, these organizations served as a reminder of worker discontent.

However, more than worker dissatisfaction threatened stability in Mexico. In 1923 the Obregón government concluded the Bucareli Agreements negotiations and received U.S. diplomatic recognition, after which Mexican nationalists viewed Obregón's role as symbolizing the undue influence the United States exercised in Mexico. Also in 1923, the last great icon of the revolutionary era was murdered. While traveling in his car back to his hacienda, accompanied by bodyguards, Pancho Villa was killed. Responsibility for his death has never been satisfactorily attributed. Theories range from the possibility that an individual was angry with Villa, to the suggestion that his murder was connected to his supposed threats to come out of retirement.

The de la Huerta Revolt

Additional instability revolved around the sensitive issue that 1924 was an election year for the presidency. As a result, different factions in Mexico jockeyed for position or influence in Obregón's selection of a candidate. Few were particularly surprised when he picked Plutarco Elias Calles as his successor. Both were from Sonora, and both had fought in the Constitutionalist army when Carranza pronounced against Victoriano Huerta in 1913.

In November 1923 Obregón's former minister of Finance, Adolfo de la Huerta, challenged Obregón's decision by announcing his own candidacy for the presidency. De la Huerta believed he was worthy of being Obregón's successor and revolted when his name was not put forward. He obtained significant support from the military. By late November rebels in Guerrero pronounced in favor of de la Huerta and were soon supported by similar actions in Veracruz. Armed with military and rebel support, de la Huerta denounced Obregón's support of Calles on December 7, 1923.

Opposition to the Calles candidacy occurred in many ways. Minister of Education Vasconcelos resigned in protest against Obregón. Many in the military, who broke with de la Huerta, had opposed Carranza's attempt to name Ignacio Bonillas as his successor in 1919. The revolt soon became bloody as opportunists, former Obregón supporters who now turned against him, and counter-revolutionaries took advantage of the instability to advance their own agendas.

Support for Obregón came from two sources—one expected, the other a surprise. The northern states, led by Sonora, backed Obregón, and soon an army advanced out of Sonora in his defense. The surprise support for Obregón was the United States. The U.S. government did not particularly favor Obregón or oppose de la Huerta, but following the Bucareli Agreements it wanted stability with its southern neighbor. Soon shipments of weapons and ammunition, even aircraft, flowed from the

United States to Obregón. Aided by the outpouring of supplies, coupled with the northern troops, Obregón ended the rebellion in less than three months.

The revolt had an unanticipated consequence for Obregón. When de la Huerta pronounced against Obregón, more than half the army (which since the end of the revolution had numbered nearly 80,000) revolted with him. Now, with his victory, Obregón ousted from the military all those who supported de la Huerta. Thus in one fairly quick move Obregón eliminated half the military, reducing a considerable amount of government expense and worry. After the de la Huerta revolt, Obregón and subsequent presidents relied on military personnel trained in military academies and those whose loyalty to the Mexican state was well established.

After stopping the rebellion, Obregón nominated Calles with no real opposition. The suppression of the de la Huerta revolt demonstrated Obregón's hold on Mexico's political power and solidified the precedent that sitting presidents would name their successor.

ECONOMIC DIRECTION UNDER OBREGÓN AND CALLES

Both Obregón and Calles continued a classic liberal economic policy adopted by Díaz. Mexico initiated a fiscal policy ensuring debt repayment, a balanced budget, and restoration of foreign capital confidence. Minister of Finance Albert Pani slashed Mexico's budgets, negotiated better debt repayment schedules, established a national banking system, implemented a tax reform policy, and pursued expenditures for public works projects.

Influenced by these fiscal reforms and aided by income from oil exports and foreign capital, Mexico spent millions developing roads and railroads. At the same time, money was spent on improving the nation's agricultural sector. Specifically, government funds were directed to assist in the development of a better irrigation system that expanded the country's arable land. Improvements occurred in virtually all these sectors, but problems with U.S. business interests threatened the achievement of these projected goals.

Calles faced numerous crises, but early on the U.S. oil interests in Mexico revealed their displeasure with the government's handling of the 1923 negotiations. Calles proved unwilling to accept the restrictions of the Bucareli Agreements negotiated in 1923. In December 1925 the Calles administration signed a petroleum law that upheld the goals of Article 27 and ignored the 1923 agreements with the United States.

From the standpoint of foreign economic influence, little changed with the revolution. An anti-foreign component can be discerned in the rhetoric of the revolution, but Mexico continued to rely on foreign capital. In fact, from 1910 to 1929 foreign investment in Mexico grew. As Jean Meyer has detailed, in 1929 foreigners invested 4.6 billion pesos in the nation; of that the United States invested 3 billion and the British invested 900 million.[4] But the dependency went beyond the role of capital and into that of market influence. In particular, the United States exerted enormous power with its trade in imports and exports with Mexico. Since the turn of the century to 1930, U.S. imports had grown from 50 to 70 percent whereas Mexican exports to the United States remained in the 70 to 80 percent range.[5]

THE CRISTERO REBELLION

In July 1926 the Calles government aggressively advanced the anti-clerical component of the constitution. Defenders of the Church responded quickly. Earlier, in 1925, a defensive organization entitled the Liga Nacional Defensora de la Libertad Religiosa (Liga) had emerged to ensure religious freedom. With Calles's action, the Liga directed the Catholic opposition; the Liga's rapid growth gave sustenance to the Catholic resistance effort. In a 1926 newspaper interview, Mexico's archbishop José Mora y del Río announced his opposition to the government's anti-clerical stance. Rather than accept the intrusive actions of the government, the archbishop suggested that practicing Catholics reject the constitution. The response by Calles was swift and aggressive. He ordered a rapid implementation of the Constitution's anti-clerical articles; thus the days of conciliatory relations between church and state ended. Foreign priests were deported, and Mexican priests had to register with the government. The Church had little room to maneuver; it had to resist the decree, otherwise its quiescence would allow the government to make ecclesiastical appointments.

With permission from the Pope, Mexico's church went on strike. Despite some reports to the contrary, this was not the first time the Church had used this weapon to express its displeasure. In Jalisco in 1919, the Church closed its doors and suspended worship services, baptism, marriage, confession, and funerals. From 1926 to September 1929 it directed a national boycott of religious services. The hope was that the boycott would generate anti-government hostility and the Calles government would bow to the pressure. But the Church overestimated the devotion of its members. Although the Mexican population was (and remains) unquestionably Catholic, the depth of devotion by its members, to the level required to generate anger against the government, did not exist.

In certain areas, however, resistance included warfare. One guerrilla campaign against the government whose members were identified as Cristeros due to their slogan "Viva Cristo Rey" (Long Live Christ the King) lasted for nearly three years. Concentrated in the west central region of the Bajío, the Cristero Rebellion remained an isolated, regional conflict. Poorly armed and led, the movement never attracted enough support or became national in scope. Despite these disadvantages, the government failed to suppress the rebellion.

Both sides employed brutal practices against each other, and as the conflict dragged on resolution appeared impossible. In 1927 the United States sent to Mexico a highly skilled ambassador, Dwight Morrow. In his capacity as U.S. ambassador he mediated between the government and the Church leadership. Morrow was not sent to Mexico specifically to mediate the crisis between the Church and State. His compassion, intelligence, and ability to speak Spanish caused many to look to him as an important figure (neutral) to mediate the conflict. Discussions lasted for another two years, concluding in September 1929 with the resolution of the conflict signified by the Arreglos (Arrangements). The Church called for its members to suspend the armed conflict in the name of the Church, and the government agreed to not enforce the Calles laws (which were not repealed) or pursue policy that threatened to destroy the Church. Although clearly a defeat for the Church and the conservative movement in Mexico, it did not mean an end to this element of Mexican society. In fact, the Mexican Right emerged from the conflict having learned a valuable lesson in how to combat the postrevolutionary Mexican state. (In its role in protecting Mexican nationalism as well as advancing a conservative position on the church, family issues, and fiscal conservatism, the Right represented a powerful challenge to liberal proposals.)

As the fighting against the Cristeros raged on, Calles had to decide on his successor for the 1928 election. Some suspected that Calles considered running again, but he would have likely faced a strong challenge from Obregón, who still retained significant support. Rather than risk a conflict, the two men hammered out an agreement in which Calles named Obregón. The constitution had to be amended allowing an individual to seek reelection if there had been a break in his term; the amendment also extended the presidential term to six years. Few protested; when two army officers voiced their opposition, Calles had them executed. In this atmosphere Obregón was the only candidate, and he "won" the election in July 1928. His celebration was short-lived because on July 17, 1928, in Mexico City he was murdered.

THE MAXIMATO (1928–1934)

Historian Frank Tannenbaum has recognized the difficulty of studying this six-year period of Mexico's history, calling it "most perplexing." When Obregón died, Calles was still president. Thus he assumed the authority to appoint Emilio Portes Gil as provisional president until elections could be held again in 1929. With Portes Gil's appointment, Mexico entered a six-year period during which three men served as president. Each man operated, rarely with any resistance, under the shadow of Calles. Beginning with the appointment of Portes Gil and following with Ortiz Rubio's landslide victory in November 1929, Calles assumed a powerful behind-the-scenes role in Mexico until 1935. With his political power he assumed the title the *jefe máximo*, and the period of his dominance became known as the Maximato. He determined political careers and ended those of anyone who opposed him.

Pascual Ortiz Rubio found governing Mexico with Calles in the background difficult, if not often impossible. Military officers ignored him; instead they received and followed orders from the *jefe máximo*. Yet despite these conditions Ortiz Rubio achieved some positive gains for Mexico. He granted autonomy to the University of Mexico, pursued a land distribution program that conflicted with Calles's views on the issue, and negotiated the resolution of the almost three-year-long Cristero rebellion. He also asserted himself as president, which further aggravated Calles, who finally grew impatient and leaked to the press in Mexico City that Ortiz Rubio had resigned. Recognizing his situation, Ortiz Rubio did just that, and Congress "elected" Abelardo Rodríguez president. Like his predecessor, he also attempted to distance himself from Calles's control, but to no avail. Unlike Ortiz Rubio, however, he did serve out his term.

The last two presidents to serve during the Maximato labored under the difficult conditions of economic instability in Mexico as the world reeled from a global economic depression. For Mexico, the consequences were devastating. Once again, its dependency on the international market created enormous problems as consumption of Mexico's exports dwindled, particularly in the areas of mining and oil. At the same time the nation's industrial infrastructure, together with its agricultural output, were weakened by the economic downturn. Moreover, the consequences of being a neighbor to the United States revealed themselves again after 1929 when the United States eliminated employment opportunities for Mexicans in the United States. The problem was compounded in the 1930s when the United States began deporting Mexicans and Mexican Americans to Mexico, ostensibly to save jobs and relief supplies for Americans during the Depression. More than 400,000 left the United States to return to Mexico at precisely the time their homeland could ill afford to absorb them into its workforce.

THE PRESIDENTIAL ELECTION OF 1934 AND THE EMERGENCE OF LÁZARO CÁRDENAS

Coming out of the well-traveled path of current politicians in Mexico, Lázaro Cárdenas arrived on the national scene in 1934. He had had an unremarkable career in the military during the revolutionary fighting, but he had the good luck to have served under Plutarco Elias Calles, who now granted him access to Carranza and Obregón. A quiet, taciturn man, Cárdenas understood the political winds and, subsequently, where to position himself. His talents and patience were rewarded with his ascension to the governor's office of Michoacan in 1928.

Later, as president, Cárdenas established the réputation that he would make himself available to the people. Apocryphal stories depicted him as willing to abandon anything to respond to the pressing needs of the people. His practice of ready availability placed the Mexican government in the position of being the chief mediator among the various camps—workers, peasants, government workers, industrialists, and landowners—and consolidating these diverse elements under the government.

Under President Lázaro Cárdenas the Mexican government became more directly involved in the nation's economy. In 1937 he authorized the expropriation of the railroad industry and placed control of the lines in the hands of labor. In the following year, under his direction, Mexico took over the oil industry. In the case of the railroad Mexico seized control of an industry controlled by domestic capital, whereas foreigners dominated the oil industry.

These actions established Cárdenas as the leading left-wing president in postrevolutionary Mexican history and at the same time advanced the rights of the laboring class. From the beginning of his presidency Cárdenas was involved with the advancement of peasants and workers. His concern about, and subsequent relationship with, labor solidified the alliance between government and the working class. His co-option of labor involved recognition of their considerable political importance. Although it was willing to cooperate with the government, labor entertained different ideas about state-directed economic development. The events surrounding the expropriation of the oil industry and the railroads united labor and the government over the theme of nationalism. These policies endeared Cárdenas to the people of Mexico; even today he remains one of the most popular presidents. In the period following the nationalization of the oil industry, Cárdenas limited his economic program. Because of what has been perceived as a moderation of his economic principles, Cárdenas was attacked for policies that protected traditional capitalist institutions.

The Mexican Labor Movement

During the 1934 presidential campaign Cárdenas urged the working class to abandon their internal conflicts and instead organize on a national level. As early as March 9, 1934, he expressed a desire to see "that the working classes would have free access to the levels of power"; to achieve this "they must organize, discipline themselves, and intensify their social action."[6] Throughout the 1920s and into the early 1930s the dominant labor union was the CROM, but internal conflicts contributed to a breakdown within the movement. It was believed that if labor could abandon its internal conflicts, a cooperative spirit would emerge and provide workers an opportunity to participate in state affairs. To achieve such solidarity two things needed to occur: Labor needed a more unified front, and Cárdenas had to eliminate former president Elías Plutarco Calles as a political opponent. His power threatened to disrupt the precarious relationship developing between labor and Cárdenas. Calles protested the June 1935 strikes as subversive, arguing that they disrupted the national economy. Meanwhile Cárdenas announced his support for the workers. His administration received the immediate support of labor leader Vicente Lombardo Toledano. In this struggle, Calles's hold on Mexican politics ended with Cárdenas the winner. Both Calles and labor leader Morones fled to exile in the United States in 1936.

Now Cárdenas was free to enunciate his labor policy. In Monterrey, on February 6, 1936, he announced a "Fourteen Points" labor policy and he declared that the government would carry out Article 123. The overall outcome was a more pro-active government intervening between labor and management to resolve labor conflicts. An important result of this mediating role was that the government positioned itself to better control labor.

Following his assertion of power over Calles and the announcement of the Fourteen Points, Cárdenas unified labor with the creation of the Confederación de Trajabadores de Mexico (CTM) under the leadership of Vicente Lombardo Toledano. Cárdenas rewarded labor for its support by encouraging workers to strike for improvements in the workplace. These strikes were often resolved in labor's favor. The relationship between the workers and the government was not new to Mexican politics, but the new atmosphere encouraged labor to believe that its concerns were being better received under Cárdenas than under previous administrations.

By 1937 conditions within the Mexican railroad industry revealed the lack of concise planning and development. For example, some areas in Mexico did not have a rail line, and the nation did not possess a standard track gauge. Also, Mexico's railroad system lacked a national network. Instead the railroads remained as they had been in the nineteenth century, designed for the extraction of goods. These factors restricted development of Mexico's economic infrastructure. The problem revealed the influence of foreign investors who were more interested in regional concerns than in Mexico's national economic development. From 1926 to 1937 the National Railways, which owned 66.9 percent of the country's railroads, made no significant improvements, and attempts to maintain existing equipment were so expensive that they were often neglected. The failure to both standardize the railway system and continue the necessary care of the lines hampered Mexican economic development. It was becoming clear that these policies were contributing to the conflict arising within the railroad industry. As U.S. government observers noted in 1937, even the government thought the railroad industry "was going more and more into the red [and] becoming practically bankrupt."[7]

By 1936 the railroad industry faced the threat of strikes. On February 18, 1936, Cárdenas exacerbated conditions between the owners and labor by encouraging workers to demand a paid day off for every six days worked. As a result workers' issues grew; not only were they clamoring for better pay, but now they also wanted a paid day off. Certainly Cárdenas's decree, as well as the statement that the government should "intervene in the class struggle on the side of labor which was the weaker party," encouraged the workers to protest their condition.[8]

These demands and Cárdenas's presence led the Union of Railroad Workers to strike against the National Railways of Mexico, Inc., beginning on May 18, 1936. Immediately the Federal Board of Conciliation and Arbitration declared the strike illegal. In a move that demonstrated the unity and strength of the railroad union, the railroad workers agreed to go back to work. One month later, after a series of meetings, the National Committee of the Confederación de Trabajadores de Mexico (CTM) agreed on a one-hour strike of all employees connected with the CTM. The strike that occurred, a half an hour in the morning and evening, demonstrated the unity and power of the CTM and announced labor's intent to strike as guaranteed by the 1917 constitution.

With the railroad conflict worsening, and the possibility of more disruptive strikes, Cárdenas invoked the 1936 expropriation law on June 23, 1937. By using this law he brought the railroad industry under national control, with the government retaining title of the industry. To placate labor, he directed workers to manage the railroads. Mexico's Senate approved the transfer of administrative control to the workers beginning May 1, 1938.

Response to the nationalization of the railroads was favorable, although there was some surprise at the idea of direct government economic intervention. The *Mexican Labor News* applauded the government action because it best served the goals of Mexico. Even conservatives recognized that expropriation of the railroads would improve the industry. These improvements not only benefited the railroads but strengthened a basic sector of the industrial infrastructure; thus national economic development was promoted. The fact that ideologically divided camps supported the nationalization is echoed in Judith Hellman's argument that the "policies that Cárdenas hoped to pursue were not revolutionary; they were reforms aimed at improving, rather than overturning, an existing situation."[9]

Nationalization of the Oil Industry

By 1935 Mexican petroleum workers demonstrated their capacity to organize and experienced local union victories. The oil workers were encouraged by Cárdenas's defiance of foreign oil interests. He wanted oil companies to pay more taxes, increase production, raise wages, and improve conditions in the workplace. With the president advocating these issues, oil workers created the Sindicato de Trabajadores Petroleros de la República Mexicana (STPRM), a coalition of twelve petroleum unions supported by railroad, electrical, and mining unions. In 1936 the STPRM joined the CTM, further expanding the influence of Mexican labor.

On May 28, 1937, STPRM struck over poor wages. Subsequently a government commission ruled that "workers' demands fell within the industries' capacity to pay,"[10] but the foreign oil companies refused to accede. However, the ruling laid the groundwork for a legal strike and enhanced the growing relationship between labor and the state. By using the proper legal channels, both labor and Cárdenas underscored their desire to maintain the status quo and operate within the existing system. However, while the oil workers' union cooperated with government officials, the state assumed more authority than labor; this increased labor's dependency on Cárdenas and subsequent administrations. By forcing labor into a dependent relationship with the state, Cárdenas followed a time-honored political tradition of co-opting potential political opponents within the system.

From the national palace on March 18, 1938, Cárdenas announced the expropriation of seventeen foreign oil companies because they were in defiance of a ruling by the Mexican Supreme Court. His announcement received immediate and harsh criticism from the international oil interests and foreign governments. His decision also underlined Mexico's intention to limit foreign influence in the nation's economy. Cárdenas justified his action on Constitutional Article 123, which protected Mexican labor, rather than on Article 27, which protected Mexican land. With this move he both nationalized the oil industry and advanced an aspect of the Mexican Revolution for labor.

Mexico's subsoil rights were preserved, the rights of labor were upheld, and—of considerable domestic importance—a strong sense of national pride was established. Historian James Wilkie has called Cárdenas's expropriation the "high point of his economic nationalism."[11] Cárdenas's allies in government and labor (in particular, CTM organizer Lombardo Toledano) viewed his expropriation measures as the "key to the economic independence and development of Mexico."[12]

Now the government was flooded with support from all sectors. The Church approved Cárdenas's actions. Voluntary contributions were raised to aid the government in repaying the oil companies for financial losses they claimed associated with expropriation. Mexico created the national controlled oil company called Petróleos Mexicanos (PEMEX) in 1938. It remains the dominant force in the oil sector, strong enough to have resisted the free market policies implemented by Presidents Carlos Salinas and Ernesto Zedillo since 1988.

Cárdenas's nationalization of the oil and railroad industries demonstrated the traditional nature of his labor policy. His administration preserved capitalism, silencing conservative critics who feared that his goal was socialism. By bringing the labor movement into the government, he ensured that the Mexican government could direct its role in the state capitalist system rather than allow a more radical labor system to emerge.

Land Reform

Cárdenas addressed the issue of land reform quickly upon assuming office. Recognizing that millions still did not own land, he followed a program designed to fulfill the promises contained within the constitution, now nearly twenty years old. During his tenure the Mexican government distributed almost 50 million acres of land—more than twice the amount distributed by all previous presidents since 1917. The bulk of the land went to *ejidos* rather than to individual landholders. The government assisted those who received land by creating the Banco de Crédito Ejidal, a lending agency that made funds available to land recipients so they could implement projects to enhance the land's productive capacity.

Critics protested Cárdenas's agrarian reform attempts, and some complaints were justifiable. For example, the president did not distribute land owned by his friends or land held by foreigners. For example, lands controlled by the U.S.-owned United Sugar Company also remained untouched. The distribution of land to the communal organizations such as the *ejidos* resulted in a decline in the nation's agricultural production, as cotton and henequen production decreased during the 1930s. Food production also declined, resulting in unhealthy rural diets; infant mortality remained high and rural income declined. In certain cases these complaints were valid, but the transfer of lands under Cárdenas definitively ended an era. His land reform measures marked the end of more than four centuries of dominance by landowners. The social gains, when compared to the economic losses, should be regarded as more important.

The Partido Revolucionario Mexicano

The Partido Revolucionario Nacional (PRN) had governed Mexico's politics since Calles established it in 1929. Cárdenas, however, saw significant changes moving across the Mexican landscape and needed a political instrument with a broader base of support for his policies. By

1938 the liberal experiment associated with Cárdenas was ending. In that same year the land distribution program slowed, and two years earlier, in 1936, the educational reforms that emphasized a socialist orientation in the classroom had ended. In truth, Cárdenas's liberal experiment reached its zenith with the nationalization of the railroad and oil industries.

With the reforms by the Cárdenas administration directed at both workers and the rural population, changes in the makeup of the official party were necessary. Moreover, Cárdenas wanted to weaken the influence of the military that had been omnipresent since the revolution. To achieve these goals the government expanded corporate membership in the national political party by creating the Partido de la Revolución (PRM). Now the membership included workers (including the CROM, the CGT, and the CTM) *campesinos*, the middle class, and, of course, the military—which was retained, but with limited influence owing to the party's expanded membership.

The irony is that this liberal president would, by the end of his tenure, lay the groundwork for a conservative instrument that ultimately controlled Mexico for the duration of the twentieth century.

NOTES

1. Alan Knight, *The Mexican Revolution*, Vol. 2 (Nebraska: University of Nebraska Press, 1986), 505.

2. Jean Meyer, "Revolution and Reconstruction in the 1920s," in *Mexico since Independence*, ed. Leslie Bethell (Cambridge: Cambridge University Press, 1991), 208.

3. John Sherman, *The Mexican Right: The End of the Revolutionary Reform, 1929–1940* (Westport, CT: Praeger, 1997), 135.

4. Meyer, "Revolution and Reconstruction in the 1920s," 211.

5. Ibid.

6. Albert L. Michaels, "The Crisis of Cardenismo," *Journal of Latin American Studies* 2 (1970): 66.

7. U.S. Department of State, *Foreign Relations Papers of the United States*, June 24, 1937 (Washington, D.C.: GPO 1939).

8. Judith Hellman, *Mexico in Crisis* (New York: Holmes & Meier, 1983), 37.

9. Ibid., 36.

10. Hobart Spalding, *Organized Labor in Latin America* (New York: New York University Press, 1977), 126.

11. James Wilkie, *The Mexican Revolution: Federal Expenditures and Social Change since 1910* (Berkeley: University of California Press, 1970), 79.

12. Dan La Botz, *The Crisis of Mexican Labor* (New York: Praeger, 1988), 73.

10

The Revolution Moves to the Right, 1940–1970

The year 1940 marked more than another election and the end of the Cárdenas era. Some have argued that 1940 saw the end of the revolutionary struggle, more specifically, that the liberal experimentation culminating with Cárdenas came to a close. The reforms he had directed were replaced, many before they could be implemented. In this new atmosphere politics had a more conservative outlook. In part, more people wanted to preserve what they had. Increasing numbers of Mexicans acquired symbols of the nation's new wealth by purchasing homes and cars, taking vacations, and enrolling their children in schools in the United States and Europe. The section of Mexican society that benefited the most from the policies that followed the Cárdenas era was the growing middle class.

From 1940 to 1970 Mexico experienced what has been called an economic miracle—a 120 percent growth in the industrial sector and a 100 percent increase in agricultural production.[1] Exactly what drove this growth remains part of a complex equation, although certainly the outbreak of World War II contributed significantly. As international trade became difficult as a result of the war-time emergency, Mexico was unable to import consumer goods that the growing middle class wanted and could purchase. Consequently the nation began to produce these goods itself, marking a transition to an import substitution growth model. Moreover, Mexican exports to the United States rose during the war. The additional income provided the financial means with which to invest in the growing industrial infrastructure.

The economic miracle, however, contained seeds of discontent. The working class felt restricted by the government's limits on labor's ability to protest or initiate a strike, and the rural population resented that land reform policies were ignored after the Cárdenas administration. By the 1960s when the government's economic policies—particularly in the area of agricultural exports—began to weaken, the government found itself incapable of taking care of the urban population. Even the middle class began to voice its displeasure with the government. For years the middle class had remained silent about the government's repressive actions, but the growing economic problems led some within the middle class to join ranks with those expressing their dissatisfaction. Ultimately the growing discontent manifested itself in the 1968 student demonstrations that were brutally suppressed by the military.

The economic policies that led to the economic miracle had their origins in the outbreak of World War II. Many of the populist programs initiated by the Cárdenas administration were abandoned at the outbreak of World War II and the election of Manuel Avila Camacho as president in 1940. Notably the land distribution programs were slowed down. The conservative direction for land reform was reinforced by an amendment to the constitution that allowed large landholders to hold their property and even add to their holdings. As a result they dominated the production and distribution of agricultural goods. By 1920, 2 percent of the farms controlled 76 percent of the land. Perhaps more significantly, these large farms concentrated on the production of goods bound for the international market. As a result, Mexico's population saw a reduction in the average per capita food consumption by the 1970s.[2]

Not all the goals promoted by Cárdenas, however, were lost. In the economic sector, the government continued to play a prominent role. The state expanded its presence in the public sector through the construction of public works projects for transportation and notably in irrigation projects to increase the productivity of arable land.

THE PRESIDENCY OF MANUEL AVILA CAMACHO (1940–1946)

The campaign for the 1940 presidential election revealed that the power held by Cárdenas had weakened by the end of his tenure. Many

Mexicans were angry and distrustful over the direction Mexico had taken since 1934, with inflation cutting across class lines. Moreover, Cárdenas's virulent anti-clericalism pushed many people into opposing the incumbent government. Initially favoring Francisco Múgica as his successor, Cárdenas ignored the critics within the Partido Revolucionario Mexicano (PRM) who feared Múgica would push for social reforms rather than continue to advance programs to enhance the economic sector. Mugica had been a reformist-minded politician aligned with the radical programs of Cárdenas, but he angered many of the nation's governors who feared that his leadership would threaten their control within their respective states.

At least two factors limited Cárdenas's ability to determine the next president. First, the Mexican economy weakened as the effects of war in Europe reached Mexico, leading to a loss of markets for Mexican exports. Second, the political right, which was finally becoming organized after more than a decade of resistance regarding the direction of the revolution, now had enough influence to dictate that the official party support a more centrist candidate. Seeking a moderate candidate and demonstrating its independence separate from the executive, the PRM officially nominated Manuel Avila Camacho in November 1939.

Avila Camacho defeated Juan Andreu Alamazán, the champion of the right, and became president in December 1940. Alamazán's candidacy, backed by the conservative political party known as the Partido Acción Nacional (PAN), represented the fears within the right that the country might continue expanding socialization programs. Moreover, many people were alarmed at the implications of the nationalization of the railroad and oil industry. And the issue about the direction of the revolution regarding religion was addressed by Camacho, who, when asked about the Church, replied succinctly, "Soy creyente, I am a believer." Many interpreted his statement as one that distanced himself from the revolutionary position regarding the Church. Laws restricting the affairs of the Church existed on the books but were not implemented; in exchange the Church learned to negotiate a delicate relationship with the government quietly tolerating the restrictions rather than speaking out against the government.

When war began in Europe in 1939, Cárdenas had refused to articulate Mexico's official position regarding the warring sides, leaving that decision to his successor. In Mexico, both political camps—the left, which included Vicente Lombardo Toledano and Francisco Múgica, and the right, represented by Juan Andreu Alamazán—announced their support for Germany. Only when Germany moved into Russia in 1941 did the Mexican left abandon its support of the Axis powers. President Avila Camacho adopted a similar position in the summer of 1941 and announced his opposition to Germany. Mexico announced its support for the war aims of the United States and its allies following Japan's attack on Pearl Harbor, and from that point on Mexican president Avila Camacho advocated, unmistakably, his position for the allies.

Alliance did not mean outright participation. Although supportive of the Allies, by early 1942 Mexico had not formally declared war. However, following the sinking of two Mexican oil tankers in May 1942, Avila Camacho requested a statement of war from Congress and received it. Thereafter Mexico provided a small military contingent for service, with the most notable contribution coming from Mexican pilots who served in the Pacific theatre of fighting.

Clearly, the most significant contribution made by Mexico—and one that had the greatest consequences for the nation's economy—was its role in supplying the Allies with war materiel. Once the Mexican Congress declared war, the nation began shipping to the U.S. war-time industrial centers supplies of lead, graphite, copper, and others that were converted into war materiel.

Relations with the United States beginning in 1942 also saw an end to the embarrassing arrangement hammered out during the early years of the Great Depression when the United States deported Mexican Americans in an effort to protect jobs for U.S. citizens. But now, with U.S. men joining the war effort, workers were needed in the United States, especially in the agricultural sector. Both Avila Camacho and U.S. president Franklin Roosevelt agreed to allow Mexican laborers (known as *braceros*) to come to the United States (the United States paid their transportation costs) and receive an agreed upon minimum wage; in addition, Mexican officials would be allowed to ensure that the rights of the *braceros* were not violated. As a result an estimated 300,000 *braceros* found work in the United States (as well as egregious examples of racism against Mexicans).

While some of Mexico's unemployed found job opportunities in the United States, in 1941 Mexico began to restrict the power of the working class through the Law of Social Dissolution. Ostensibly established to defend Mexico from fascist subversives, the law broadly stipulated that anyone engaged in activity deemed threatening to society faced certain jail time. This law remained on the books for three decades and was often used against dissident elements advocating "reformist or revolutionary" ideas. Such controlling laws were enhanced by revisions in government policy toward the national labor organizations. During the war years employers possessed the power to more easily fire workers and impose restrictions on public employees. Labor leaders, including Vicente Lombardo Toledano, maintained that workers associated with the Confederation of Workers of Mexico (CTM, formed in 1936) should not strike for fear that such actions would have a negative effect on the Allied war effort. Despite his support for the government's actions, Lombardo Toledano was removed and replaced by Fidel Velázquez as head of the CTM. Velázquez adopted a more conservative approach in advocating for labor. Paralleling Velázquez's conservatism the government moved more aggressively against strikes, determining with greater frequency that many strikes were illegal.

THE PRESIDENCY OF MIGUEL ALEMÁN VALDÍS (1946–1952)

A lawyer, a millionaire from real estate deals, a former governor of Veracruz, and secretary of Gobernacíon (Government) under Avila Camacho, Miguel Alemán Valdís made clear his pro-industrial growth position with the statement, "What was good for business was good for Mexico." He also represented the new direction politics was taking in Mexico, being the first president to have not fought during the revolution. His ascension to office came at the behest of the ruling apparatus established in 1946 to replace the Partido Revolucionario Mexicana. The new party, the Partido Revolucionario Institucional (PRI), mirrored the new directions within the nation's agricultural and industrial sectors. The PRI favored preservation of the large haciendas rather than the revolutionary goal of land distribution, and it supported the expansion of industrial growth to manufacture products that had previously been imported.

Alemán's immediate entourage was young, well educated (often in the United States), and frequently united on many issues, thus they were not weakened by the political infighting that had divided other governments. In particular, the Alemán faction was united in its goals to oust leftist elements in Mexico, especially those affiliated with the communists. The concern with communists reflected the new direction within the government that had adopted an anticommunist stance that could effectively isolate the left. At the same time this position provided a rallying cry that appealed to capitalists, conservative union interests, and those concerned with polarization of international events between the United States and the Soviet Union.

Alemán's administration pursued the economic growth model of import substitution industrialization. In this capacity the state arbitrated between big business and the workers as well as between big business (privately owned companies) and state-owned companies. Public works projects became a cornerstone of Alemán's economic model. Dams were constructed along the nation's major river systems, including the Colorado, the Papaloapan, and the Rio Grande. The goals of these dam projects were to control flooding, expand the production of arable land, and produce electricity. Roads were built and improved to link the domestic market in Mexico and facilitate the movement of goods within and outside of the country. The international airport in Mexico City also underwent substantial expansion to improve transportation in and out of Mexico and demonstrate the enhanced level of growth. Not all of the government's efforts were directed solely toward the economic sector, however. In a symbolic demonstration of support for education, the government began construction on a new campus for the National University in Mexico City. These projects and the subsequent economic growth during and after World War II have been regarded by many observers as the beginning of the Mexican miracle.

As a balance to the expansion in public works, but also with an eye toward economic growth, investments were directed to an expansion of irrigation systems in the countryside. As Peter Smith has pointed out, the irrigation systems represented the new economic philosophy in Mexico in that they "emphasized productivity and profit."[3] Under the "green revolution" that followed, the primary focus was to assist the large, mechanized, commercial farms—especially those in the north. Small farmers and farming communities in the southern part of the nation did not receive a proportional degree of assistance, a situation that has influenced recent dissident actions in the southern state of Chiapas.

As dissension grew within the separate agricultural sectors in the country, the national government established the Confederación Nacional Campesina (CNC) to negotiate between disparate farming elements in the north and south. The CNC remained a subordinate agency to the official party (the PRI), indicating that the government in essence controlled the level of discourse about discontent among factions in the country.

At this point political hopes in the nation rested on the hope that democratization programs established during the alliance with the United States in World War II would benefit Mexico. The government, however, began to exercise even greater power—particularly over potential political rivals.

One of those affected was the intellectual leader of Mexico's labor movement and former secretary of the CTM, Vicente Lombardo Toledano. After being removed from leadership of the CTM, in 1948 he sought to establish a new political party that would rival the authority of the institutionalized political party, the PRI. In 1948 railroad workers protested against wage cuts that resulted from the peso devaluation, and in the following year Lombardo Toledano established the Union General de Obreros y Campesinos de Mexico (UGOCM). The Alemán government responded by declaring a UGOCM strike illegal and refusing to allow the UGOCM to officially register. Failure to receive official recognition by the government did not deter the UGOCM from being a loud voice of dissent regarding the government's actions toward labor.

Alemán continued to ensure a compliant labor force when in 1948 his government placed Jesús Díaz de León at the head of the National Railways Workers Union. Díaz de León was nicknamed "El Charro." His nickname soon became synonymous with the term *charrismo*, which was associated with the perception that official union leaders were antidemocratic, anticommunist, violent, and corrupt. Many saw the *charro* leaders as willing to sell out the union membership, because the state controlled the various officials of the CTM (the urban workers' union) and the CNC (the rural workers' union) through financial rewards and access to politicians. This form of co-opting had roots in the practices associated with the Confederación Regional Obreros de Mexico (CROM) and its notorious leader, Luis Morones (see Chapter 8). From the outset the recognized unions had state assistance in controlling the actions of potential rival labor groups. Indeed, state dominance of the CTM and the CNC made the labor organizations mere rubber stamps when they "approved" government appointments of labor officials.

Serving as president during the buildup of the cold war, Alemán oversaw the continuation of friendly relations with the United States. U.S. president Harry Truman visited Alemán in Mexico City and engendered real popularity with the public by visiting the monument to the Niños Heroes. Alemán also traveled to the United States, becoming the first sitting Mexican president to do so. These exchanges kept the two neighbors allied in the increasingly polarized world of the cold war, but benefits occurred in other ways as well. As a result of Mexico's friendly relations with the United States, loans from international lending agencies were made available to Mexico and U.S. tourists began to travel there in ever greater numbers, adding to the available dollars for the nation's continued industrial expansion.

But the growth had negative consequences as well, not the least of which was growing corruption. As the number of millionaires grew substantially, money left Mexico to be deposited in foreign banks. Revolutionary goals suffered as well. Like his predecessor, Alemán abandoned the land reform measures granted by the constitution and established laws to protect landholders instead. Peasant organizations that protested were targeted by government troops as well as the private armies used by the landowners to maintain their dominance in the countryside. A potential ally of the peasants, the labor movement had been effectively quieted under Alemán. As long as Mexico's economy continued on its dramatic path, the middle class remained quiet. Indeed, the increasingly repressive behavior of the government depended on a strong economy. Later, in the 1960s when the economy weakened, a considerable number of disaffected groups joined together to protest the actions of the government.

THE PRESIDENCY OF ADOLFO RUIZ CORTINES (1952–1958)

The 1952 election demonstrated that not everyone tolerated the repressive actions of the government. An opposition movement emerged with Miguel Henríquez Guzmán as the candidate. Known as the Henriquista movement, it soon encountered opposition from the institutionalized party, the PRI. Alemán responded by placing his support behind Adolfo Ruiz Cortines, who had served as secretary of Government. The official labor party, the CTM, led by Fidel Velázquez, immediately announced its support of Ruiz Cortines. Not surprising, with the president's support and the PRI's control of the electoral process, Ruiz Cortines easily won.

Ruiz Cortines soon faced numerous problems, not the least of which were the reputation of former president Alemán and the image of the PRI. Alemán and his cronies had been criticized for corrupt practices that netted them great wealth. As a consequence, Ruiz Cortines portrayed himself as a hardworking, fiscal conservative while simultaneously distancing himself from Alemán and his close subordinates. To establish his own reputation, Ruiz Cortines extended the right to vote to women and pushed through a series of laws that addressed the issue of public corruption and responsibility of public officials.

Fiscal problems remained an important issue for Ruiz Cortines, especially as the cost of living began to rise in Mexico. In response the government artificially lowered the retail cost of beans and corn. Many businessmen reacted harshly to this action, regarding the government intervention as an unnecessary move in an arena reserved for business. Their dissatisfaction manifested itself in a variety of ways, the most destructive of which was reduced investment within Mexico's economic infrastructure and capital flight out of the country. Not surprisingly, the government actively courted businesses to keep their money both in the country and engaged in the economy.

In April 1954 the government responded to a demand by businessmen that the peso be devalued from 8.65 to 12.50 pesos to the dollar. Thereafter investment in production increased, resulting in immediate growth in the nation's economy. Initially the Mexican labor movement supported the decision, as it led to more jobs for workers even as their immediate purchasing power declined. Ruiz Cortines rewarded the loyalty of the national labor organizations by proposing a 10 percent compensatory raise.

The raise, however, was not enough to placate labor. The UGOCM argued it was not sufficient; and Fidel Velázquez, head of the CTM, threatened a general strike unless a 24 percent raise was given. In a move that raised his political stock, Adolfo López Mateo, secretary of Labor, intervened. Workers received a 20 percent pay raise—less than what they had demanded, and less than what they actually lost in real purchasing power. But the raise appealed to many workers, and consequently work stoppages did not occur.

The actions by López Mateo revealed what Peter Smith calls the reality in Mexico—the "velvet glove sheathed the iron fist."[4] This was evident later in the decade when the railroad workers associated with the Sindicato de Trabajadores Ferrocarrileros de la República (STFRM) announced their opposition to the decision to devalue the peso. Within the STFRM emerged a more radical faction led by Luis Gomez and Valentin Compa, both of whom appealed to a strain of radical nationalism within the STFRM and who opposed the *charro* elements within the nation's labor movement. Railroad delegates from the STFRM reported in 1958 that Mexico's workers had suffered a 40 percent decrease in purchasing power since the peso was devalued ten years earlier. In response, some called for a series of escalating work stoppages unless the government addressed the situation. The government responded quickly and decisively by calling the strike illegal, authorizing the army to seize the railroads, and having the police imprison those associated with the strike. One of the more outspoken proponents of the STFRM position was Demetrio Valleja, who was arrested and served sixteen years in prison.

There were other problems that the oppressive measures of the government could not address. For example, the population had doubled from 16 million in 1934 to 32 million in 1958. The resulting strain on the agricultural system would become apparent by the beginning of the 1960s, and this strain would soon affect the middle class. Accompanying the dizzying rate of population growth was the movement out of rural areas to the cities. Many people hoped to find work (a myth still playing out in Mexico) but soon learned that the number of available jobs was far smaller than the number of people flowing to the cities. Before long, more than the agricultural system was strained by the population growth. In many cities—Mexico City being the gross example—the basic services of water, electricity, sewage, and drainage proved incapable of dealing with the demand.

These problems did not go unnoticed. In one of his last addresses to the nation, President Ruiz Cortines recognized that much in Mexico needed to be improved upon. The educational system had failed to educate the masses; poor medical facilities continued to be a problem except for the wealthy; and as the flight to the cities suggested, poverty remained widespread. Despite Mexico's economic miracle the wealth had failed to trickle down to the people, either in real income or in social services. Such conditions suggested it might be time to return to the liberal goals enunciated by the document of the revolution (the constitution) or face expressions of internal dissent.

THE PRESIDENCY OF ADOLFO LÓPEZ MATEOS (1958–1964)

In this election the official party, the PRI, had to factor in the element of women voting for the first time. Moreover, it had to recognize the strength of the opposition party, PAN, and its candidate, Luis H. Alvarez, who had received the blessing of the Catholic Church. Although many Mexicans had issues to complain about, they proved once again reluctant to change political parties—especially to one that was decidedly pro-clerical.

In the end the successful election of the official PRI candidate, Adolfo López Mateos, represented the continued strength of the official party. Also, the PRI managed to choose a candidate who was acceptable to the various factions within PRI, ranging from former Cardenistas to those aligned with Alemán. López Mateos campaigned vigorously and in doing so revealed the contrast between himself and his predecessor, Ruiz Cortines. López Mateos was 47 years old in 1958, nineteen years younger than Ruiz Cortines. Many people noted his youth, energy, and appearance. The number of women voting increased the overall number of votes, and their electoral involvement reflected an interest in issues related to Mexican youth. López Mateos emerged as the candidate who promised to deliver social programs that had been neglected since the end of the war. By no means the exclusive area of the youth, these were becoming increasingly critical issues favored by those who disapproved of the conservative shift of Mexican politics during the post-Cárdenas years.

López Mateos received much applause from those on the left when he declared shortly after assuming office that he viewed himself "on the extreme left within the Constitution." The statement had enormous implications for the nation and the office of the president. From a political standpoint, the comment was a wise move because it isolated many groups on the left. For those who favored the land distribution reforms identified with the Zapata declarations issued during the revolutionary struggle, López Mateos was viewed as an important government official who appeared supportive of their goals.

In the atmosphere of the cold war, Mexico moved to demonstrate its independence. Its position in the international arena was reinforced when the Cuban revolution, led by Fidel Castro and Ernesto Che Guevara, took over Cuba. Much to the dismay of the United States, the López Mateos government announced that Mexico wanted to uphold the principles of self-determination and nonintervention. As a consequence, Mexico was seen as operating outside the smothering influence of the United States. In Mexico, the opposition to U.S. policy manifested itself in less diplomatic ways. For example, in the National Congress legislators openly criticized U.S. actions. Following the U.S.-directed Bay of Pigs invasion in 1961 and the subsequent embarrassment to the United States, demonstrations took place in Mexico protesting the U.S. behavior. Only during the October 1962 missile crisis did the Mexican government align itself with the United States by supporting its blockade against Cuba.

The Bay of Pigs invasion was a failed attempt by the United States to stop the Castro-led Cuban revolution. The United States supported and trained Cuban exiles to invade Cuba at a northern beach called the Bay of Pigs. When the U.S.-trained force landed on the Cuban beach, they were immediately defeated.

The Cuban Missile Crisis was caused by the refusal of the John F. Kennedy administration to allow the Soviet Union to establish missile launch sites in Cuba. To enforce this position, the United States imposed a naval blockade around Cuba; this denied the Soviets the ability to further the development of these missile sites. Ultimately the Soviets capitulated to the U.S. demands, but not before tensions between the United States and the Soviets threatened a nuclear attack.

López Mateos's support from the Cárdenistas came as no surprise, as the president not only continued but increased the role of the state in the nation's economy. Government spending as measured as part of gross national product grew from 10.4 to 11.4 percent under López Mateos. In particular, the government expanded its role in foreign-controlled corporations, most notably in electricity and the film industry. That policy endeared him to the more conservative factions that had favored increased government involvement and had clearly pushed Mexico's postwar economic miracle. At the same time, López Mateos did not forget the elements on the left that had been clamoring for distribution of land, one of the cornerstones of the postrevolutionary demands by the left. More than 23 million acres of land was distributed to approximately 300,000 campesinos.[5]

State intervention occurred in a variety of other areas beyond the economic sector. In response to the rapid population growth that revealed a tremendous shortage of adequate housing, especially in urban areas, the government embarked on an extensive campaign to build subsidized housing. The new housing plans included schools, clinics, and child care facilities. So rapidly were some cities growing that López Mateos took the unprecedented move of encouraging industries to locate in places other than Mexico City.

The government also stepped up support for public education. Like other projects initiated with great fervor right after the promulgation of the constitution, educational programs had received decreasing attention. But under López Mateos education became the largest expenditure in the nation's budget, with the construction of new school buildings as well as the distribution of free textbooks. However, critics from both the left and right criticized the government's role in the preparation of textbooks. Those on the right were angered by the anti-clerical direction taken during and after the revolution and the poor light in which the Catholic Church was being portrayed. Those on the left found the celebration of the revolution's success overplayed when the textbooks failed to point out the areas in which the revolution promised much but failed to deliver.

As Mexico and the world moved into the increasingly unstable decade of the 1960s, the nation enjoyed the leadership of López Mateos whose youth, charisma, and style were widely appreciated. His successor, however, did not possess these attributes

THE PRESIDENCY OF GUSTAVO DÍAZ ORDAZ (1964–1970)

Selected by the PRI to succeed López Mateos in the 1964 presidential election, Gustavo Díaz Ordaz had the historical misfortune to follow a popular president and serve during incredibly turbulent times. Moreover, he was extremely conservative and, as events would demonstrate, intolerant. During the López Mateos administration he had served as secretary of Government and carried out a ruling under which the internationally famous Mexican muralist David Alfaro Siqueiros was jailed on the dubious charge of sedition. Although López Mateos had pardoned Alfaro Siqueiros in 1964, Díaz Ordaz carried into his tenure negative associations with his role in the incident.

The new president had climbed the political ladder within PRI, first through the state machinery in Puebla and then on the national scene when he was selected by López Mateos to serve as secretary of Government. It was this office that positioned him for the nomination as presidential candidate in 1964. Díaz Ordaz was a mestizo with dark skin, which prompted revelations that race was still a touchy issue in Mexico. Nothing revealed this more than the outpouring of critical jokes following his election—none more savage than the phrase identified with Díaz Ordaz: "Anyone can become president."

The newly elected president sought to maintain cordial relations with the United States while at the same time continue the independent position established by López Mateos. Yet once again events in the Western Hemisphere tested the resolve of Mexican independence toward the United States and the nature of their relations. In 1965 when the United States occupied the Dominican Republic in response to an alleged communist coup, Mexico, along with other Latin American countries, did not recognize the action. Four years later the Díaz Ordaz government criticized the U.S. government, now led by Richard Nixon, for its policy of intercepting drugs along the U.S.-Mexican border because the actions initiated by the U.S. government slowed the flow of commerce between the two nations. Although neither government viewed these issues as potentially serious threats to their relations, for Mexico they were examples of a growing willingness to act independently of the United States and not be viewed—either domestically or internationally—as subordinate to its northern neighbor. As it turned out, both Mexico and the United States at the end of the 1960s faced serious domestic threats to their governments. In 1968 the Mexican's government brutally suppressed a student protest in the capital, and the U.S. government was facing a divided populace over its actions in Vietnam. Consequently foreign relations between the two neighbors received little attention.

In the arena of political reform the Díaz Ordaz government acted in the traditional heavy-handed manner of its predecessors. In the last year of his term, López Mateos had supported a reform law granting five seats in the Chamber of Deputies to any political party that received 2.5 percent of the total votes cast in the national election. The policy allowed opposition parties access to the national political system without actually winning an election. Moreover, the actions by PRI were regarded as an opportunity to expand the democratic process, although in reality the policy was another example of the government co-opting opposition movements. By bringing the opposition parties into the Chamber of Deputies and regulating the number of opposition seats available, the government appeared to be granting democratic opportunities—but on a rigorously controlled schedule.

Once Díaz Ordaz assumed office, the democratic aspirations of opposition movements came face to face with the reality of presidential power. Díaz Ordaz lacked the political savvy of his predecessor and was regarded as a president who lacked any sense of political subtlety. His dealings with the PRI—in particular with Carlos Madrazo, its new president—in 1964 revealed his heavy-handed ways. Madrazo, former governor of Tabasco, was a liberal reformer who sought to continue the democratization programs initiated under López Mateos in 1963. These included increased participation for women and for the rank and file within the party, and limits on regional political bosses. To no one's great surprise, the regional bosses and their political machines resisted and began calling for Díaz Ordaz to have Madrazo replaced. In a move that revealed that the democratic policies had run their course, the president fired Madrazo after less than two years in office. In addition, the PRI began to engage in contemptuous behavior toward the opposition candidates and their parties. Mayoral elections in 1967, won by PAN candidates, were deemed invalid because of problems in the vote-counting process. The impunity with which the government was stealing elections demonstrated to many that the goals of the revolution were being threatened and that the PRI did not care about individuals, but looked to the government as a means to deliver personal wealth and serve political ambitions. Before long, anger against the government exploded as Mexico City made preparations to host the 1968 Olympic Games.

Like many outbursts of discontent, the student-initiated protests in 1968 had roots in longstanding dissatisfaction. In Mexico specifically, the students expressed dissatisfaction with the directions being taken by the PRI in regard to the goals of the revolution and a broad discontent toward the ruling system. Their complaints had historical precedent. In 1934, at the University of Guadalajara, students initiated a strike that ended only after the governor of Jalisco called in the military. Thereafter students brought down a statue honoring President Alemán in Mexico City. Increasingly the PRI used a device—the *granaderos* (riot police)—that responded quickly and with severely repressive measures. These actions aroused the anger of many people, not just students. In 1964 medical interns struck in Mexico City over Christmas bonuses that were not forthcoming and complained about conditions in the workplace as well. The government initiated some attempt to resolve their concerns, but in the following year doctors joined the interns in protesting the conditions. This time the government responded with the *granaderos* to halt the strikes.

Into this arena came the 1968 Olympics, held in Mexico City, and the eyes of the world community focused on both a Latin American nation and a developing nation. To meet the demands for athletic venues, housing, and transportation, Mexico embarked on a construction schedule that soon resulted in 24-hour work schedules to prepare Mexico City for the games. Critics charged that the extensive preparations were pulling much-needed funds away from internal improvement projects needed more urgently by the nation and the people. However, spokesmen from PRI argued that the Olympics would generate sufficient funds to justify the costs for hosting the Games. This was the immediate background to the protests that began in July and culminated in October 1968 on the eve of the opening of the Olympic Games.

On July 22 and 23 police were called out to respond to what was regarded as minor street fighting between students from two different schools. In the conflict one student died and some teachers were beaten. Three days later students gathered to celebrate the anniversary of Fidel Castro's July 26 attack on the Moncada Barracks. For many radicals, the Moncada Barracks attack by Castro and his compatriots in 1953 marked the beginning of the Cuban revolution; as a result this has remained an important event and date for those who identified with the revolution. Again the police were called, and the casualties mounted with four killed and hundreds wounded. In this atmosphere student protests escalated to seizing school buildings and fighting the police by using Molotov cocktails while the police responded with bazookas. By the end of the month students throughout Mexico City had formed a National Strike Council, which organized strikes on a national level.

August and September 1968 saw more student actions met by increasing government repression, which caused a radicalization of previously neutral groups. Now the students were supported by the lower classes that also had experienced negative consequences of government authoritarianism, repression, and corruption. As the games neared and the costs mounted, even government bureaucrats joined the protests as they grew angry over unpaid wages and the expectation that they should remain at their jobs during the athletic contests. All of a sudden these were not simply the protests of dissatisfied students who feared that their education would not lead to adequate jobs. Nothing illustrated the breadth of participants more than the August 27, 1968, demonstration that took place in the Zócalo, the plaza in front of the National Cathedral in downtown Mexico City. An estimated half-million people filled the plaza in the largest anti-government demonstration in the nation's history. Armed soldiers, supported by tanks, broke up the protest early in the morning of August 28.

Amid this potent mix of discontented elements a rally was called for October 2, 1968, in the Plaza of Three Cultures (Tlatelolco) in Mexico City. This meeting served as a venue to protest—among other things— the military occupation of the National University in September, the continued use of the *granaderos*, and the excessive expenditures for the upcoming Olympic games. Some 5,000 people (a small number in comparison to previous demonstrations) had gathered in the Plaza to hear speeches when the army arrived. Exactly what happened depends on one's political viewpoint; emotional debate still rages about the event. But it is fairly clear that the demonstrators did not leave when requested by the military officials, and soldiers moved in armed with tear gas, billy clubs, armed rifles with fixed bayonets, and automatic weaponry. The government later claimed the students were armed and encouraged the army to take the actions that it did. By any definition, however, it was a one-sided massacre of the demonstrators. Autopsy reports indicated that people died from gunshot and bayonet wounds. Official reports eventually listed the dead at 43, but the number was surely much higher. Noted Mexican journalist Elena Poniatowska suggests that 325 were killed, whereas some Mexican observers have maintained that more than 500 died. Hundreds, perhaps thousands, more were arrested, and some have been listed as disappeared. Estimates of the wounded have soared as high as 2,500.[6] Nothing had occurred of such magnitude by the government since the days of the Porfiriato.

Since that day in October 1968 there have been serious questions about the role of the PRI, the repressive nature of the government, and the direction of the revolution. It is significant that the events at Tlatelolco divided the Mexican populace between supporters and opponents of the PRI. And Díaz Ordaz has always had to deal with the fact that he was president when government troops opened fire on demonstrators.

Meanwhile, the problems in the political arena masked the fact that the nation's economic system faced significant problems as well. The peso had become weak in comparison to the U.S. dollar, and with trade deficits rising the government began borrowing abroad, resulting in an indebtedness of approximately $4.2 billion by 1970. The agricultural aspect of the economic miracle had ended with the realization that Mexico had to import foodstuffs. In both urban and rural areas unemployment and, equally debilitating, underemployment was rising. As the decade of the 1970s approached and Mexico faced a search for a new president, the country also faced serious questions about its future on economic, political and social levels.

NOTES

1. James D. Cockcroft, *Mexico: Class Formation, Capital Accumulation, and the State* (New York: Monthly Review Press, 1990), 150.

2. Ibid., 177.

3. Peter Smith, "Mexico since 1946," in *Mexico since Independence*, ed. Leslie Bethell (Cambridge: Cambridge University Press, 1991), 340.

4. Ibid., 349.

5. Ibid., 353.

6. Elena Poniatowska, "Massacre in Mexico," in *Twentieth Century Mexico*, ed. W. Dirk Raat and William H. Beezley (Lincoln: University of Nebraska Press, 1986), 264.

11

The Search for Stability, 1970–1999

Mexico entered a new stage of its postrevolutionary history following the events at Tlatelolco plaza in 1968. Mexican writer and critic Carlos Fuentes viewed the massacre at Tlatelolco as the birth of a new Mexico as it was revealed that the only method available to challenges to the government was the forceful suppression of dissent.[1] By itself the event was a significant demonstration of the repressive nature of the official party and its government leaders. According to Mexican journalist Elena Poniatowski, Tlatelolco did not have a specific ideology, but rather reflected the breadth of dissatisfaction and impatience that had been expressed since the days of the revolution.[2] In light of the governing elites' inability or unwillingness to respond to pressing public problems, groups were established to respond to the needs of the peasants, the urban poor, and the politically disfranchised. As noted Mexican intellectual Octavio Paz realized, the problems facing Mexico required a prominent role on the part of the people. Paz noted in 1975 that "the real remedy is not to be found in a reform from the top downward, but rather from the bottom upward, a reform strongly backed by an independent popular movement."[3]

Since 1968 Mexico has witnessed a growing movement to address the people's perceptions of the wrongs facing the nation. Independent political parties, separate from the PRI and finally recognized in the 1980s, have formed to provide political opportunity for those outside the official party. The economic crisis of the early 1980s provided another opportunity for criticism of the government. In 1985, following the disastrous earthquake that struck Mexico City, grassroots organizations were established to provide basic aid when the PRI was clearly unable to give it. The growing divisions in Mexico were illustrated by the successful campaign of Cuauhtémoc Cárdenas in the 1988 presidential election. After electoral fraud by the PRI was discovered, Cárdenas' "stolen victory" caused many to question how much longer the PRI could survive if it continued its traditional practices of corruption, violence, and repression.

The year 1994 saw Mexico enter the long-debated North American Free Trade Agreement (NAFTA). While some were celebrating this economic achievement, people in the southern state of Chiapas revolted in a call for goals that harked back to the days of the revolution. Their identification with one of the revolutionary icons, Emiliano Zapata, was significant. The guerrilla movement that emerged out of Chiapas is known as the Zapatista Army of National Liberation (EZLN).

In responding to these challenges the PRI has used the traditional practices of violence, co-optation, bribery, and lies. Yet cracks in the façade of its omnipresent power are growing. The revelation of the depth of corruption within the Salinas family associated with the drug trade and implicated in recent political murders has validated many charges that the government has served as an opportunity for its own players to become wealthy and corrupt. Despite the continuation of old practices and revelations of corruption and charges of criminal activity at the highest governmental level, Mexico continues to push forward the goals of the revolution and the hope of more equitable conditions for its populace. The next century may well reveal that the revolutionary struggle of this past century will be attained.

THE PRESIDENCY OF LUIS ECHEVERRÍA (1970–1976)

The legacy of the Tlatelolco massacre continued well after the events of October 1968. On the anniversary of the attack in 1969, terrorist actions ripped through Mexico as guerrilla groups exploded bombs in the offices of newspaper publishers and government buildings. In 1970 the search for President Díaz Ordaz's successor concluded with the naming of Luis Echeverría. He had served as secretary of the Interior in the Díaz Ordaz administration and thus had been considered responsible for the military actions in the Plaza of Three Cultures. Despite the policies carried out during his presidency, Echeverría continues to be remembered as the individual responsible for orders that resulted in the government massacre of students in 1968.

Echeverría represented the new order in Mexican politics that appeared after 1970—politicians who were better trained as bureaucrats than savvy political operatives. The name used to popularly describe this new breed of politician was "technocrat." Their loyalty was to the political party—the PRI—and the individuals who enabled them to manipulate this machinery.

Once safely in the presidential office, Echeverría followed his own political agenda. His actions, including the way he dressed, surprised many people. Prior to taking office he had dutifully worn a coat and tie, but following the election he switched to the more informal shirt called the *guayabera*, normally worn in the Yucatán or the Caribbean. The nature of his rule became personal, copying in many ways the populist manner of Cárdenas. Echeverría understood the need to resolve the social problems dividing the country and to strengthen the weak economic sector. In an attempt to reverse the negative association of his connection with the massacre at Tlatelolco in 1968, he released student political prisoners in 1971. He soon moved to the left in the political spectrum, particularly as he pursued policies to assist the rural and urban poor. As inflation began to occur in the early part of his tenure, Echeverría's administration created artificial price controls to keep down the cost of basic goods. These efforts were accompanied by a rise in wages to help workers cope with inflation. The response from the private business sector was to move capital out of the country.

The discontent of the 1960s did not disappear in the face of the violent repression that occurred in 1968, yet early in Echeverría's tenure the guerrilla movements and acts of violence declined. Mexico had become so quiet that in 1971 communist David Alfaro Siqueiros, who had been earlier jailed for acts of "social dissolution," praised the Echeverría government for moving toward "a progressive and advanced state."[4] The peace would be short-lived, because the winter of 1971–1972 revealed that the events of 1968 had not been forgotten. Mexico was gripped by an outburst of violent actions, principally bank robberies and kidnappings. The robberies, so the rumors went, were carried out to fund the development of a revolutionary movement. The kidnappings were of prominent officials, none more so than the president's father-in-law, José Guadalupe Zuno Hernández. Zuno, former governor and caudillo of Jalisco, was seized in 1974 and held for ransom. Foreigners were also targeted, including a U.S. State Department official stationed in Guadalajara, a British foreign office representative, and the daughter of the Belgian ambassador to Mexico.

As these actions took place Lucio Cabañas, a former schoolteacher, created his own army in the state of Guerrero. Cabañas's forces soon began attacking military installations, carried out the assassinations of government officials, and kidnapped Guerrero's senator, Rubén Figueroa. It would take a military force estimated at more than 10,000 to finally stop Cabañas and his movement. The government announced that it had aggressively ended the guerrilla actions of Cabañas, arguing that domestic stability had been achieved. However, cynical individuals concluded that Cabañas would soon be replaced, arguing instead that the problems facing the government remained to be solved.

One event forced the business community to take a radical position that created a sense of independence for its role in the nation's economy. In September 1973 urban guerrillas killed Eugenio Garza Sada, head of the Monterrey Group, on the streets of Monterrey. Garza Sada led an organization estimated to have been responsible for 20 percent of Mexico's industrial output.[5] Outraged about the rising levels of violence and angered about the political direction taken by the Echeverría government (in particular its position toward strikes and land distribution), the Monterrey Group pulled together a powerful coalition of Mexico's business community and declared itself independent of government interference. With this move the business sector broke a long-established relationship between the business community and the government.

Echeverría meanwhile sought to expand his base of support, in particular by looking to the younger generation. He lowered the voting age to 18 and also lowered the age requirements for holding public office. The president brought increasingly younger individuals into important government positions; these men became known derisively as the *efebrocracia*, or "youthocracy." Echeverría hoped to use this voting bloc to sustain his reformist policies and counter the entrenched authority of the PRI as well as power possessed by the Monterrey business group.

Echeverría's populist efforts reminded many of those associated with Cárdenas, which stirred deeply rooted emotions both for and against what Cárdenas had attempted. Also reminiscent of the former president, Echeverría pursued improvements in the productive capacity of the nation's agricultural sector. Although his goal was to increase food supplies and achieve a decreased dependence on foreign agricultural imports, he also wanted to quiet discontent within the peasant associations. Thus he embarked on an agrarian distribution program. One component was the recognition that in 1970 Mexico imported nearly 700,000 tons of corn, so he ultimately distributed more than 12 million hectares of land to promote domestic production. These actions angered the private landholders, who viewed his policies as a threat. When peasants seized land in the state of Sonora, the response was predictable: Conservative landholders rallied support from their conservative industrial peers to oppose the action. As Echeverría's administration drew to a close, the president acted independently by upholding the legality of the land seizures.

The challenges from the rural elements and independent movements within the industrial elite paled in comparison to the economic problems pressing on the country. By 1973 inflation had reached 20 percent, marking the end of the Mexican miracle. Because it became difficult for Mexico to export products to the international market, a rising imbalance between imports and exports occurred. This imbalance revealed the weakness of Mexico's economy, in that much of the nation's industry relied on government protection.

Rising inflation was accompanied by declining outputs in electricity, steel, and oil. In the face of these challenges Echeverría enacted programs to expand the state's role in the economy. In 1973 laws were passed that enabled the state to regulate the role of foreign corporations (but unlike the policies implemented under Cárdenas, not to eliminate the foreign presence). In recognition of inflationary problems, government spending rose from 8 to 12.5 percent of the nation's gross domestic product (GDP). As under Alemán, monies poured into school construction, housing projects, and agricultural development. In fact, agricultural projects, soon accounted for 20 percent of the national budget.[6] The increased government spending brought an increase in GDP, yet the rise in GDP hid an ugly reality: Funding for these government programs came from deficit spending and multilateral loans. The Echeverría government had to resort to foreign capital because the private business community made clear its opposition to restructuring the tax codes.

Even with this substantial growth, for the first time since 1954 rumors circulated that the peso needed to be devalued. As the rumors mounted and were countered by the government, the wealthy elite began to send their money out of the country. Disparaged as being unpatriotic, these individuals became known as *sacadólares* (dollar extractors); nothing, however, stopped the capital flight.

By 1976 it was clear that expanded government services and subsidies had not achieved economic stability or thwarted inflation. Instead, Echeverría's actions had contributed to a rise in the nation's debt. Increasingly he faced criticism from the domestic press and intellectuals. Noted Mexican historian Daniel Cosío Villegas wrote essays chastising the president's policies, something that had not been done to a sitting president in years.[7]

Nothing dramatized the failures of the past six years more than the decision in the fall of 1976 to devalue the peso. Beginning on August 31 the government let the peso "float" to a natural level that dropped from 12.50 to 19.90 (to the dollar) by September 12. A month and a half later the government again "floated" the peso, and it dropped to 26.50 to the dollar. In two months Mexico's currency lost more than 50 percent of its value. The Mexican miracle had indeed ended.

Accompanying the fiscal instability were threats of violent repercussions throughout Mexico. Rumors flew around the country that various individuals would be threatened. Soon these threats could not be dismissed. In August 1976 Margarita López Portilla, wife of president-elect José López Portilla, was attacked by terrorists in Mexico City. She escaped unharmed, although one of her bodyguards was killed. As the peso continued to weaken, more rumors of politicians being targeted were heard; in this atmosphere it was not easy to dismiss the rumor that a military coup was being considered.

Instead the nation prepared for the upcoming inauguration of José López Portilla. Echeverría had startled Mexican political observers in 1975 by suggesting that "public opinion" should be considered in the evaluation of the presidential selection process. In doing so he laid the groundwork for a more democratic process. Several candidates emerged at the same time the PRI called for a government plan that the official candidate would uphold. Soon the selection process revealed the heavy-handed role of the PRI and the president. In September 1975 José López Portilla, Echeverría's secretary of the Treasury, was announced as the next candidate. Labor announced its support for the official candidate, with the *campesinos* association, the CNC, adding its support. Many suspected that Lopez Portilla was selected because Echeverría could easily manipulate him. As with previous elections, the contest in July 1976 was a foregone conclusion. The farcical nature was enhanced by PAN's inability to present a candidate of its own.

THE PRESIDENCY OF JOSÉ LÓPEZ PORTILLA (1976–1982)

Given the instability at the end of Echeverría's tenure, incoming president López Portilla sought to end the violence, limit corruption, and create a more cooperative relationship between government and those advocating substantial government reforms. In this effort he followed a well-established policy of political reform. New parties were allowed to appear, so the communists and socialists fielded parties; it became easier for new parties to register; the number of seats in the Chamber of Deputies grew; and all parties were given access to the media.

As before, the political concerns masked the more pressing problem of economic uncertainty. The import subsidization policy that had driven Mexico's economic miracle ended during Echeverría's reign. Now López Portilla had to wrestle with the antagonistic relationship between government and industrialists as well as address the issue of land seizures by peasants. Consequently many people viewed the economic future with trepidation.

The economic concerns soon became less pressing with the discovery of new oil reserves. Oil was discovered in Tabasco, Chiapas, and offshore sites in the Gulf of Mexico. Since the end of the nineteenth century Mexico had been producing enough oil to supply domestic needs, and during both world wars its oil exports had risen, but Mexico had never become a major international player in the oil industry. All this began to change in the 1970s. New reserves had been found while Echeverría was president, but the discoveries continued to mount at a dizzying pace under López Portilla. By 1980 Mexico claimed to have 5 percent of the world's oil reserves and 3 percent of its natural gas reserves. Oil production more than tripled under López Portilla, so that Mexico soon became the world's fourth leading producer of oil. Not only did the nation experience a rise in oil production, but the price of oil rose at the same time. Earnings rose even more dramatically than oil production, with revenues growing from approximately 500 million pesos to more than 6 billion by 1980.

These discoveries and the revenue they generated profoundly influenced Mexico. The nation's confidence rose dramatically with the recognition by López Portilla that there are two types of countries, those that have oil and those that do not—"We have oil." Under López Portilla, Mexico challenged the United States in the international arena. For example, Mexico did not participate in the U.S.-led boycott of the 1980

Olympic Games, and it granted recognition to rebel forces in El Salvador in 1981.

Although oil emboldened Mexico within the international community, it created escalating problems in the nation's economy. Flush with its rising wealth from oil, the López Portilla administration initiated steps to enhance the economy, increase employment opportunities, and reduce the balance of payments deficit that had grown during the 1970s. As a consequence Mexico became increasingly dependent on oil and the international market. In the countryside, oil revenues were targeted to help increase agricultural productiveness and eliminate the need for food imports. López Portilla created the Mexican Food System (Sistema Alimentario Mexicano (or SAM) to direct agricultural production goals. Significant results were achieved, but many critics pointed out that the numbers were artificially inflated due to substantial rainfall that followed a prolonged drought. Even with the direction of SAM and substantial financial support from the World Bank, Mexico still imported foodstuffs.

The importation of food paralleled the rise in other imports and revealed a serious problem within the oil-driven economy. Flush with money, Mexico continued to import heavily and thereby failed to lower the balance of payments. By 1979 the debt constituted more than 30 billion pesos per year; these numbers remained essentially the same over the next two years. Parallel to the commercial deficit, government spending also grew. During the Echeverría years government spending amounted to approximately 7 percent of the GDP, but by the end of López Portilla's tenure in 1982 it had risen to more than 18 percent. To meet these climbing costs Mexico turned to foreign lending agencies for financial support, using oil as collateral. During López Portilla's administration Mexico's debt nearly tripled from 30 to 80 billion pesos. At the same time inflation skyrocketed to 100 percent by 1982 from an average of 20 percent in 1975. As a result, purchasing capabilities became increasingly difficult.[8]

Now Mexico began losing capital, as investors looked to foreign investment opportunities. Those who did not choose to invest simply deposited their money in foreign banks; regardless of the method, money was flowing out of Mexico. In 1982 the López Portilla government attempted to address the economic uncertainty and, in doing so, made it worse. He revealed his understanding of the nature of the problem when he instructed the nation's banks to "float" the peso, as Echeverría had earlier done, but the consequences were equally damaging. The peso quickly dropped from 26 to 45 pesos to the U.S. dollar and by summer reached between 75 and 80 pesos to the dollar.

International lending agencies recognized the problem and started to address the possibility of Mexico defaulting on its loans. Meanwhile López Portilla, like Echeverría, blamed forces outside of the government. He complained about the *sacadólares*, accused the banks of theft, and denounced those who were growing wealthy by manipulating the economic instability. In this mindset López Portilla in September 1982 made the rash decision to nationalize the nation's banking system and artificially established the peso at 70 pesos to the dollar. Although the left approved the action, the decision weakened the long-standing relationship between the state and private (both domestic and foreign) capitalists. Moreover, the nationalization of the banks meant that the state, already economically weakened, now had to shoulder the economic burden of the private banks.

López Portilla left office like Echeverría did: with the economy worse than when he assumed office and the populace angry that during the economic crisis the president had grown wealthy. Some feared that the economic problems might actually threaten the nation's social stability.

THE PRESIDENCY OF MIGUEL DE LA MADRID (1982-1988)

In this political and economic atmosphere Miguel de la Madrid was inaugurated in December 1982. During his campaign and in his inaugural address he commented on the need to lay the groundwork for renovating the nation's moral character, improving democratic opportunities, and increasing the power of the judicial and legislative branches; such comments reflected the traditional liberal position. But in 1982 his words apparently had some consequence, as the number of people voting increased. Enrique Krauze, in *Mexico: A Biography of Power*, writes that the turnout demonstrated the public's support for de la Madrid's declaration for the "moral renovation of society."[9] The people and increasingly the media were paying attention. In 1983 the press repeatedly reported on the excesses of the previous administration. Charges were even leveled against government officials for their connection to the drug trade in Mexico. Mexico City's police chief, among others, was implicated.

The new president surrounded himself with political analysts and economists who became known as "technocrats." Armed with their knowledge of economic issues, the government moved quickly and decisively. The international financial community led by the International Monetary Fund (IMF) established conditions to address the nation's economy. Mexico reduced its expenditures in GDP and eliminated artificial price controls on many goods. Again in an attempt to achieve financial stability, the de la Madrid administration "floated" the peso and watched it drop to 150 pesos to the dollar in 1983. This proved to be a temporary stop in the decline. From 1983 to 1986 the peso went on a virtual free-fall, reaching 800 pesos to the dollar; 1987 saw the continuation of the same trend as it moved to the unbelievable exchange rate of 2,300 pesos by December 1987.

The impact of this downturn had devastating consequences on the majority of the population, especially as the country's foreign debt mounted at a similarly drastic pace. The government implemented measures that included restructuring the debt payment schedules, but various factions argued for halting all debt payments. The government chose not to consider this potentially devastating course of action because future loan arrangements would have been difficult to obtain.

Inflation continued to run between 70 to 80 percent; by 1986 it rose above 100 percent; and it reached a high of nearly 160 percent by 1987. Yet real wages rose only one-third that amount. With the loss of artificial price supports the price of basic goods skyrocketed and inflation led to a decrease in individual purchasing power, plunging many people into real economic uncertainty. The growing complaints by workers, both urban and rural, raised the possibility of strikes and began to threaten the relationship between organized workers and the government. This situation became dangerous in the ensuing years as the nation attempted to respond to the Mexico City earthquake of 1985, mounting inflation, growing political opposition movements, and the emergence of guerrilla operations, most notably the one in Chiapas.

To counter the government's debt, decrease expenditures, and meet the demands of international lending agencies, Mexico instituted a number of economic austerity measures. Spending programs for development projects were curtailed, public businesses were sold back to private owners, and at one point President de la Madrid went so far as to eliminate certain federal government positions.

To make matters worse, on September 19, 1985, at 7:00 A.M. an earthquake registering more than 8 on the Richter Scale struck Mexico City. More than 20,000 died and the number of homeless rose to over 200,000.

In the face of this crisis the de la Madrid administration could have responded in a strong, capable, and caring way. Instead the government failed. The Ministry of Foreign Affairs declared it would not request aid; it specifically rejected aid from the United States. The lack of concern on the part of the government was evident when the army was sent in to Mexico City not to aid in rescue attempts, but to protect factories. It was widely reported in the days after the earthquake that the military assisted factory owners in retrieving their machinery rather than in removing the bodies of dead factory workers.

The devastation to many buildings exposed the government's failure to enforce building codes related to earthquakes, for which Mexico City is well known. Critics argued that the lack of enforcement of such codes was indicative of corrupt practices in all levels of government. The government-built public housing complexes, constructed to house the rapidly growing population of Mexico City, were some of the most badly damaged. Mexico City's police headquarters also suffered extensive damage. When much of the building collapsed, torture chambers were revealed whose existence the government had routinely denied.

Recognizing the government's failure to respond, people in Mexico City began to organize. Students, workers, and women banded together in teams to provide rescue, food, clothing, shelter, and medical supplies. As journalist Luis Hernandez Navarro wrote, "the people got organized and responded to the double challenge of a destroyed metropolis and paralyzed authority."[10] Out of the disaster emerged the realization that a viable civil society existed in Mexico. This revelation also caused many to consider why they needed a centralized state that so obviously could not care for its people. As a consequence the opposition movements pointed to the government's shortcomings and advanced candidates for the greater goal of defeating the PRI.

Soon other charges, wholly separate from the events in Mexico City, were leveled against the government. For example, critics suggested that government officials either condoned Mexico's role in drug trafficking or, worse, benefited from the trade. As the drug problem mounted, relations between Mexico and the United States worsened. Historically the long border between the two nations had witnessed the movement of goods and people despite the efforts of customs agents on each side. Individuals in the United States blamed Mexico for the supply of drugs, while Mexico blamed the United States for the demand to consume drugs. It became fashionable among conservative critics and politicians in the United States to blame all the problems of drug trafficking on

Mexico. Pressure mounted in the United States to tighten control along the border to limit the flow of goods and, inherently, the flow of people, who were increasingly regarded as a threat to the U.S. economic infrastructure.

THE PRESIDENCY OF CARLOS SALINAS DE GORTARI (1988–1994)

The 1988 election year served notice to the PRI that its decades-long dominance was being threatened. Opposition parties had grown throughout the 1980s in response to calls for increased democratization, which some political officials had been making since the end of World War II. Arguably, however, the greatest stimulus to the expansion of political parties was the poor response by the federal government following the 1985 earthquake.

PAN put forward its candidate, Manuel Clouthier, who had become wealthy as an industrialist. His position reflected concerns put forward by both political camps but was primarily conservative. He called for an increased role of the private sector in the nation's economy, improved relations with the United States, and—like all candidates—an end to the corruption surrounding the electoral process.

The liberal opposition candidate had name recognition and had climbed the political ladder within the PRI. Cuauhtémoc Cárdenas, son of Lázaro Cárdenas, had served ably within the PRI, as his ascension to the gubernatorial seat of Michoacán testified. In 1988 the younger Cárdenas became an outspoken leader calling for increased democracy, especially within the PRI. Rather than challenge him, a coalition of opposition political parties formed to back his campaign. With the support of the Frente Democrático Nacional, Cuauhtémoc Cárdenas became the "populist" candidate who saw a historic opportunity and seized it.

Despite growing predictions of the demise of the PRI, such claims were grossly exaggerated. President de la Madrid selected another "technocrat" in the figure of the official candidate, Carlos Salinas de Gortari, who had been de la Madrid's secretary of Budget and Planning. Although he held a doctorate in economics from Harvard, Salinas had never served in an elected office and thus knew little about the electoral process. Past PRI candidates had not needed these skills, but 1988 was a different election year. Campaign coverage was extensive, and the opposition candidates—especially Cárdenas—were extensively reported.

As July 1988 neared, it became increasingly clear that the PRI was being challenged and watched as never before.

The election was held on July 6, 1988, and as results began trickling in PRI officials began to realize that they might lose. Their response reveals that the election was probably very close and they were probably losing. Although people had voted on tickets placed in ballot boxes, computers were utilized for the final count so the results could be tabulated and announced quickly. As the tally of votes grew for Cárdenas, officials announced that there had been a problem with the computers and that they were being temporarily shut down. When the computers came back on line, the results showed that Salinas had won with just barely over 50 percent of the votes. The narrow margin of victory allowed PAN to expand its influence with the PRI, since both parties are in closer political and economic agreement than their rhetoric suggests. Nothing dramatized this new arrangement more than the decision by PAN and PRI to burn the ballot boxes and ballots that had been seized by the military during the uncertainty over the election outcome. Their agreement precluded anyone ever knowing the actual election result. Immediately critics protested that the election had been stolen. Moreover, unlike in years past, people took to the streets all throughout Mexico, angry over the egregious behavior of the government; in some places the military was required to bring order, but not without the loss of life.

The drama of the new atmosphere in Mexico was revealed in September 1988 prior to Salinas's assumption of office. In the wake of the July election, various challenges to the process were heard. PRD representative Porfirio Muñoz Ledo publicly challenged President de la Madrid about the supposed fraud. Muñoz Ledo's action served as a reminder of the changing face of Mexico's politics and, as Enrique Krauze writes, revealed a growing unwillingness to accept the government's fraudulent behavior.[11]

Once installed as president, Salinas moved quickly to insure stability against the hostility expressed toward the electoral fraud that guaranteed his victory. In many areas the PRI faced calls for reform, and for Salinas—and ultimately the nation—the nature of reform would define Mexico's views toward the revolution. Debate had long focused on whether the revolution was dead or alive, especially in terms of the chronic issues related to the Catholic Church, organized labor, and land. Salinas's policies resulted in a systematic abandonment of much of what had been promised during the revolution.

Salinas's decision regarding the peasants and revolutionary goals related to land demonstrated how far the president was willing to go in addressing the nation's responsibilities. He argued that the original goal of land distribution, to create a sense of equity, had to be abandoned in light of the more pressing need to increase economic productivity in the agricultural sector. For the first time the government revised the language of Article 27; specifically, a peasant had the option to continue keeping his land in the *ejido* or sell it. The government maintained that any changes in Article 27 were designed to benefit the peasant. In reality, however, the privatization of *ejidos* made possible the acquisition of such lands by wealthy Mexicans or foreign agri-businessmen.

Another important symbolic target was the Church. In many ways Salinas continued the process of relaxing the implementation of the anticlerical language of the Constitution of 1917 that had begun with president Avila Camacho. Priests were once again free to express their opinions and exercise their right to vote; ecclesiastical education was permitted, free from potential government intervention; and the Church could once again own property. Nothing dramatized this new direction more than the historic visit to Mexico by Pope John Paul II and the exchange of diplomatic representatives between Mexico and the Vatican in 1992. The Pope followed up this visit with a return to Mexico in January 1999.

Trained in economics, the president and his administration rapidly moved to stabilize the nation's financial status. Within four years after coming to office, Salinas could brag that inflation had been reduced to a reasonable rate of 20 percent, the budget had been balanced, and there was even a surplus. The selling of public enterprises continued, with Mexico emerging as one of the leading Latin American nations promoting privatization. The government sold off as much as 85 percent of the industries previously acquired, including the government-owned banks acquired under de la Madrid. (However, as Dan La Botz points out in *Democracy in Mexico*, the Salinas government limited the number that actually purchased controlling interest in these formerly state-owned enterprises.[12]) A few industries remain sacrosanct, and Salinas wisely did not move to privatize them; the leading example was PEMEX, the government-controlled oil industry. PEMEX was the darling of Mexico's nationalized industries. So highly positioned was PEMEX's status that it resisted calls for privatization even after the devastating explosion in Guadalajara in 1992, caused when petrol leaked into the city's sewer system from the nearby PEMEX facility.

In order to ensure relative acceptance of his economic policies, Salinas needed support from the peasantry; the revisions of the land ownership policy guaranteed he had their support. He also needed support from labor. Here he took a more traditional approach by demonstrating un-equivocally the authority of the state over labor. Shortly after coming to office the president arrested the head of the powerful oil workers union, Joaquín Hernández Galicia, who had been a prominent supporter of Cár-denas. In an aggressive raid in January 1989, police and soldiers arrested Hernández Galicia and fellow union officers at their offices or homes. Salinas defended this action by maintaining that the men had used their position to steal from union coffers and also engage in weapons traffick-ing. A little more than a month later the government again cracked down on corruption by ordering the arrest of the head of Mexico's largest bro-kerage business. Virtually all unions that did not behave in a manner deemed acceptable to the government faced state action; unions of teach-ers, miners, dock workers, and telephone company workers all faced government-imposed restrictions.

NAFTA: The North American Free Trade Agreement

Salinas's legacy in economics includes the arrangements that led to the North American Free Trade Agreement (NAFTA) with the United States and Canada. On January 1, 1993, U.S. president George Bush, Canadian prime minister Brian Mulroney, and Mexican president Salinas signed the historic agreement that ensures free trade among the three nations. The U.S. Congress approved the measure in the following November. The agreement freed up the movement of money and goods among the three participants and marked the beginning of a reduction in tariffs among them. In particular, the hope was that more money would flow into Mexico, thereby creating more job opportunities and better wages. But in agreeing to this plan Salinas exposed Mexico to free market com-petition with the world's most powerful economy. Nevertheless NAFTA marks a significant shift in Mexican politics. In 1980 the López Portillo government had refused to join the General Agreement on Tariffs and Trade (GATT) because it was viewed as a threat to Mexico's national sovereignty. The United States, still known in Mexico as the "colossus of the north" (as it has been called since the nineteenth century), contin-ued to be distrusted by many. More optimistic observers, however, pointed to the possibility of better jobs, higher wages, access to more sophisticated environmental protection devices, and even more open politics because of U.S. demands for open business practices.

The concern with the United States is warranted. Under NAFTA, Mexico's agricultural sector faces unfair conditions when it competes with the United States, which has a distinct advantage in terms of natural resources, research development infrastructure, technology, and subsidies. To stem the tide of U.S. influence, Mexico must improve the productive capacity of its agricultural sector. Failure to do so may result in increased dependence on trade with the United States, causing a widening trade deficit in agricultural products.

NAFTA's ultimate impact in the industrial sector is also questionable for Mexico. At the core of the imbalance is the role of cheap labor, popularized with the opening of the *maquiladoras* (manufacturing plants) along the U.S.-Mexican border. In the *maquiladoras* Mexicans work for very low wages—often under $5 a day in unfit labor and health environments—and face roadblocks to unionization, which was guaranteed to them by the 1917 constitution. As in the agricultural sector, Mexico's advanced research and development systems are not as developed as the U.S. or Canadian ones.

NAFTA symbolizes the profound change in Mexico's economic policies, because it indicates that the neoliberal policies represented by Carlos Salinas emerged victorious over the traditional populist and nationalist concerns that influenced Mexico's economic decisions for so long. Whether NAFTA provides the economic opportunities that many have envisioned remains to be seen, but the devaluation of the Mexican peso in 1985 that led to higher food costs has served as an ominous reminder that Mexico is the weakest economic partner in NAFTA.

Salinas celebrated his negotiation with NAFTA by nominating Luis Donaldo Colosio as the official PRI candidate for the 1994 presidential election. Trained as an economist, Colosio had assisted Salinas in the reform policies of the PRI. Colosio became president of the PRI and in 1989 signaled his reformist approach by accepting the victory of the opposition party, PAN, in the gubernatorial election in the state of Baja California Norte. After receiving the nomination, he repeatedly commented that he wished to win the election fairly rather than by using corrupt electoral practices.

Chiapas

For the newly nominated candidate, the sitting president, and the observing world the events of January 1, 1994, were shocking, embarrassing, and exhilarating. On that day a relatively unknown guerrilla movement calling itself the Zapatista Army of National Liberation (Ejército Zapatista de Liberación Nacional, or EZLN), numbering approximately 12,000, seized control of three cities—Margarita, Ocosingo, and San Cristóbal de las Casas—in the southern state of Chiapas. The Mexican army responded aggressively by employing helicopter gun ships, aircraft, and ground troops against the attack, resulting in more than 145 deaths and estimates of the wounded numbering in the hundreds.

For many in Mexico the attack and its leader, self-styled Sub-Comandante Marcos, were a surprise. Although the government had had information about the formation of the group, the suddenness of its attack—on the day of the official implementation of NAFTA—was an embarrassment. Suddenly the image of an articulate guerrilla leader who smoked a pipe, wore a ski mask, and had an Internet website became wildly popular in Mexico. Images of Sub-Comandante Marcos, believed to be Rafael Sebastián Guillén Vicente, were printed on T-shirts and sold on the streets of the capital. He had come out of the movement known as the Front for National Liberation that emerged in the 1980s as one of many guerrilla movements whose roots reached back to 1968. The EZLN leadership proclaimed its movement to an indigenous organization that had no ties to the guerrilla actions of the previous decade. Calling for social justice and the implementation of a democratic government, it demanded that Salinas step down as president.

Coming out of Chiapas, shaped by what Marcos called "five hundred years of poverty and exploitation," the movement focused a great deal of attention on what had not been achieved within the revolutionary rhetoric. Salinas's attack against Article 27 had serious repercussions in this predominantly rural region. Now, with the announcement of the NAFTA accord, many feared that they could no longer compete against the economic might of the United States and its farmers. Employing the rhetoric of failed revolutionary promises and aligning the movement with the indigenous past, Sub-Comandante Marcos soon talked of the revolutionary movement becoming a nationwide phenomenon.

Within the government calls were heard to unleash military might against the rebel forces. Probably cognizant of the symbolic past of Tlatelolco and conscious of the international focus on Mexico as a result of NAFTA, Salinas did not give the military free reign. Instead he issued a call for amnesty to the guerrillas on January 12, 1994. With elections coming up in 1994, the government had to respond cautiously in the atmosphere of calls for democratic reform and the international community paying close attention. Yet when amnesty calls and attempts at negotiations failed, the military was employed in a limited action whose military power nevertheless far outstripped that of the EZLN guerrillas. As a result the EZLN was forced out of the cities they had seized in January and fled into the surrounding jungles, where the government could contain the rebels. On more than one occasion there have been reports of violently repressive actions in which dozens of citizens in Chiapas were murdered.

The governments of Salinas and his successor, Ernesto Zedillo, have both employed the dual tactic of negotiation followed by aggressive military use; both have used the air force in bombing and strafing tactics against the people in Chiapas. In 1998 the government again carried out military strikes against several communities, the most egregious being at Acteal in March resulting in at least 45 deaths. As late as January 1999 men portraying themselves as police killed four Indians, including a 4-year-old girl, near the city of San Cristóbal, Chiapas.

The events in Chiapas shocked and disturbed many people in Mexico, as reports revealed practices similar to that of the Porfiriato. The new PRI candidate, Luis Donaldo Colosi, found the events particularly influential in how he regarded political reform. In a March 1994 speech he expressed negative views of a Mexico that was still part of the third world, repressive, and unable to adequately provide for the population. Resolution of these problems, he claimed, would occur through increased democracy and a separation of the PRI from government policy. It was a bold speech that was viewed as an attempt to distance himself from the president and the PRI.

As Mexicans continued to discuss the rebellion and violence in Chiapas, the nation faced another disturbing action when Colosio was assassinated following a speech in Tijuana in March 1994. Immediately conspiracy theories were discussed in Mexico and in the international community; many kept coming back to the idea that the government had been involved. Later that year another political assassination occurred when the Senate majority leader, José Francisco Ruiz Massieu, was shot in Mexico City in September. Like Colosio, Ruiz Massieu had advocated democratic reforms within PRI and improved relations with opposition parties. Again charges swirled around the nation that the PRI was connected with both murders. José Francisco Ruiz Massieu's brother, Mario Ruiz Massieu, worked in the attorney general's office and in a macabre twist of events was named by President Salinas to investigate his brother's death. Evidence published in Mexican and international papers implicated Raúl Salinas, brother of Carlos Salinas, for conspiring in the murder of Ruiz Massieu.

THE PRESIDENCY OF ERNESTO ZEDILLO PONCE DE LEÓN (1994–   )

After Colosio's assassination Salinas had to name a new candidate and chose Ernesto Zedillo Ponce de León, another technocrat educated in the United States in economics. But this selection revealed acute divisions within the PRI, as some members hesitated to support Zedillo's nomination. More significant, the PRI and Zedillo faced a substantial opposition challenge from the Party of the Democratic Revolution (PRD) represented by Cuauhtémoc Cárdenas, and from PAN's representative, Diego Fernández de Cevallos. The split within the PRI and the presence of opposition candidates led to a decision to hold a political debate among the three candidates. Scheduled for May 12, 1994, the debate attracted a huge television audience. Many observers viewed the debate as evidence of democratization taking place in Mexico, albeit carefully controlled by the government in that it dictated the schedule. The debate gave Zedillo great exposure and, through Diego Fernández's articulate attacks against the other candidates, demonstrated that a more open political discourse was indeed taking place.

The election was held in August 1994, with Zedillo winning just over 50 percent of the vote. The Mexican government proclaimed the elections the fairest in the nation's history, and foreign governments echoed this position. Mexico permitted nearly 1,000 individuals to observe the election. They maintained that even though the election was more fair than previous ones, instances of intimidation, corruption, difficulty with registering voters, and threats of reprisals for those who did not vote for PRI undermined the official claims of a truly fair election.

Zedillo took the oath of office in December 1994 and immediately had to deal with Salinas's corrupt legacy (which soon consumed the nation's attention) and the economic problems threatening the country. The economy, which had stabilized under Salinas's leadership, was now collapsing. Zedillo's decision to devalue the peso exacerbated the economic decline. The steps taken in the devaluation process were poorly planned and came as a surprise to many in both the domestic and international financial communities. In a rapid sequence of events the peso fell to 12 percent of its value and then quickly dropped to 50 percent. As a consequence the Mexican stock market collapsed, the nation faced an economic depression, and capital again was sent abroad.

As the economic crisis deepened, Zedillo turned to the United States and the Clinton administration for financial assistance. More than $50 billion was raised from international lending agencies, with the United

States providing $20 billion alone. Although the bailout stemmed a complete financial collapse, it did not resolve the rising interest rate in Mexico for loans that reached 100 percent, nor did it halt the rising unemployment that saw 800,000 Mexicans lose their jobs in the first six months of 1995. It also failed to stop the loss of workers' purchasing power, which decreased by an estimated 40 percent in 1995.[13]

Accompanying the economic instability, in March 1995 Raúl Salinas, brother of Carlos Salinas, was charged with conspiracy in Ruiz Massieu's murder. Raúl Salinas's access to his brother was well documented, and thus many Mexicans began to assume the president had also been involved. The authorities who arrested Raúl Salinas implied that the president had participated in attempts to cover up the murders of Ruiz Massieu and Colosio. Soon the Salinas brothers were linked to other unsolved murders in Mexico—including the death of Cardinal Juan Jesús Posadas Ocampo, who had been gunned down outside Guadalajara's airport. The corruption connected with the Salinas family soon included accusations of involvement with drug trafficking. Formerly the arena of shadowy drug lords, now the nation's highest-ranking political officer and the official party were connected with narco-traffickers. The suspicions about Raúl Salinas's connection with the death of Ruiz Massieu were confirmed in January 1999 when he was found guilty; he now faces fifty years in prison.

When Zedillo came to power he called for political reform, as had previous presidents. But in light of his razor-thin victory in the 1994 presidential election and the nation still being sensitive about the fraudulent 1988 election, he made cautious moves toward reform. Soon Mexico's Congress began responding to calls from the Zedillo administration, as well as pressure from the international community, to make political reform a component of future commercial agreements. In July and August 1996 Congress presented a series of proposals that included new distribution patterns of congressional seats, spending limits, and most significant, a proposal to allow citizens of Mexico City to vote for the mayor and City Council representatives. Further indication of the new policies accepted by the PRI was the fact that PAN won victories in the gubernatorial elections in Guanajuato, Jalisco, and again in Baja California Norte.

The dramatic manifestation of PRI's decline was the victory by PRD candidate Cuauhtémoc Cárdenas in the 1997 mayoral election in Mexico City. A significant outcome of that midterm election was PRI's loss of a majority in the Congress for the first time in sixty-eight years. Enormous celebrations took place in Mexico City and elsewhere in the country in recognition of the symbolic defeat of the PRI. Before long, pundits and politicians, including President Zedillo, sounded the death knell of the PRI. Zedillo stated that "after these elections, no one can ever again refer to the PRI as the only party, the state party or an appendage of the government."[14] Others responded to the PRD victory in a more cynical fashion. When asked about his view of the 1997 elections, one cabdriver in Guadalajara responded by saying, "es mucho teatro" (it's much theater).

Zedillo's dire predictions were reinforced in the 1998 gubernatorial election in the northern state of Zacatecas in which the PRI lost to the rival PRD. The PRI, however, remains a powerful presence in Mexico's political infrastructure; its seven-decade period of dominance means it will be difficult to dislodge. Clearly it must operate in a more open, honest manner because the electorate has demonstrated a willingness to consider rival parties.

Poised on the eve of the next century Mexico's government faces age-old problems, always in the context of the status of the revolution and its goals. Even Presidents Salinas and Zedillo have spoken of the end of the revolutionary experiment. Their free market economic policies are one indication of this trend. Moreover, the opportunity for opposition parties to participate in the political arena augurs well for the nation's goals of democratization.

NOTES

1. Carlos Fuentes, *A New Time for Mexico* (New York: Farrar, Straus, and Giroux, 1996), 75.

2. Elena Poniatowski, *Massacre in Mexico* (Columbia: University of Missouri Press, 1975).

3. Octavo Paz, quoted in Elena Poniatowska, *Massacre in Mexico* (Columbia: University of Missouri Press, 1975), xvi.

4. Barry Carr, "The Fate of the Vanguard under a Revolutionary State: Marxism's Contribution to the Construction of the Great Arch," in *Everyday Forms of State Formation: Revolution and the Negotiation of Rule in Modern Mexico*, ed. Gilbert M. Joseph and Daniel Nugent (Durham: Duke University Press, 1994), 345.

5. Dan La Botz, *Democracy in Mexico: Peasant Rebellion and Political Reform* (Boston: South End Press, 1995), 59.

6. Peter Smith, "Mexico since 1946," in *Mexico since Independence*, ed. Leslie Bethell (Cambridge: Cambridge University Press, 1991), 370–371.

7. Roderic Ai Camp, "Political Modernization in Mexico," in *The Evolution of the Mexican Political System*, ed. Jaime E. Rodríguez O. (Wilmington, DE: Scholarly Resources, 1993), 248.

8. Enrique Krauze, *Mexico: Biography of Power—A History of Modern Mexico, 1810–1996* (New York: HarperCollins, 1997), 763.

9. Smith, "Mexico since 1946," 379–380.

10. *Los Angeles Times*, September 4, 1997. Special thanks to Ms. Melanie Hannon for this quote.

11. Krauze, *Mexico: Biography of Power*, 776.

12. La Botz, *Democracy in Mexico*, 230–231.

13. Ibid., 119.

14. *Washington Post*, July 13, 1997.

Notable People in the History of Mexico

Lucas Alamán (1792–1853)   As a historian, Lucas Alamán provided a conservative critique of some of the early pivotal moments in Mexico's history. His more popular works *History of Mexico* and *History of the Mexican Republic*, provided him with a vehicle to make known his conservative viewpoint. He favored independence for Mexico but rejected the liberal goals of a republican government. Instead he wanted a monarchical style government, preferably with a Bourbon monarch. Recognizing that his views were in the minority, he served in different republican governments as minister of the Interior and minister of Foreign Affairs. He was also conservative in the economic arena. He called for a central banking system to assist industrial development in Mexico, while at the same time allowing the government to renegotiate the country's foreign debt. Alamán was one of the lone voices warning about the threat presented by the United States; his fears were validated in the U.S.-Mexican War (1846–1848), which he accurately depicted as U.S. aggression. Mexico's loss to the United States and other failures convinced him that liberal leadership was the problem. Thus he supported Antonio López de Santa Anna's return in 1853 as a military dictator. He died that same year before he could see the error of his judgment regarding Santa Anna.

Cuauhtémoc Cárdenas (1934–   )   Son of the highly regarded former president Lázaro Cárdenas, Cuauhtémoc moved beyond his father's political shadow in the 1988 presidential campaign when he broke with PRI and ran as the candidate for the opposition party, Frente Democrático Nacional. Many Mexicans have long believed he won the campaign but lost to the fraudulent PRI electoral machinations. In 1997 Cárdenas won the Mexico City mayoral election as the candidate for the PRD. His long-time presidential ambitions may depend on his performance as mayor of the world's largest city.

Lázaro Cárdenas (1895–1970)   Elected as president in 1934, Cárdenas climbed to power in the traditional manner in Mexico. During the violent years of the revolutionary struggle he rose to the rank of general and supported both Alvaro Obregón and Plutarco Elias Calles. His connection with these early presidents was rewarded when Calles supported Cárdenas's election as governor of Michoacán in 1928. As governor, Cárdenas revealed his reformist ideas by supporting educational reforms, peasant and labor associations, and land distribution programs. These policies became cornerstones of his presidential reformist policies. As president, he carried out many of the revolution's more progressive goals, thereby building a populist reputation. Cárdenas distributed more land to peasants than any other president since the revolution. His nationalization of Mexico's railroads in 1937 and the oil industry in 1938 enhanced his populist reputation and secured him a place in the minds of many Mexicans as a defender of Mexican nationalism.

Venustiano Carranza (1859–1920)   Born to a privileged landowner who had participated with Benito Juárez in the War of the Reform, Venustiano Carranza continued the family ranching business. Failing to obtain Porfirio Díaz's support for his run as governor of Coahuila, Carranza thought he had been slighted by the caudillo. As a result, Carranza sided with Francisco Madero in 1910 and was rewarded by being named provisional governor of Coahuila in January 1911. He became an important military supporter of Madero, and in this capacity he participated in the May 1911 negotiations at Ciudad Juárez resulting in Díaz's exile. Following Madero's assassination in February 1913, Carranza pronounced against Victoriano Huerta in his Plan de Guadalupe. The plan announced support for the 1857 constitution and named Carranza as the leader. Because of their adherence to the constitution, Carranza and his supporters became known as the Constitutionalists. By 1916 he had solidified enough control to call for a constitutional convention, which resulted in the creation of the 1917 constitution that still exists today. He became the first post revolutionary president elected in 1917 but was killed in 1920 when he attempted to name his successor in the presidential election of that year.

Hernán Cortés (1485–1547)   There are no statues or monuments celebrating the legacy of Cortés in Mexico. Instead he is regarded as a villain. As leader of the Spanish conquest over the Aztecs in 1521, Cortés served as the symbol of Spanish cruelty, power, and dominance over the Indian population. He and his men departed from the Caribbean island of Cuba in 1519, arrived at the present-day site of Veracruz, and began to march inland to the Aztec capital, now Mexico City. Harnessing both luck and cruelty, and exploiting the internal divisions within the Aztec empire, Cortés and his conquistadors destroyed the Aztecs by 1521. The conquest laid the foundation for the beginning of a new race and nation. Cortés's union with his interpreter, Doña Marina, symbolically marked the beginning of the mestizo race in Mexico (the by-product of European and Indian blood) with the birth of their son, Martín Cortés.

Sor Juana Inés de la Cruz (1651–1695)   One of the brightest lights in literature during Mexico's colonial era was the woman Sor (Sister) Juana Inés de la Cruz. She was brought to the vice-regal court as a young girl and soon amazed the court with her talents. Considered an intellectual prodigy (she was writing poetry by the age of 15), she was also regarded as a woman of remarkable beauty. For unknown reasons she abandoned the court at age 18 to enter a convent. As a nun she was free to pursue intellectual endeavors and continue her writing. An explanation for her abandonment of the vice-regal court may perhaps be found in her writing: She frequently criticized women's lack of status and lamented failed romantic relationships. She died at age 44 from an epidemic that struck Mexico City.

Porfirio Díaz (1830–1915)   He followed the traditional path to power in Mexico by ascending the ranks of the Mexican military. He made his reputation as a successful army officer at the historic Battle of Puebla (Cinco de Mayo) in 1862 when the French were defeated in their early attempts to occupy Mexico. On the basis of his military success he sought the presidency in 1872 but was defeated. In 1876 he became president by pronouncing against Sebastian Lerdo, who Díaz protested had come to office by violating the constitutional provision of "No Reelection"; that is, no sitting president could be reelected. As dictator he disregarded this provision and dominated Mexico for the next thirty-five years. During his dictatorship (known as the Porfiriato) Mexico took important steps toward modernization and industrialization at the end of the nineteenth century. However, these two processes were costly in their consequences for the land and the people. His ruthless dictatorship ended only after the Mexicans revolted in 1910, leading to his removal from office and forced exile in May 1911.

Juan Diego (Sixteenth century)   Juan Diego, an indigenous convert to Catholicism, has been mythologized as having seen the Virgin at the Aztec site of Tepeyac, which is where the Aztecs worshipped the mother of gods, Tonantzin. On five different occasions the Virgin appeared to Diego as a dark-skinned woman and spoke to him in Nahuatl, the Aztec language. The connection of this image to the Aztec religion assisted the mass conversion process of the Indians. According to legend the Virgin instructed Juan Diego to build a shrine to honor her on the hilltop formerly associated with an Aztec goddess. Diego arranged a meeting with a skeptical Bishop Juan de Zumárraga, who became convinced after Diego produced his cloak imprinted with the image of the Virgin. Regardless of the validity of the story, God was viewed as having chosen Mexico and its people to benefit from the appearance of the Virgin. The Virgin of Guadalupe represents the fusion of the two cultures; soon the Virgin came to symbolize the idea of liberty.

Father Miguel Hidalgo y Costilla (1753–1811)   The son of a Creole hacienda owner, Miguel Hidalgo y Costilla was born into a world of relative comfort. Following graduation from school he entered the priesthood and was ordained in 1778. Soon Hidalgo was acting in ways that disturbed the Church. He challenged the vows of clerical celibacy by openly having a mistress. He gambled, danced, called the king a tyrant, and challenged the supremacy of the papacy from Rome. As his behavior became impossible to ignore, he was brought before the Court of the Inquisition in 1800 but was acquitted. In 1803 he became the priest at Dolores, where he continued his nontraditional ways by assisting parishioners in learning practical economic skills that challenged the restrictive economic reforms established by the Bourbons. Soon he joined a literary debating society that examined the relationship between Mexico and Spain. It was not long before the group began considering independence and their discussion reached the authorities. When the group's members received word of their impending arrest Father Hidalgo raced to the church, where he rang the bell to call out his parishioners and announce his opposition to bad government. His call on September 16, 1810, known as the Grito de Dolores (Shout from Dolores), is regarded as marking the birth of Mexico's independence. Hidalgo soon found himself in charge of an unruly mob that attacked the elites, creating terror in central Mexico. Soon royal forces were sent to arrest Hidalgo, who was captured in March 1811. Found guilty of heresy and treason, Father Hidalgo died before a firing squad in July 1811.

Agustín Iturbide (1783–1824)   Symbolic of the early caudillo who readily shifted political allegiance to obtain political gain, Augustín Iturbide helped Mexico achieve independence in 1821. He had climbed the ranks through the colonial militia by suppressing the independent efforts of Father Hidalgo and José María Morelos; in fact, Iturbide assisted in the capture and execution of Morelos in 1815. Not known as an outstanding military leader, Iturbide emerged as the choice of both conservatives and liberals who wanted to break with Spain in 1820 in order to ensure Mexico's post-independence future. Together with Vicente Guerrero, Iturbide issued the Plan de Iguala in 1821 establishing the framework for Mexico's break with Spain. When Mexico's attempt at early self-government revealed the depth of divisions in the nation, Iturbide staged a demonstration whereby he was asked to become constitutional emperor of Mexico. His reign, and Mexico's experimentation with an empire, lasted less than one year. In 1823 military officers, in a practice that would become quite common in Mexico's early history, pronounced against Iturbide. He fled into exile, knowing that if he returned he would be killed. Overestimating his popular support in Mexico, Iturbide returned in 1824 and was executed.

Benito Juárez (1806–1872)   Juárez was the prominent leader of the liberal movement that began with the revolution de Ayutla in 1855. A Zapotec Indian born in Oaxaca, he became an orphan at age 3, served as a book-binding apprentice at 12, and completed law school by the time he was 25. He followed the traditional path of many lawyers when he entered municipal politics in Oaxaca City, and from there he soon became governor of Oaxaca. While in exile to escape Santa Anna, Juárez and others pronounced against the caudillo with the Plan de Ayutla in 1854. Contained in the pronouncement were the reformist plans of the liberal faction that Juárez led until his death in 1872. The reformist goals were written into law with the 1857 constitution that sparked a three-year civil war between liberals and conservatives. The liberals won in 1861 but had to defend Mexico from 1862 to 1867 while the French occupied Mexico. During both military struggles Juárez was the spiritual leader of the liberal side.

Frida Kahlo (1907–1954)   A unique presence in the twentieth-century art world, Kahlo was horribly injured in a bus crash at age 18 and lived with severe pain for the remainder of her life. During her convalescence she began to paint as a way to escape the pain and boredom. It soon became apparent that she possessed talent in drawing. Encouraged by friends and her own boldness, she visited the well-known artist Diego Rivera to obtain his opinion of her work. Their visits soon moved beyond an appreciation of artistic talent. At age 20 she married Diego Rivera, opening the door to the world of the intellectual avant-garde. They had a tumultuous marriage that ended in divorce and remarriage a year later; their second marriage lasted until her death in 1954. Kahlo ultimately established a strong reputation in the art world and mounted numerous solo exhibitions. Her solo exhibitions were an attempt to distance herself from those who suggested her talent reflected her relationship with Diego Rivera. Her art focused on surreal examinations of traditional Mexican interpretations that had gained popularity in the years following the revolution.

Antonio López de Santa Anna (1794–1876)   Santa Anna was the epitome of the nineteenth-century caudillo in Mexico. His mercurial career spanned the first four decades of Mexico's independence. He traversed Mexico's political spectrum from hero to villain, liberal to conservative, dictator to president, all with dizzying speed. From 1821 to 1854 he occupied the president's office on eleven different occasions. His military success paralleled his experiences in the political arena. He defeated the rebellious Texans in 1836 at the Alamo but soon signed away the Texas territory to gain freedom following his capture. He defeated the French in 1838 but lost part of a leg in the process. When his army failed against the United States in 1847 he surrendered his military rank and fled the country, as Mexico was losing the war and ultimately half of its territory. Despite these losses on the battlefield and his schizophrenic behavior in the political field, he remained enormously popular and was repeatedly invited to lead the nation. Exiled in 1855, he was later allowed to return; in great irony, he died a relatively unknown man in 1876.

Francisco Madero (1873–1913)   The son of a wealthy family from the state of Coahuila, Madero found himself at the front of the Mexican Revolution in 1910. Educated at the best schools in Mexico, as well as in Berkeley, California, and Paris, Madero returned to run the family business and soon adopted a sympathetic view of workers. Responding to comments by President Porfrio Díaz in 1908, Madero published *The Presidential Succession in 1910*. This book propelled him into the leadership of the anti-reelectionist camp that opposed Díaz's reelection in 1910. Because of his growing political popularity, he was arrested and jailed in 1910 while the election took place. After the election Madero escaped to the United States, where he pronounced against Díaz in the Plan de San Luis Potosí. This action marked the beginning of violent military action that ultimately defined the Mexican Revolution from 1910 to 1920. Madero was officially elected president in October 1911 and faced the awesome task of negotiating with the multiple factions seeking to direct the course of change. Like many revolutionaries who acquire power, Madero pleased few and angered many. These conditions led to a coup against him early in 1913 and his murder in February 1913.

Doña Marina (Sixteenth Century)   When the Spanish arrived on the Yucatán coast, the local Indians gave them a number of women. One was an Indian woman whom the Spanish named Doña Marina. (Some have given her the nickname La Malinche, meaning the woman who betrayed her people.) Her role in the conquest proved quite valuable. Possessing the ability to speak one of the Mayan dialects as well as Nahuatl, the language of the Aztecs, she interpreted so the Spanish could "speak" with the Indians they encountered on the way to the Aztec capital Tenochtitlán. Later Doña Marina became the lover of Hernán Cortés and they had a child, Martín Cortés. He represented the multiracial society that defined Mexico through the blending of the two races—the mestizo.

Moctezuma II (?–1520)   In 1502 Moctezuma II came to power as a result of historical accident: the death of his brother on the battlefield. Initially Moctezuma had studied for the priesthood while his brother trained to lead the Aztecs in war. After the brother's death, Moctezuma II came to the throne of an empire that included between 11 and 20 million people. His empire contained elements that resisted Aztec domination, not the least of which was the group known as the Tlaxcalans. This group proved a valuable ally of the Spanish when they arrived in 1519. Twice

Moctezuma's forces attempted to defeat the Tlaxcalans and lost. Although he was aggressive in his attempts against these dissident elements, Moctezuma was much less so following the arrival of the Spanish. Initially believing the Spanish to be incarnations or representatives of an ancient Aztec deity, Moctezuma hesitated to aggressively move against them. When they arrived at the Aztec capital they imprisoned him, but he continued to rule in captivity. Soon his capitulation to Spanish dominance resulted in his loss of power among his people. Used one last time by Cortés to quiet Aztec discontent, his people ultimately stoned him to death.

José María Morelos y Pavón (1765–1815)   Morelos inherited the leadership of the independence movement following Father Hidalgo's execution in 1811. Morelos's forces were better trained than those under Hidalgo, resulting in less egregious violations to lives and property. Utilizing an effective guerrilla campaign, Morelos's forces encircled Mexico City by 1813. From this position he held a meeting at Chilpancingo, where independence was formally declared and provisions for a constitution were discussed. These discussions reflected nineteenth-century liberalism in calling for universal male suffrage, an end to slavery, abolishment of government monopolies, elimination of caste systems, and equal justice. While the delegates at Chilpancingo were debating, the Spanish counterattacked and soon had the guerrillas on the run. Morelos was captured in 1815. Like Hidalgo, he was tried for heresy and treason and was executed.

Quetzalcóatl   One of the ancient deities worshipped by various Indian groups in Mesoamerica and adopted by the Aztecs, Quetzalcóatl occupies an important place in Mexico's history. Legend has it that while in competition with rival gods for influence, Quetzalcóatl, a light-skinned deity who wore a beard, humiliated himself after becoming intoxicated; he then fled to the east, marking his way by shooting arrows through small trees (making crosses) and promising to return. Hernán Cortés and the Spanish explorers arrived in the year the Aztecs believed Quetzalcóatl would return. Because the Spanish arrived from the east, light-skinned, bearded, and carrying the sign of the cross, many Aztecs—including Moctezuma—thought they had some connection to the ancient deity. The resulting hesitancy of the Aztecs to repel the Spanish has been seen as an opportunity for the Spanish to make alliances with other Indian groups and may explain why the much more numerous Aztecs did not quickly crush the Spanish.

Diego Rivera (1886–1957) One of Mexico's great muralists of the twentieth century, Diego Rivera first started studying to be an artist at age 15. As a painter he employed the style of cubism and postmodernism after traveling to Paris in 1911. His themes dramatized the pre-Columbian Mexican heritage, the role of the farmer and laborer, and the costumes of popular Mexico. His celebrations of Mexico's culture and people led to the decision by Secretary of Education José Vasconcelos to employ Rivera to paint murals on school buildings. His murals depicting the Indian in Mexico's history criticized both Spain's and post-independence Mexico's treatment of the Indian.

Carlos Salinas de Gortari (1949–) Mexico's president from 1988 to 1994, Carlos Salinas symbolizes the corruption that has pervaded Mexico's political system, specifically the Partido Revolucionario Institucional (PRI). Trained as an economist in the United States at Harvard University, Salinas slowly climbed the bureaucracy of the PRI and received the presidential nomination in 1988. Believed to have won the 1988 election through corruption and fraud, Salinas nonetheless embarked on his vision of reforms for Mexico. His reign culminated with Mexico's adoption of the North American Free Trade Agreement in 1994. Despite his success in the economic sector his tenure was marked by violence, rumors of association with Mexico's drug trade, and corruption. His brother has recently been found guilty in a conspiracy to kill a former high-ranking officer in the PRI (Salinas's former brother-in-law), Francisco Ruiz Massieu) and has been connected with the drug trade. Harshly criticized in Mexico's press and the international press, Salinas currently lives in self-imposed exile in Ireland.

Sub-Comandante Marcos (?–) Believed to be Rafael Sebastián Guillén Vicente, he is the charismatic leader of the Ejército Zapatista de Liberación Nacional (EZLN) rebellion that broke out in January 1994 in the southern Mexican state of Chiapas. Photographed wearing a ski mask and frequently smoking a pipe, Sub-Comandante Marcos has called for the expansion of democracy, equitable land rights for the indigenous population, and other conditions promised by the 1917 constitution but as yet undelivered for the people of southern Mexico. Criticized for spreading revolutionary propaganda to the remainder of the country, Sub-Comandante Marcos nevertheless remains an important symbol of protest in Mexico.

Pancho Villa (1878–1923)   Born Doroteo Arango, probably in 1878, in what is now the state of Durango, he was orphaned at a young age. Needing to support his family he began working on a nearby ranch, where he shot a man who attempted to rape his sister. He barely escaped with his life into the nearby canyons, where he began his career as an outlaw in 1891 at the age of 13. What followed remains open to debate, but he apparently changed his name to Francisco Villa and began working as a miner. Soon he drifted toward more criminal activity including cattle rustling, bank robbery, and murder. His ability to avoid capture by the Rurales (a national police force) helped shape his colorful reputation among many in Mexico. He joined the Madero revolutionary movement in 1910. After Madero's assassination in 1913 he sided with the Constitutionalists led by Venustiano Carranza. Soon, however, Villa split with the Constitutionalists and lost a military engagement in 1915, which ultimately limited his role to the periphery of Mexico's revolutionary struggle. He claimed attention in 1916 and 1917 when he attacked U.S. border towns, resulting in the United States sending troops into Mexico in an attempt to capture him. The failure of the troops only added to his popularity. In 1919 he negotiated a truce with the Carranza government and retired to his hacienda in Durango. Four years later he was assassinated. Villa emerged as a significant revolutionary icon in Mexico—especially in northern Mexico, where his name still evokes respect.

Emiliano Zapata (1879–1919)   In many ways Emiliano Zapata has evolved as one of the more important revolutionary icons. He emerged from the state of Morelos, where he had been a farmer and horse trainer. Elected as representative of his village in 1909, he soon became an ardent proponent of land reform. He supported the revolutionary actions of Francisco Madero, who sought the presidency against Porfirio Díaz in 1910, because Madero had promised to pursue land reform policies. When it became clear that Madero was abandoning his promises, Zapata pronounced against him in 1911. From 1911 to 1919 Zapata struggled to achieve the singular goal of bringing about land reform. In 1919 President Venustiano Carranza became a target of Zapata for his failure to implement the land reform measures promised in the 1917 constitution.

Treacherously deceived by one of Carranza's generals, Zapata was killed in 1919. His name and goals live on, as the current rebellion in Chiapas is named for him.

Juan de Zumárraga (1468–1548)   As the first bishop and archbishop of Mexico, Zumárraga arrived in Mexico in 1529 with the purpose of protecting the Indian population from the excesses of the Spanish. Initially checked by more powerful secular leaders in the colony, Zumárraga protested from the pulpit and in letters to Spain. Although his power remained poorly defined, he nevertheless worked out an important relationship between the civil government and the Catholic Church in the colony. Zumárraga and numerous other clerics organized the massive conversion of the Indian population to Christianity and attempted to educate the Indians to read and write. Zumárraga was flexible toward the converting Indians in their attempts to identify in Christianity certain elements of their previous forms of worship. Nothing dramatized this more than his role in the creation of the myth surrounding the Virgin of Guadalupe in 1531.

Bibliographic Essay

I have limited the following bibliographic essay to works in English on Mexico's history.

An important starting point for anyone interested in Mexican history is Leslie Bethell's edited work in the Cambridge Latin American History series. More specifically, five books—*Colonial Spanish America*, Leslie Bethell (Cambridge, 1987); *The Independence of Latin America*, ed. Leslie Bethell (Cambridge, 1987); *Spanish America after Independence c. 1820–c. 1870*, ed. Leslie Bethell (Cambridge, 1987); *Latin America: Economy and Society, 1870–1930*, ed. Leslie Bethell (Cambridge, 1989); and *Mexico since Independence*, ed. Leslie Bethell (Cambridge, 1991)—introduce the reader to the leading historians of Latin America and Mexico. Although some titles suggest a greater emphasis on Latin America than on Mexico, they introduce key issues that help explain Mexico's complex history. James Cockcroft, *Mexico: Class Formation, Capital Accumulation, and the State* (New York, 1990), is an interesting read of Mexico's sweeping history. Enrique Krauze, *Mexico: A Biography of Power, a History of Modern Mexico, 1810–1996* (New York, 1997), examines some of Mexico's leading historical figures.

Mexico's early peoples are examined by Elizabeth P. Benson in her edited work, *The Olmecs and Their Neighbors* (Washington, DC, 1981).

Robert M. Carmack, Janine Gasco, and Gary H. Gossen contribute to this area of study in *The Legacy of Mesoamerica: History and Culture of Native American Civilization* (Englewood Cliff, NJ, 1996). Other significant works on Mexico's pre-Hispanic history include Michael Coe, *Mexico: From the Olmecs to the Aztecs* (London, 1994); Robert MacNeish, *The Origins of Agriculture and Settled Life* (Norman, OK, 1991); and Michael D. Coe, Linda Schele, and David Friedel, *A Forest of Kings: The Untold Story of the Ancient Maya* (New York, 1990). Eric Wolf's *The Sons of the Shaking Earth: The People of Mexico and Guatemala—Their Land, History and Culture* (Chicago, 1974), is a classic examination of the rise of early civilizations in Mexico.

A more detailed analysis of the Aztecs includes Nigel Davies, *The Ancient Kingdoms of Mexico* (New York, 1982); Miguel Leon-Portilla, *The Broken Spears: The Aztec Account of the Conquest of Mexico* (Boston, 1992); Inga Clendinnen, *Aztecs: An Interpretation* (New York, 1991); Mary G. Hodge and Michael E. Smith, ed., *Economies and Polities in the Aztec Realm* (Austin, 1993); and R. C. Padden, *The Hummingbird and the Hawk* (New York, 1970). A rich examination of the conditions faced by the Aztecs following the conquest is found in Charles Gibson, *The Aztecs under Spanish Rule* (Stanford, CA, 1964).

The classic account of the conquest from the Spanish point of view is Bernal Díaz del Castillo, *The True History of the Conquest of New Spain* (New York, 1966). Despite some recent suggestions questioning his role with the conquest, this book remains an important insight into the Spanish actions during the conquest. An important read about conditions in Spain is John H. Elliott, *Imperial Spain, 1469–1716* (New York, 1962). More recent analyses include John K. Chance, *Conquest of the Sierra: Spaniards and Indians in Colonial Oaxaca* (Norman, OK, 1989); and Hugh Thomas, *Conquest: Montezuma, Cortés, and the Fall of Old Mexico* (New York, 1993). One of the more traditional, Eurocentric accounts of the conquest is William H. Prescott, *History and Conquest of Mexico* (New York, 1967; there are many editions of this work). An important analysis of the conquistadors is Bernard Grunberg, "The Origins of the Conquistadores of Mexico City," *Hispanic American Historical Review* 74 (1994).

Alfred W. Crosby examines the environmental consequences when the New World met the Old World, beginning at the end of the fifteenth century and the arrival of Columbus. In his detailed study Crosby explains how the "exchange" between these regions had both positive and negative consequences. See Alfred W. Crosby, *The Columbian Exchange: Biological and Cultural Consequences of 1492* (Westport, CT: Greenwood Press, 1972).

Numerous works examine the consequences of Spanish rule on the indigenous population. Benjamin Keen and Juan Friede edited *Bartolomé de las Casas in History: Toward an Understanding of the Man and His Work* (DeKalb, IL, 1971). Nancy M. Farriss, *Maya Society under Colonial Rule: The Collective Enterprise of Survival* (Princeton, 1984), provides a critical look at how the ancestors of the Mayas responded, and Charles Gibson, *The Aztecs under Spanish Rule: A History of the Indians in the Valley of Mexico* (Stanford, CA, 1964), evaluates the Aztec perspective. More recent examinations of the Aztecs include Ida Altman, "Spanish Society in Mexico City after the Conquest," *Hispanic American Historical Review* 71 (1991); and James Lockhart, *The Nahuas after the Conquest: A Social and Cultural History of the Indians of Central Mexico, Sixteenth through Eighteenth Centuries* (Stanford, CA, 1992).

A host of impressive works has detailed the colonial era in Mexico, discussing everything from politics to the economic sector. An important analysis of the colonial economy is provided by Woodrow Borah, *Early Trade and Navigation between Mexico and Peru* (Berkeley, 1954). Meanwhile François Chevalier continues to evaluate the economy by focusing on the role of the hacienda in *Land and Society in Colonial Mexico: The Great Hacienda* (Berkeley, 1963). Peter Bakewell examines the colonial economy in his study of the role of the mining sector found in *Silver Mining and Society in Colonial Mexico: Zacatecas, 1546–1700* (Cambridge, 1971). The methods of labor control used by the Spanish are examined in Susan M. Deeds, "Rural Work in Nueva Vizcaya: Forms of Labor Coercion on the Periphery," *Hispanic American Historical Review* 69 (1989); Lesley B. Simpson, *The Encomienda in New Spain* (Berkeley, 1960); and William B. Taylor, *Landlord and Peasants in Colonial Oaxaca* (Stanford, CA, 1972).

Further examinations of the colonial economy include John E. Kicza, *Colonial Entrepreneurs: Families and Business in Bourbon Mexico City* (Albuquerque, 1983); James Lockhart, "Encomienda and Hacienda: The Evolution of the Great Estate in the Spanish Indies," *Hispanic American Historical Review* 49 (1969); Richard Salvucci, *Textiles and Capitalism in Mexico: An Economic History of the Obrajes, 1539–1840* (Princeton, 1988); Eric Van Young, *Hacienda and Market in 18th Century Mexico: The Rural Economy in the Guadalajara Region, 1675–1820* (Berkeley, 1981); Guy C. P. Thomson, *Puebla de los Angeles: Industry and Society in a Mexican City, 1700–1850* (Boulder, 1989); David Brading, *Haciendas and Ranchos in the Mexican Bajío: León, 1700–1860* (Cambridge, 1978); Richard B. Lindley, *Haciendas and Economic Development: Guadalajara, Mexico, at Independence* (Austin, 1983); and Margaret Chowning, "The Consolidación de Vales

Reales in the Bishopric of Michoacán," *Hispanic American Historical Review* 69 (1989). A consequence of Spanish colonial rule is considered in Christon Archer, *The Army in Bourbon Mexico, 1760–1810* (Albuquerque, 1977); Linda Arnold, *Bureaucracy and Bureaucrats in Mexico City, 1742–1835* (Tucson, 1988); Brian Hamnett, *Roots of Insurgency, Mexican Regions, 1750–1824* (Cambridge, 1985); Susan Deans-Smith, *Bureaucrats, Planters and Workers: The Making of the Tobacco Monopoly in Bourbon Mexico* (Austin, 1992); Brian Hamnett, *Politics and Trade in Southern Mexico, 1750–1821* (Cambridge, 1971); and Nancy M. Farriss, *Crown and Clergy in Colonial Mexico, 1759–1821* (London, 1968).

The controversial issue of race in colonial Mexico has been examined by John K. Chance, *Race and Class in Colonial Oaxaca* (Stanford, CA, 1978); Louisa Hoberman, *Mexico's Merchant Elite, 1590–1660* (Durham, 1991); Asunción Lavrin, ed., *Sexuality and Marriage in Colonial Latin America* (Lincoln, NE, 1989); Rodney D. Anderson, "Race and Social Stratification: A Comparison of Working-Class Spaniards, Indians, and Castas in Guadalajara, Mexico, in 1821," *Hispanic American Historical Review* 2 (1988); Magnus Mörner, *Race Mixture in the History of Latin America* (Boston, 1967); and Cynthia Radding, *Wandering Peoples: Colonialism Ethnic Spaces, and Ecological Frontiers in Northwestern Mexico, 1700–1850* (Durham, NC, 1997).

Social behavior in the colonial era has been evaluated in William H. Beezley, Cheryl E. Martin, and William E. French, *Rituals of Rule, Rituals of Resistance: Public Celebrations and Popular Culture in Mexico* (Wilmington, DE, 1994); William B. Taylor, *Drinking, Homicide and Rebellion in Colonial Mexican Villages* (Stanford, CA, 1979); Lesley B. Simpson, *Many Mexicos* (Berkeley, 1959); Patricia Seed, *To Love, Honor, and Obey in Colonial Mexico: Conflicts over Marriage Choice, 1574–1821* (Stanford, CA, 1988); Steve J. Stern, *The Secret History of Gender: Women, Men, and Power in Late Colonial Mexico* (Chapel Hill, NC, 1995), and Michael C. Scardaville, "Alcohol Abuse and Tavern Reform in Late Colonial Mexico City," *Hispanic American Historical Review* 60 (1980).

Contributing factors to the move for independence are considered in John Tutino, *From Insurrection to Revolution in Mexico: Social Bases of Agrarian Violence, 1750–1940* (Princeton, 1986); Timothy Anna, *The Fall of Royal Government in Mexico City* (Lincoln, NE, 1978); and Jaime Rodríguez O., ed., *The Independence of Mexico and the Creation of the New Nation* (Los Angeles, 1989).

An examination of the post-independence period is found in Charles A. Hale, *Mexican Liberalism in the Age of Mora, 1821–1853* (New Haven,

1968); Michael P. Costeloe, *Church and State in Independent Mexico: A Study of the Patronage Debate, 1821–1857* (London, 1978); and Timothy Anna, *Forging Mexico, 1821–1835* (Lincoln, NE, 1998). Contemporary examination of post-independence Mexico can be found in Joel Poinsett, *Notes on Mexico* (London, 1825); and H. G. Ward, *Mexico in 1827* (London, 1828). An impressive number of authors have studied Mexico in the years after 1821, as Mexico searched to create a viable, independent nation. Suggested readings for this topic include: Richard Sinkin, *The Mexican Reform, 1855–1872* (Austin, 1979); Peter Guardino, "Barbarism or Republican Law: Guerrero's Peasants and National Politics, 1820–1846," *Hispanic American Historical Review* 75 (1995); Douglass Richmond, ed., *Essays on the Mexican War* (College Station, TX, 1986); Jan Bazant, *Alienation of Church Wealth in Mexico: Social and Economic Aspects of the Liberal Revolution, 1856–1875* (Cambridge, 1971); David A. Brading, "Liberal Patriotism and the Mexican Reforma," *Journal of Latin American Studies* 20 (1988); Brian Hamnett, *Juárez* (London, 1994); and Charles A. Hale, *The Transformation of Liberals in Late Nineteenth Century Mexico* (Princeton, 1989).

I mention one important Spanish source for readers. Daniel Cosio Villegas directed a team of historians who compiled archival material from the United States, Europe, and Mexico on the period from 1867 to 1910. The result of this effort is the thirteen-volume work *Historia de México* (Mexico, 1958–1972).

An impressive array of works examines the era of Porfirio Díaz's dictatorship. See John Coatsworth, *Growth against Development: The Economic Impact of Railroads in Porfirian Mexico* (DeKalb, IL, 1980); James Cockcroft, *Intellectual Precursors of the Mexican Revolution, 1900–1913* (Austin, 1968); Thomas Benjamin and William McNellie, eds, *Other Mexicos: Essays on Regional Mexican History, 1876–1911* (Albuquerque, 1984); Mark Wasserman, *Capitalists, Caciques and Revolution: The Native Elite and Foreign Enterprises in Chihuahua Mexico, 1854–1911* (Chapel Hill, NC, 1984); Rodney D. Anderson, *Outcasts in Their Own Land: Mexican Industrial Workers, 1906–1911* (DeKalb, IL, 1976); William K. Meyers, *Forge of Progress, Crucible of Revolt: The Origins of the Mexican Revolution in La Comarca Lagunera, 1880–1911* (Albuquerque, 1994); Paul Vanderwood, *Disorder and Progress: Bandits, Police and Mexican Development* (Wilmington, DE, 1992); John Womack, *Zapata and the Mexican Revolution* (New York, 1968); and Heather Fowler-Salamini and Mary Kay Vaughn, eds., *Women of the Mexican Countryside, 1850–1990: Creating Spaces, Shaping Transition* (Tucson, 1994).

The study of the Mexican Revolution continues to benefit from extensive and frequently innovative research. Two early examinations, but still influential works, are Frank Tannenbaum, *The Mexican Agrarian Revolution* (Washington, DC, 1929); and Marjorie R. Clark, *Organized Labor in Mexico* (Chapel Hill, NC, 1934). Although previously mentioned, John Womack, *Zapata and the Mexican Revolution* (New York, 1968), remains one of the classic examinations of issues shaping the activism of the peasants. John M. Hart, *Anarchism and the Mexican Working Class, 1860–1931* (Austin, 1978), evaluates the role of workers in the revolutionary process. Ramón Eduardo Ruiz argues that the revolutionary process was not all that radical in *The Great Rebellion: Mexico, 1905–1924* (New York, 1980). Alan Knight's *The Mexican Revolution,* 2 vols. (Lincoln, NE, 1986), remains one of the most influential and comprehensive studies of the revolution. Charles C. Cumberland, *Mexican Revolution: Genesis under Madero* (Austin, 1952), and Charles C. Cumberland, *Mexican Revolution: The Constitutionalist Years* (Austin, 1972), provide enjoyable reads for this immensely complex topic.

Robert Quirk, *The Mexican Revolution, 1914–1915: The Convention of Aguascalientes* (Bloomington, IN, 1960), and E. Victor Niemeyer, *Revolution at Queretaro: The Mexican Constitutional Convention of 1916–1917* (Austin, 1974), provide insight into the two revolutionary conventions that met in the years between 1910 and 1917.

Important works on some of the key players in the revolution are Douglass W. Richmond, *Venustiano Carranza's Nationalist Struggle, 1893–1920* (Lincoln, NE, 1984); Linda Hall, *Alvaro Obregón, Power and Revolution in Mexico, 1911–1920* (College Station, TX, 1981); and Friedrich Katz, *The Life and Times of Pancho Villa* (Stanford, CA, 1998). John Womack, *Zapata and the Mexican Revolution* (New York, 1968), again serves as a reminder of ways in which a historian can bring to life a historical character.

In the years following the revolution the state exercised dominance over a number of institutions. Jean Meyer, *The Cristero Rebellion: The Mexican People between Church and State, 1926–1929* (Cambridge, 1976), examines the struggle shaped by the anti-clerical language of the 1917 constitution. Jim Tuck also addresses the Cristero Rebellion in *The Holy War in Los Altos: A Regional Analysis of Mexico's Cristero Rebellion* (Tucson, 1982). John W. F. Dulles, *Yesterday in Mexico: A Chronicle of the Revolution, 1918–1936* (Austin, 1960), details some of the complex issues dividing the nation. Educational reforms addressed in the 1917 constitution are examined in Mary Kay Vaughn, *Cultured Politics in Revolution: Teachers, Peasants, and Schools in Mexico, 1930–1940* (Tucson, 1996).

The Cárdenas era has received critical attention recently. See Marjorie Becker, *Setting the Virgin on Fire: Lázaro Cárdenas, Michoacán Peasants, and the Redemption of the Mexican Revolution* (Berkeley, 1996). John W. Sherman, *The Mexican Right: The End of Revolutionary Reform, 1920–1940* (Westport, CT, 1997), details the formidable role of the right during the Cárdenas administration. Robert P. Millon, *Mexican Marxist: Vicente Lombardo Toledano* (Chapel Hill, NC, 1966), examines this union leader and his relationship with Cárdenas.

Works focusing on the postwar years in Mexico examine the complex issue of democratization and the potent opportunity for change. See Barry Carr, *Marxism and Communism in Twentieth Century Mexico* (Lincoln, NE, 1992); and Susan Eckstein, *The Poverty of Revolution: The State and the Urban Poor in Mexico* (Princeton, 1977). Elena Poniatowska, *Massacre in Mexico* (New York, 1975), examines the events at Tlatelolco in 1968. See also Samuel Schmidt, *The Deterioration of the Mexican Presidency* (Tucson, 1991); and Edward J. Williams, *The Rebirth of the Mexican Petroleum Industry* (Lexington, MA, 1979). Jonathan Brown and Alan Knight, eds., examine the oil industry in the years before and after World War II in *The Mexican Petroleum Industry in the Twentieth Century* (Austin, 1992). See also Roderic Ai Camp, *Crossing Swords: Politics and Religion in Mexico* (New York, 1997). An early examination of the Zapatista movement is George A. Collier, *Basta: Land and the Zapatista Rebellion in Chiapas* (Oakland, CA, 1994). See also Joe Foweraker and Ann L. Craig, eds., *Popular Movements and Political Change in Mexico* (Boulder, CO, 1990); Dan La Botz, *Democracy in Mexico: Peasant Rebellion and Political Reform* (Boston, 1995); Daniel Levy and Gabriel Székely, *Mexico: Paradoxes of Stability and Change* (Boulder, CO, 1983); and Stephen D. Morris, *Political Reformism in Mexico: An Overview of Contemporary Mexican Politics* (Boulder, 1995); Tom Barry, *Zapata's Revenge: Free Trade and the Farm Crisis in Mexico* (Boston, 1995), continues the examination of the Zapatista movement and what this rebellion represents.

Index

About the Author

BURTON KIRKWOOD is Professor of History at the University of Evansville, in Evansville, Indiana.

Other Titles in the
Greenwood Histories of the Modern Nations
Frank W. Thackeray and John E. Findling, Series Editors

The History of Japan
Louis G. Perez

The History of Israel
Arnold Blumberg

The History of Spain
Peter Pierson

The History of Germany
Eleanor L. Turk

The History of Holland
Mark T. Hooker

The History of Nigeria
Toyin Falola

The History of Brazil
Robert M. Levine

The History of Russia
Charles E. Ziegler

The History of Portugal
James M. Anderson

The History of Poland
M. B. Biskupski